Critical Muslim 34

Artificial

Critical Muslim is published quarterly by C. Hurst & Co. (Publishers) Ltd. on behalf of and in conjunction with Critical Muslim Ltd. and the Muslim Institute, London.

All editorial correspondence to Muslim Institute, CAN Mezzanine, 49–51 East Road, London N1 6AH, United Kingdom.
E-mail: editorial@criticalmuslim.com

C. Hurst & Co (Publishers) Ltd., 41 Great Russell Street, London WC1B 3PL

ISBN: 978-1-78738-405-7 ISSN: 2048-8475

To subscribe or place an order by credit/debit card or cheque (pounds
sterling only) please contact Kathleen May at the Hurst address above or
e-mail kathleen@hurstpub.co.uk

Tel: 020 7255 2201

A one-year subscription, inclusive of postage (four issues), costs £50
(UK), £65 (Europe) and £75 (rest of the world), this includes full access
to the *Critical Muslim* series and archive online. Digital only subscription is
£3.30 per month.

Critical Muslim

Subscribe to Critical Muslim

Now in its ninth year in print, *Critical Muslim* is also available online. Users can access the site for just £3.30 per month – or for those with a print subscription it is included as part of the package. In return, you'll get access to everything in the series (including our entire archive), and a clean, accessible reading experience for desktop computers and handheld devices — entirely free of advertising.

Full subscription

The print edition of *Critical Muslim* is published quarterly in January, April, July and October. As a subscriber to the print edition, you'll receive new issues directly to your door, as well as full access to our digital archive.

United Kingdom £50/year
Europe £65/year
Rest of the World £75/year

Digital Only

Immediate online access to *Critical Muslim*

Browse the full *Critical Muslim* archive

Cancel any time

£3.30 per month

www.criticalmuslim.io

CM34

SPRING 2020

CONTENTS

ARTIFICIAL

C Scott Jordan	INTRODUCTION: CERTIFICATE OF AUTHENTICITY	3
Jeremy Henzell-Thomas	ARTIFICIAL DEFINED	15
Abdelwahab El-Affendi	FAKING UNBELIEF	31
Robert Irwin	ANCIENT MECHANICAL HORRORS	39
John Sweeney	AI AND COVID-19	51
Emre Kazim	DIGITAL ETHICS	61
Colin Tudge	IS IT BAD TO BE ARTIFICIAL?	67
Christopher B Jones	FOUR EARTHS	83
Esra Mirze Santesso	FAUX FEMINISM	103
Hassan Mahamdallie	THE ENGLISH ROSE WHO WASN'T	117
James Brooks	PROMISES, PROMISES	127
Liam Mayo	THROUGH THE SEA GLASS	141

ARTS AND LETTERS

Naomi Foyle	SHORT STORY: THE MARCH	155
Shah Tazrian Ashrafi	SHORT STORY: HUNGRY SEASON	177
Mozibur Rahman Ullah	FOUR POEMS	185

REVIEWS

Marie Michalke	GHETTO STORIES	199
Arsalan Isa	A CIRCUS OF BOYS	207

KHUDA BUSHQ   COVID-19 ENTERTAINMENT   213

ET CETERA

SAMIA RAHMAN   LAST WORD: ON THE DISAPPEARING
              NORMAL   225

THE LIST   TOP TEN SPARKS FOR THOUGHT ON AI
              BY WENDY SCHULTZ   232

CITATIONS   240

CONTRIBUTORS   259

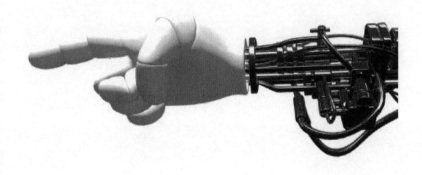

ARTIFICIAL

INTRODUCTION: Certificate of Authenticity *by C Scott Jordan*
ARTIFICIAL DEFINED *by Jeremy Henzell-Thomas*
FAKING UNBELIEF *by Abdelwahab El-Affendi*
ANCIENT MECHANICAL HORRORS *by Robert Irwin*
AI AND COVID-19 *by John Sweeney*
DIGITAL ETHICS *by Emre Kazim*
IS IT BAD TO BE ARTIFICIAL? *by Colin Tudge*
FOUR EARTHS *by Christopher B Jones*
FAUX FEMINISM *by Esra Mirze Santesso*
THE ENGLISH ROSE WHO WASN'T *by Hassan Mahamdallie*
PROMISES, PROMISES *by James Brook*
THROUGH THE SEA GLASS *by Liam Mayo*

INTRODUCTION:
CERTIFICATE OF AUTHENTICITY

C Scott Jordan

It was the kind of song that demands to erupt to life from the cacophony of battling frequencies that result when twisting the tuning nob of an old radio. That aural taste of the 'old times' even translates to the advanced digital music players of today.

Oh, and there we were all in one place
A generation lost in space
With no time left to start again

So come on Jack be nimble, Jack be quick
Jack Flash sat on a candlestick
'Cause fire is the devil's only friend

Don McLean's *American Pie* was the 1971 song that everyone knows, but few know all the lyrics to. Except for my dad, who knew every word. It's a hell of a story laced with historical reference and colourful allusions. The only definitive bit we know is that the 'day the music died' was 3 February 1959 when a plane crash killed rock and roll legends Buddy Holly, Ritchie Valens, and 'The Big Bopper' J.P. Richardson. Beyond that, McLean refused to further elaborate on the song's meaning and I'll be damned if that isn't the way of a true artist. That spirit tethers me to the song. Perhaps my father fancied him as the music-and-joy-delivering god-protagonist engaged in maintaining the dance that would save our mortal souls as he went toe to toe with the devil. Upon reflection the tune is at its heart a song about change. Ironically it has a feedback loop of nostalgia built into it, much as American popular culture seems to have the same specialisation. The song was written to memorialise the end of post-war America as the 60s and 70s rolled in, but really the song alludes to the new change just ahead, the uncertain (and probably dystopic) future that would come to be known as the 1980s. Yet, oddly enough change itself changes in this song. The end of post-war America was one event, the plane crash mentioned above, yet the death of the 70s was to be much slower. Drugs take a long time to clear the system. Free love dies hard. Charles Manson and his Helter Skelter race war failed, but had the Civil Rights movement succeeded? The move from Elvis to the Beatles is as traumatic as the move from the darkness of winter to the brightness of summer. This song was the epic poem of the death of my father's childhood and the painful baptism of adulthood that constituted his 1980s. It was nostalgia that could prepare him to cope with change. And here I am thinking of how 9/11 was my adulting baptism and how that was only the beginning of what has only been the constant always-already change that we live today. With each succeeding crisis, I long for the pleasant bits of the last one. Sure it was terrible, but at least I could leave the house.

McLean's song is a tragedy. I suppose nostalgia must always be. The song ends with a toast, a submissive last hurrah to the end of the age of music. Everything ages and all men must die. The whole thing is rather anticlimactic as the midpoint of the song gets so catchy and energetic, but the song ends the same way a good party ends, with awkward silence and no clue what to do next. But I feel the song begs the listener to stop listening, to go and carry on with their own life. It is fun to sing this song and recall the history it celebrates, but here is the chorus, now bugger off. As winter gives way to spring, this song doesn't so much end as await the next verse, that which is to be written by us and subsequent generations.

As I sat down to write my father's eulogy, I thought about the generational rift between him and me. I've noted it in previous writings, but it brought about a new notion that has been bubbling about in my head in the couple of months that have passed since his death. Before those gathered at his funeral, I made the comment that if I was to describe my father in one word, it was that he was authentic. I was both surprised and filled with a bit of joy as I received nods and positive reactions to the statement from the assembled mourners. Yet almost immediately following it and to this very moment I wonder what exactly that means.

I, along with many of you, have had a great deal of time to think on matters under the various movement restrictions that have sprung up in response to the COVID-19 pandemic. COVID-19 leaves a special mark on this issue of *Critical Muslim*, it is the elephant in the room sitting on the couch that's going to inform more than a lot of writing that will come in its wake. This particular issue is a snapshot of a time in history, half aware and half unaware of the global impact the virus would come to have. This particular introduction has the advantage of having been written from a place where reflection on the event can occur. Other pieces were written before things went viral, some as events unfolded in real time, so the way the virus is covered in this issue is particularly beautiful. Samia Rahman closes this issue with a thoughtful reflection from when the COVID-19 crisis unfolded through to when the UK went into total lockdown, even with the Prime Minister, a victim of the scourge himself. COVID-19 reveals and shines additional light on the postnormal state our world continues to rapidly descend into. Rahman, a sceptic of postnormal times, is faced with the reality of a world that will not be the same. Her scepticism is pushed to its limits as she resists the urge we all have for a return to normal as we are continually asked to #StayHome. She calls to mind the myriad issues we face that remain waiting on the horizon for us to resolve. She also grapples with the rest of us as the infrastructure provided by Silicon Valley rapidly moves into becoming essential in day-to-day life under Covidy times. E-commerce is the great enemy of small and independent business and the death of the working class. Yet it is the reason the global economy has not totally collapsed following this March and April of true discontent. The crisis has also nudged many of us to give unprecedented control to authority. We rely on vapid individualism to unite us in a communal effort to battle this plague. It would almost appear no one is innocent of having either bent or completely discarded our principles. Under these circumstances, how can we ever hope to be authentic?

The now infamous year 2016 was the scariest year in history, that is until 2017–2020 occurred. Donald Trump, Brexit, and the fake-news-industrial complex showed that democracy is just as susceptible to being hijacked or corrupted as any other system of governance or framework we choose to hang power on. John Sweeney writes from a world held hostage by COVID-19. Times of crisis, such as this pandemic, 'make abundantly clear, there is certainly an opportunity to promote more engagements that critically and creatively focus on navigating uncertainty, rather than attempting to "manage" risk, at a variety of scales within and beyond government.' He explores how in conjunction with the greater occurrence of postnormal times, the radical changes we are faced with in our day-to-day give us a chance to look deeper at the flaws in democracy and the way we approach AI. AI after all might be a key factor that contributes to our breaking through to the dawn after the COVID-19 crisis. Yet many issues need to be discussed, debated, and transcended before we run blindly into the futures, those that may fit our preferences and those, both knowingly and unknowingly, that may not fit what we truly desire. Even the desperate prayer for everything to go back to normal and return to business as usual should be taken with a more critical lens.

I think the quandary provoked by authenticity underlies the same discussion Rahman and Sweeney are having. As our world is brought to its knees before a microscopic element of the natural world, we find ourselves hiding in the increasingly artificial world we have created. Plugged-in, with apps and the internet of things maintaining a pseudo continuation of society we now see, upon the precipice, the loss of our natural world and even the loss of our authentic selves. Our social media feeds become the private confessional booths of the reality TV shows we always thought our interesting lives warranted being produced. Christopher Jones harkens back to an old-school (dare I say authentic) form of environmentalism that brought about the Gaia theory. Well within his rights to present a 'hate to say it, but I told you so' tone, Jones doesn't waste time pointing fingers, but instead looks to the future and presents us with four scenarios. Each one set to a different degree of how artificial we can make this planet, looking for hope in increasingly hopeless times. That is the hidden spirit of postnormal times. For when Ziauddin Sardar first spoke of it, he left us with the ground work for a solution, which can be found in creative imagination.

We can tackle the issue of the artificial by placing it in the ring with its apparent opposite, authenticity. Interestingly, both of these concepts can be framed within the fear they promote. Why do we fear the artificial? Why do we fear that we may not be authentic? Exploring these polar ideas under the lens of fear works as a sort of check and balance. Fears are never simple. Often, they can become infinitely complex when studied. For fear may be of one particular thing. Consider a spider. But often fear comes with a history, or at least a pedigree. In lieu of a proper lineage, fear can also spawn from associated ignorance, or ignorance of where it comes from, even ignorance derived directly from the very thing itself. Fear of spiders can be fear of a spider's potential abilities. But it may be a fear of something spiders represent from networks, to predatory behaviours, even to things that are just different. Unknown. Particularly in relation to two opposing fears, such as that of the artificial and that of the authentic, we may find them more intimately connected than we are comfortable with. As we investigate these two ideas, let us really test their flexibility to see if they might become something very different or even non-existent in postnormal times.

The contemporary world has no shortage of things that scare us to death, artificial and authentic play an interesting role in global anxiety. In parsing out their pedigree, we might just figure out what makes them so frightening. Right off the bat, a point of order needs to be made. The adjective 'artificial' in today's context has us all pining to add 'intelligence' to the cold lonely word. While AI is an essential talking point, which is addressed at length in this issue, there is a deeper world to explore behind the idea of artificial. There's more to it than homicidal robots. Ironically, this divisive term has some of its old roots in common with the idea of togetherness and harmony. Despite our notions of artificial being a relatively new, or even futuristic, notion, Jeremy Henzell-Thomas lays out an etymology that takes the word back to ancient times. He writes an impressively neutral journey through the branching of language that takes us to artificial intelligence, a term only coined in the 1950s, and its meaning today. Leave it to human history to take the simple concept of bringing two things together and see it out to a contemporary debate on masters and slaves. It is a strange origin for a horror story where humanity and the artificial go back and forth helping each other to be better together, until a fear is birthed that one might be better than the other. The existential problem arrives when we step back and see that the artificial and the human are both 'created things'. Our beliefs, our histories, the assurances we give ourselves to get through the day drive us to believe the only way the fear of the artificial can be overcome is via the Thunderdome. Two constructs enter. One construct exits.

In these strange and anxious times, it is important to take stock of how our fears inform and construct the narratives and the stories we tell. Since narrative can have such a strong impact on the decisions and actions we take, it is imperative to reverse engineer this process. In doing this we can critically analyse our fears and give ourselves a more sophisticated lens to face what we are afraid of. At its root, it is just a simple exercise of knowledge building, but actually it is not just another volume of 'what we know', it is going through, clearing ignorance, and if not diminishing uncertainty, definitely making clear what it is that we know we don't know.

If we don't set these pieces up correctly, we risk walking into a minefield. Just as our brains notice we are watching the cliché horror film suspense build up prior to a jump-scare, we instinctively avert our gaze. The things that scare us, often scare us so much that we are driven to abandon rationality in the hope of a quick solution. So, let us turn on the lights, check under the bed, in the wardrobe, and confront the monster directly.

Why do we fear the artificial? I believe the answer to this question is, perhaps ironically, the reason we love the artificial. It might just be better. But how can better be bad? Leave it to the hyperbolic capitalism of today to turn everything into an advertisement. Ever notice how all marketing campaigns compare their product to the 'other guys'? Our product does everything theirs does, but ours does it better, or faster, or for half the price. How might human beings look on an Amazon product comparison? Could artificial intelligence be better than human intelligence? What about cybernetic augmentation? And let's not just limit this to bodies and information, artificial is practically a fad. Maybe you don't fear the artificial, but do you fear a fake? Fake identities and fake ideologies carry half the baggage and make you fit in a crowd. Fake lives are so much easier to manage, no?

I would argue that the fear and love of the artificial is driven by a survival vestige that one might hope we would have been able to transcend by this point. This instinct derives from the primal fear of the loss of supremacy. Nobody wants to be left behind. This is why each period of human existence is thought to be the best it had ever been. This fear drives progress and pushes us to be better, which is not a bad thing. But as the tragedy of the commons goes, all good things can be abused. This same drive propels the myth of race, fundamentally the desire to be better than the Other. While we squabble over which geographical origin point, glorified god, or skin pigment concentration makes us better than them, a truly new entity sits on the horizon ready to upend the whole history. Unifying us all in our mutual obsolescence.

And the few who can see the torch in the cave for what it really is, what do they do? They construct more fake things. There's the tragic flaw of the human race. We are master tool users and so what do we do when threatened? We build more tools of course. So, we find ourselves in a farce of building tools to subdue other tools. But really, colonialism and globalisation were perfect practice for this final asinine battle. But perhaps there are places where one most definitely could not fake it until they make it. Universal truths, such as religion. Yet, as Abdelwahab El-Affendi explains, religion becomes not only a great locus of mimicry, it also tends to be a place where the art of fakery is perfected. 'Religion should be the last place fakery should thrive. After all, God knows everything. There is no place to hide from Him. If you fake it, He would know.' But it is this very assumption which shakers and movers throughout history have hidden behind as they played out their nefarious games. Religion, often a unifying symbol of humanity and love is used to divide, spread hate, and even pit others against each other in never ending cycles of evil and destruction. In the realm of the artificial, it would appear nothing is sacred. When we realise the weapons we build can be used against us, we turn to thought. We construct narratives, fake histories, and propaganda to keep those endorphins flowing so we can sleep at night as we set the stage for our own Armageddon. Populism is cranked into hyperdrive and, fearing the robot overlord poised to overtake us, we double down on our own supremacy. We tell stories of how British was always British. We ask people to speak American. We say, if it's European, it must be better. We ignore any skeletons we unearth when making the next luxury apartment complex. We cast any alternative as fake news. Even pitted against our own snuffing from existence, united in that truth, we cling to the differences because that story is how we keep the killer robots at bay. Unless we can use those killer robots to further racial supremacy over an Other. Even if a more multicultural and pluralistic world may, in fact, be better, we ignore it for fear of having lost that supremacy.

Spinning lies for survival, or at least the survival of supremacy, is all too familiar in the realm of scientific knowledge. James Brooks tracks the intoxication of science news by PR departments painting scientific insights as sexy propaganda. The resulting offspring are unrealistic expectations and bogus public promises. 'Fake news starts with a lie and strives to make it credible; science PR takes a genuine event and extrapolates it to fantastical end-points.' Perception and reality are torn asunder and no one can verify what is true. Myths are advanced, such as scientific progress is always good, alongside problematic realities, such as scientific progress both warns of and simultaneously creates climate change. Brooks rests his hope on this having to eventually reach a breaking point. But will it happen soon enough for us to change our ways?

Despite the fact that this fear can be taken to fanatical lengths and reveal motivation for some evil acts, it is not necessarily a shameful fear. Particularly coupled with the fact that most films about AI and robots in the future end with human subjugation or humans being such horribly flawed creatures that their annihilation is actually in their own moral self-interest. The seriousness of this fear resides in whether or not the stakes are the end of the human race, which, all other opinions aside, I think most agree would be at least tragic. The question we must ask is if coexistence is possible. And this question, to many is the defining question not just concerning the discussion of the artificial, but with application to various social ills.

As our mechanistic boogie man comes out from the shadows of nightmare into reality, instead of considering whether or not we might be able to cope with and live parallel to the artificial, we about face and turn to the mirror. In our reflection, we hope to find that one thing that separates us from the monster, the authentically human and definitely non-monster part of us. Heaven forbid we become the monster. Is that really the worst thing that could happen? And is authenticity all it's cracked up to be?

When you really look at the conceptualisation behind the word authentic, it is incredibly problematic. But how? Well, it would appear at face value that everyone wants to be authentic. Right? Since nobody wants to be fake. Right? Well, putting authenticity up against artificial is a tough competition. While artificial dates back to ancient times. Authenticity is rather a new idea. Yet, they both have a pervasive nature that allows them to infect ideas before and after their indoctrination into popular parlance. Interestingly, authenticity is the estranged half-brother of individualism. As the entire history of Western philosophy is more or less a story of 'how to deal with the Other', artificial was there from the start. As early thought was largely characterised by common thought, the individual was not required for there to be someone outside of the tribe and thus different. It was not until we started asking 'what am I?' Suddenly, 'what am I' was accompanied by the fear that I may not be authentically what I *ought* to be.

This was not the concern of a strictly communalist worldview as there is reinforcement from your network and any challenges from the outside must obviously be wrong or artificial. Once the Pandora's box of individualism is open, you can't help but see the I, even if you think communal worldviews are groovy. Because then you suddenly have such problematic thoughts as, am I being authentically a part of the greater whole. This sounds oddly familiar to fundamentalist arguments for the infallibility of capitalism. As long as we all act selfishly in our own self-interest, being unified in that objective, we magically, selfishly act in the common good. Let's just hope we are all using the same moral glue to hold that flimsy argument together.

The concept of authenticity has continued to muck things up as we progress through human history. Jean Jacques-Rousseau got the ball rolling in speaking on authenticity as a realisation produced through introspection. A process where we discover our innermost motivations. These motivations come in conflict with external or public motivations. In public discourse we negotiate our inner motives with the motives outside of us in a process that appears to make us less authentic. So, in public we become artificial. Oh, what fun Rousseau would have had with social media! This equating of authenticity with, essentially, 'human nature' destines the concept to being eaten alive by the eighteenth and early nineteenth century thinkers. Kierkegaard brings the idea back into the light. Because of the tragedy of the commons, if we try to find authenticity in ourselves alone, we are doomed to despair as society runs rampant, forcing us into horrid inauthenticity. Keeping authenticity a relational matter, instead of it being a relation of ourselves into ourselves, he argues that we should see ourselves in relation to God to find authenticity. But bringing it to God wasn't the easiest thing to swallow in the rapidly secularising Europe of the nineteenth and twentieth centuries. Enter Martin Heidegger who gives us one of the better philosophical treatments of authenticity.

In his magnum opus *Being and Time*, Heidegger relates authentic being to time. The word authenticity actually comes from one of Heidegger's many invented words, *Eigentlichkeit*. Roughly the word translates to something that is truly my own. This implies that authenticity is something that we have to take ownership over. Thus, authenticity requires action and the agency to go out and get it. The authentic, bringing it back to time, is the relation between where we are, which encompasses where we came from, and where we can potentially go. For Heidegger, the inauthentic is the default setting of the world. We, as being-in-the-world, act and so take ownership of our being, all of this is a sort of negotiation with the self, the world, and even Others. Both as a descriptor and normative base, we authenticate the world in our actions. Here we can unify our fear of being inauthentic and our fear of the artificial. By reflecting and acting in a shared world we authenticate, which is artificial as it is a construction, but if we see that as our human nature, sprinkle in some religion and ethics, maybe we can live together on this Earth without this fear of no longer being supreme? Yet, as it so happened, one of Heidegger's first acts after publishing *Being and Time* was to join the Nazi Party. Oops, but that doesn't mean we can't do better.

Although the pursuit of authenticity seems thus far to be a pretty treacherous journey, I think seeing it as a negotiation might make it an important tool for navigating postnormal times. But we mustn't lose sight of the fact that postnormal times are problematic times. And if we are to accept Heidegger's examination of authenticity, it creates a serious predicament for our scrutinising artificial and authenticity. These two fear harbingers seem to collide, and in their derailment, lose their meaning. And the clean-up becomes a very confusing mess. Yet not entirely foreign under the purview of postnormal times. Recall complexity, chaos, and contradictions. These among the other tenets of postnormal times need to be accounted for as we go about authenticating the world. I believe contradictions are key here.

To be authentic does not mean to be free from contradiction. That may not be possible in the contemporary world. After all, it is brought to the forefront of our minds by the COVID-19 pandemic. We, as humans, are complex, and so simple solutions will not do. This is why we have to be weary of nostalgia. It can lead us towards a new type of romanticism that Liam Mayo warns us about in his scathing criticism of modernity. He notes how the modern period set in motion an artificialisation that does not turn back unmotivated. It replaces the old world in cold, calculated steel and drains essential elements of what it is to be human as modernity eats its own tale attempting to be authentic. The world rendered is unable to cope with change, let alone the changing change of postnormal times. This is the internal problem of Don McLean's song. He sings of how America longs for 'old time' values yet partakes in the radical freedom of the 1970s. The simple slogan, 'Make America Great Again' carries on the American dream of having the cake and getting to eat it as well. This simplistic lens of historical investigation is doomed to fail on launch. As Heidegger suggests, the process of authenticating ourselves needs be a negotiation between the past and what may come. This will result in contradictions. It is in transcending these contradictions that we find the authenticity we so desire. And it's a construct. It's artificial, but it is something many have argued that only humans can do. The authentic is artificial. Kint is Söze.

In a touching tribute, Hassan Mahamdallie challenges us to see people beyond the pictures that remain after they have passed. Defining physical features, skin colour, hair, and even the expressions we flash all give us a snapshot of a reality. 'In reality,' Mahamdallie writes, 'Maureen exists not in some narrow trickle of nativist exclusivity, but as a unique combine in a churning current of working-class identities, forever mixing, merging and transforming, often below the surface, mostly unremarked upon and unrecognised, but no less real for all that.' It is an actuality that may have existed but upon reflection is now artificial as in the eye of the beholder, we lose sense of the great complexity that our fellow human beings are. Our lives are increasingly controlled by algorithms which simplify our complexity to 'likes' and other inputs. Blips of data. And with that they do a remarkable job of predicting our temporary nominal needs, but I think they will find themselves hard pressed to comprehend the complexity of humanity, let alone mimic or recreate it.

Yet we lean into this. In the same breath we buy our own artificialisation in the inauthentic of double lives and cry out protest against it. This comes in the form of our alter cyber egos or even the persons we find ourselves playing in public versus in private. And when we are motivated to reconsider it all, the two ideas, artificial and authentic are too contradictory to negotiate. And don't the alternative sound so much nicer? This brings to mind the 1991 R.E.M. song 'Shiny Happy People'. This song is one of the rare few that gains a great deal of depth through its music video. The song on its own is pretty indistinguishable from the general dissonance of the happy-go-lucky peace-time 1990s Western world. Although, maybe it's just a bit too giddy. And you'd be wise to look into it. The music video seems to perpetuate your initial feelings on the song as the band R.E.M. sing 'gold and silver shine!', dancing in a deranged fashion in front of a sequence of hand-drawn landscapes. The over-the-top sincerity of the jovial jam is only made more ridiculous by the anarchy that was 90s Western fashion. But then, suddenly the song pauses, and the beat becomes sober and the video focuses on the background, which was always fake, but now all the more so as we are shown the sad looking old man, pedalling a bicycle device that is causing the landscapes to rotate. Happiness it would appear is the construct of efficient unhappy labour. Having taken in a huge gulp of reality, instantaneously the music speeds back up and the band is joined by a random and diverse crowd that dances with them for several stanzas making sure to keep the act up, no need to focus on the reality. We can all just be 'shiny happy people holding hands'. Though in times of COVID-19, we may want to keep the hand holding to a strict minimum.

Perhaps the greatest tragedy is that such contradictions trade fear for comedy. After all, Karl Marx said we should agree with Hegel on the duplicate repetition of history, 'the first time as tragedy, second as farce'. But which one are we on? Which one is the real one? Either way, these conflicts lack the attention they drastically need. And despite the fact that most people are walking contradictions, it seems to be a severe minority who embrace it and transcend the deference. Persons of contradiction are rarely appreciated, let alone understood. The world seems to demand too much structure and logic, but now as we wait in our isolations, we see all of that beginning to crumble.

What we need most is a change of perspective. We live multiple lives. Built realities and realised fantasies. Our constructs have become our crutch in the natural world. COVID-19 run rampant; we may try to see how we can continue on in our own negotiated authentic way through the new avenues provided by technology or even those brought about by embracing a new perspective or idea. The lines between what is authentic and what is artificial are blurring, so why not embrace this strange change. And whether you are reading this in confinement or the fresh, free air of public, we can take comfort as we are all writing the next verse of Don McLean's song. Maybe the music can live again and we can move beyond the fake. And maybe for the first time, be something truly real.

ARTIFICIAL DEFINED

Jeremy Henzell-Thomas

The word *artificial,* like many other words, is a mixed bag, best conceived of as a semantic continuum encompassing positive, neutral and negative connotations. An exploration of the etymology and historical development of the usage of the word can greatly increase our understanding of its more complex nuances, ambiguities and shifts in meaning and, therefore, prevent us from falling into prescriptive, dogmatic or monolithic conceptions which confine it within a single meaning.

In discussing Artificial Intelligence (AI), the term coined in 1956, we may be tempted to paraphrase the 'Four legs good, two legs bad' refrain of George Orwell's *Animal Farm* as 'Natural good, artificial bad' especially in the light of the fears of the late Stephen Hawking that AI 'could spell the end of the human race.' Speaking at MIT in 2014, Tesla and SpaceX leader and innovator Elon Musk, though hardly a technological pessimist, also called AI humanity's 'biggest existential threat' and compared it to 'summoning the demon'. We will return to such fears and reservations about 'transhumanism' and 'dehumanisation' in due course, for they are shared to a varying degree by so many who are justifiably concerned about the future of humanity, but I first want to anchor the subject in the actual word *artificial* by excavating its roots.

Going back as far as possible to its earliest known (or hypothetical) roots, the word *artificial* comes from Indo-European *ar-* + *dhe-*. The root *ar-* had the sense of 'joining' or 'fitting together', very much like the modern sense of an orderly, congruent and aesthetically pleasing arrangement of parts, as in its Greek derivative *harmonia*. The root *dhe-* had the sense of 'to set down, put, make, shape' (as in its derivative *thesis* and all its relatives, for example, *hypothesis, prosthesis, synthesis, thesaurus).* These senses come through in its Latin derivatives: *artificialis* 'of or belonging to art', from *artificium* 'a work of art; skill; theory, system,' from *artifex* 'craftsman, artist, master of an art', from *ars* 'skill, art' + *-fex* 'maker', from *facere* 'to do, make'. The original sense of the 'skill' required to 'join things together' is retained in the English word *artisan*.

Further etymological excavation reveals that the *ar*- root is not only the source of Greek *harmonia* but also produced the Greek word *areté*, which is usually translated as 'virtue' although it is not a specifically moral term. It was used to refer not only to human skills but also to inanimate objects, natural substances and domestic animals. A good knife had the virtue (*areté*) of being able to cut well 'by virtue of' its sharpness. The term denoted any sort of excellence, distinctive power, capacity, skill or merit, rather like Latin *virtus,* which, like the Greek, also had the sense of bravery and strength. The Italian word *virtuoso* preserves the sense of exceptional skill. The connotation of excellence in the word *areté* also comes through in the related word *aristos,* 'fittest, best'.

Homer often associates *areté* with courage, but more often with effectiveness. The person of *areté* uses all their faculties to achieve their objectives, often in the face of difficult circumstances, hardship or danger. One heroic model is Odysseus, not only brave and eloquent, but also wily, shrewd and resourceful, with the practical intelligence and wit (in the sense of quick thinking) of the astute tactician able to use a cunning ruse to win the day.

Although the Latin word *virtus* comes from *vir*, 'man' (source of *virility* or manliness), itself originally from the Indo-European base *wi-ro*, 'man', Homer uses the word *areté* to describe not only male Greek and Trojan heroes but also female figures, such as Penelope, the wife of Odysseus, who embodies *areté* by showing how misfortune and sorrow can be stoically endured to an excellent degree. Such is the virtue of *sabr* (patient endurance) in Islamic tradition, in the same way as the aesthetic sense of refinement the Greeks also associated with *areté* converges at one level with that of Arabic *ihsan*, 'doing what is good and beautiful', behaving in an excellent manner. In Islamic ethics and spirituality, *ihsan* embraces the aesthetic, moral and spiritual dimensions of a beautiful and virtuous character (*akhlaq* and *adab*). In the same way, the concept of 'beauty' expressed by the word *husn* transcends what is merely decorative in appearance and encompasses not only the aesthetic sense of beauty in its homage to the 'due measure and proportion' with which all of creation is endowed, but also the intimate equation between what is beautiful and what is good. In this sense, great art always transcends artifice.

In the original Greek of the New Testament, *areté* is included in the list of virtues for cultivation in Christian moral development, and is associated primarily with the moral excellence of Jesus. It figures in the celebrated 'Admonition of Paul' in *Philippians* 4:8: 'Finally, brethren, whatever is true, whatever is honourable, whatever is just, whatever is pure, whatever is lovely, whatever is gracious, if there is any excellence (*areté*), if there is anything worthy of praise, think on these things.'

While in modern English, usage of the word *artificial* can still carry an essentially neutral sense of simply being caused or produced by human agency (e.g. social, political, medical, nutritional) it has progressively taken on some ambiguous and even negative connotations. The sense of 'made by man, contrived by human skill and labour' (from the early fifteenth century) could also carry the implication of 'unnatural, lacking in spontaneity'. From the sixteenth century it could refer to anything made in imitation, or as a substitute for, what is natural. The meaning 'full of affectation, insincere' is from the 1590s and 'fictitious, not genuine, sham' from the 1640s.

A striking embodiment of the connotation of insincerity is the Artificial Smile (also called Pretend Smile, Fake Smile, Phony Smile, or False Smile). The Body Language Project describes this as 'a feigned smile where the orbicularis oculi muscles surrounding the eyes play no part and the lips are only stretched across the face with the help of the zygomatic muscles surrounding the mouth. The tell-tale cue in the fake smile is the lack of crow's feet. The teeth are often bared, with a tense jaw and the lips show asymmetry.' Such a fake smile, where the eyes play no part, shows others that one is not sincerely expressing approval or happiness. It is used to appear cooperative and to appease others in a polite way, whilst showing that one is not really on board with another person or their ideas.

The negative connotations of *artificial* come through unambiguously in the related word *artifice*.' Although this originally meant something made with technical skill (an 'artefact') it has come to mean 'artfulness' in its negative sense of a clever trick, cunning ruse, tactical manoeuvre, ploy or stratagem. The same ambiguity can be found in the word *fabrication*, which can mean either something man-made or a lie. There is a revealing semantic correspondence here with the word *craft* in English. This originally meant 'strength' or 'power' in Germanic, but it also developed the additional sense of 'skill' in Old English, probably because of the way in which skill (as in the forging of weapons) was an obvious source of power. The pejorative sense of 'crafty' as deviously 'artful' or 'cunning' may have arisen from the influence of the church in rejecting any association of power with pre-Christian pagan culture. 'The Craft' can be used to refer to sorcery, as much as to the society of Freemasons. In the same way, the word *cunning* itself did not always mean 'skilfully deceitful' (as in the wiles of the devil), but simply meant 'knowledge' or 'ability', as preserved in the words *can* and *canny,* or Scots *ken.*

The varying connotations of *artificial* are easily illustrated in modern usage. At the positive end of the continuum, artificial replacements (prostheses) for limbs and joints developed in orthopaedic surgery have been a godsend to countless disabled people. They are among the world's truly great inventions. I speak from experience, having had a hemiarthroplasty to replace my upper left arm after a recent accident. I remember the joy my mother expressed at the age of 80 when knee replacements enabled her to return to active work in the garden she so loved, and the relief experienced by my daughter when she had hip replacements as a young woman as a result of congenital hip dislocation that caused her severe pain and progressive immobility. Prosthetic arms and hands have now advanced to the point where they give individual control of all five fingers. In the same way, the transformational benefits of artificial hearing aids, spectacles and dentures can hardly be disputed. Dentures used to be called false teeth, and it's interesting to note that the word 'false' carries no negative connotation in this context.

AI will also bring numerous other medical benefits. Major developments are being hailed in almost daily reports. Recently, news came through of how an AI algorithm was used to discern a powerful antibiotic (halicin) that kills some of the most dangerous antibiotic-resistant strains of bacteria in the world. These include Acinetobacter baumannii and Enterobacteriaceae, two of the three high-priority pathogens that the World Health Organization ranks as 'critical' for new antibiotics to target. Another example of the major impact of AI on healthcare is the better detection of cancer through improved radiology. A recent article in *The*

Lancet reports that the performance level of an AI algorithm in detecting breast cancer on mammograms was significantly higher and much faster than that of radiologists without AI assistance.

When it comes to complex human organs, artificial replacements are much more elusive. An artificial replacement for the heart remains a long-sought 'holy grail' of modern medicine. The demand for organs always greatly exceeds supply, so a functional synthetic heart would be a boon by reducing the need for heart transplants. The heart, however, is not merely a pump, and its subtleties defy straightforward emulation with synthetic materials and power supplies. Severe foreign-body rejection limited the lifespan of early human recipients to hours or days. A new concept of an artificial heart was presented in *the Journal of Artificial Organs* in 2017 by Nicholas Cohr and colleagues. This 'soft artificial heart' (SAH) was created from silicone with the help of 3D printing technology. The goal was to develop an artificial heart that imitates the human heart as closely as possible in form and function. This sounds promising, but the stark reality is that this SAH prototype only manages to achieve 3000 beats in a hybrid mock circulation machine. The working life of a more recent Cohrs prototype (replacing silicone with various polymers) was still limited, according to reports in early 2018, with that model providing a useful life of one million heartbeats, or about ten days in a human body. Since then, Cohrs and his team have been striving to develop a model that would last up to fifteen years, but Cohrs admits that it cannot be predicted when a working heart which fulfils all requirements and is ready for implantation would be available.

As for artificial brains, in an article in *Futurism,* Lou Del Bello proclaims that 'Scientists Are Closer to Making Artificial Brains That Operate Like Ours Do.' He claims that a new superconducting switch could soon empower computers to make decisions in much the same the way we do, essentially turning them into artificial brains. The switch 'learns' by processing incoming electrical signals and generating appropriate output signals, and this is held to mirror the function of biological synapses in the brain which allow neurons to communicate with each other. What is more, the performance of this synthetic switch surpasses its biological counterpart, using much less energy than our brains and firing signals much faster at one billion times per second, in comparison to fifty times per second for natural synapses. Researchers are confident that the new artificial synapse may eventually power a new generation of artificial brains capable of improving on the current capabilities of AI systems. This enhanced capacity would include the ability to deal with ethical conundrums that impinge on decision-making. For example, the development of driverless cars needs to factor in the imperative for the AI driver to resolve the moral dilemma of having to decide whether to prioritise the safety of its own passengers or others who might be involved in a collision. Such challenges highlight only too clearly how far there is to go before an artificial brain is capable, if ever, of encompassing the full range of faculties residing in the human brain. Just as the heart is much more than a mechanical pump, so the brain should not be reduced to a mere calculating machine.

It would be useful at this point to consider other instances of the 'artificial' that carry ambivalent implications with a varying degree of balance between pros and cons. Take the practice of 'artificial insemination' (first recorded in the lexicon in 1894). This common practice in animal breeding and a fertility treatment for humans has brought many obvious benefits, although it has to be said that the rise of dependency on assisted reproductive technology (ARTs) also has some potentially negative social implications, including the pressure placed on couples to conceive. Where parenthood is culturally mandatory, childlessness becomes socially unacceptable.

As in the case of ARTs, it is not easy to assess the extent to which the benefits of artificial aids are offset by negative consequences. Artificial lighting is a case in point. Despite its numerous benefits, it is exerting pervasive, long-term stress on ecosystems, from coasts to farmland to urban waterways, many of which are already suffering from other, more well-known forms of pollution. As *Solarspot* warns, the constant glare of artificial lighting can have adverse effects on physical and mental health. Ninety percent of our light sources now use LED (light-emitting diode) lighting, and this includes a blue spectrum that is more intense than it is in natural sunlight. The blue light emitted at peak emission from smartphones, tablets and computers can disrupt natural sleeping and waking patterns (the circadian rhythm). Exposure to too much artificial light also can have a negative effect on memory and lead to a build-up of neurotoxins, with increased risk of breast and prostate cancer. It can also degrade eyesight through macular degeneration not only in older people but also in children.

Varying degrees of pros and cons are also associated with such things as artificial sweeteners, flavourings and colourings. In the US, the Food and Drug Administration (FDA) have approved six artificial sweeteners – saccharin, acesulfame, aspartame, neotame, sucralose and stevia – all of which help to combat obesity, metabolic syndrome, and diabetes (all risk factors for heart disease). Nevertheless, overstimulation of sugar receptors from frequent use of these hyper-intense sweeteners may limit tolerance for more complex tastes and can make you shun healthy, filling, and highly nutritious foods while consuming more artificially flavoured foods with less nutritional value. Participants in one heart study who drank more than twenty-one diet drinks per week were twice as likely to become overweight or obese as those who didn't drink diet soda.

As for artificial flavourings and colourings, defenders claim that they must pass strict safety testing, but there is growing concern about their potential health risks, and not only amongst 'organic purists.' In particular, the effect on children's development and behaviour is a topic of ongoing discussion. The health risks related to the consumption of artificial food additives include allergic reactions such as anaphylaxis, food hypersensitivity, and the worsening of asthmatic symptoms. Azo-dyes, a group of food colourings commonly used to add bright colours to edible products, contain chemical substances that when metabolised by intestinal bacteria may become potentially carcinogenic. As is so often the case, the gravity of such risks is difficult to evaluate because any toxic effects depend on the amount of colouring ingested, which typically is of negligible amount, and in any case the azo-dyes also tend to be poorly absorbed into the blood stream. Concern has also been raised as to a possible link between food additives and neurological development, including attention deficit hyperactivity disorder (ADHD) in children, although no conclusive evidence had been found to date.

This brings us to Artificial Intelligence. As might be expected, there is a wide divergence in perceptions of its benefits and risks. On the plus side, as an article for World Economic Forum by Julia Bossmann claims, 'intelligent machine systems are transforming our lives for the better, optimising logistics, detecting fraud, composing art, conducting research, providing translations' and so on. She confidently predicts that 'as these systems become more capable, our world becomes more efficient and consequently richer.' On the minus side, we have doom-laden prophecies of a dystopian future, or even the extinction of humanity. It is likely that most people would occupy the middle ground in a broad continuum of views, neither being taken in by a utopian vision of AI as a panacea to increase efficiency and reduce the ever-increasing complexity of modern life, nor persuaded by the fearful predictions of Stephen Hawking and Elon Musk. After all, Hawking's relationship with AI was far more complex than the oft-cited soundbite that it could 'spell the end of the human race.' As Ana Santos Rutschman, associate professor with the Center for Health Law Studies at Saint Louis University, explains, 'the deep concerns he expressed were about superhuman AI, the point at which AI systems not only replicate human intelligence processes, but also keep expanding them – a stage that is at best decades away, if it ever happens at all.' The fact that we need to avoid a one-sided evaluation of AI is pointedly highlighted by the irony that, as Rutschman notes, Hawking's very ability to communicate his thoughts and feelings depended on basic AI technology.

The 'One Hundred Year Study on Artificial Intelligence' launched by Stanford University in 2014, highlighted various concerns, but so far it has identified no evidence that AI will pose any imminent threat to humankind. The 'top nine ethical concerns' that 'keep AI experts up at night' identified by the World Economic Forum include Unemployment (What happens after the end of jobs?), Humanity (How do machines affect our behaviour and interaction?), and Singularity (How do we stay in control of a complex intelligent system?). There is also increasing concern about the threat of 'data colonialism', by which major world powers might exert domination over the less powerful, and enact total surveillance arising from the monitoring of every aspect of a citizen's life to a degree that previous totalitarian regimes could only dream of. In 1978, Zbigniew Brzezinski was already describing the 'technotronic era' as one involving the gradual appearance of a stringently controlled society, 'dominated by an elite, unrestrained by traditional values', with the technological means to impose almost continuous surveillance over every citizen. Advances in facial recognition technology make such mass surveillance even more attainable, although politicians and police forces are quick to justify this technology on the grounds that it improves public safety by reducing crime.

At the World Economic Forum (WEF) in Davos in January 2020, Sundar Pichai, CEO of Alphabet Inc. (one of the world's biggest companies valued at $1 trillion) and its subsidiary Google LLC, stated that AI 'has tremendous, positive sides to it, but is has real negative consequences.' His message, however, was mainly upbeat. Asked what kept him awake at night, Pichai replied, 'I worry that we turn our backs on technology. I worry when people do that they get left behind. It is our duty to drive this growth in an inclusive way.' History shows, however, that advances in technology do leave people behind. The Luddites, the nineteenth century radical faction which destroyed textile machinery as a form of protest against the replacement of their skills by machines, did not manage to prevent the rapid expansion of the 'dark satanic mills' which so appalled William Blake as a sign of the social, moral and spiritual devastation wrought by the industrial revolution. Bringing the same narrative of the 'left behind' up to date, Jean Schradie's very recent study, *The Revolution That Wasn't: How Digital Activism Favors Conservatives* unearths the way in which digital technology, far from being the democratising and levelling force that it was expected to be, has actually become another weapon in the arsenal of the wealthy and powerful. This is because digital platforms like Google and Facebook work better for top-down, well-funded, well-organised movements which favour conservatives rather than liberal, progressive or leftist groups.

So, should we be scared of artificial intelligence? The futurist, Bernard Marr, identifies what he considers the six greatest risks relating to AI that we ought to be thinking about. The first is the development of autonomous weapons with a mind of their own, which, once deployed, will likely be difficult to dismantle or combat. The second is AI's power for social manipulation, as was all too evident in the way Cambridge Analytica misused the data from fifty million Facebook users to try to sway the outcome of the 2016 U.S. presidential election and the U.K.'s Brexit referendum. 'By spreading propaganda to individuals identified through algorithms and personal data, AI can target them and spread whatever information they like, fact or fiction.' Thirdly, there is the risk of invasion of privacy and social oppression that I have already discussed in relation to the exponential growth in surveillance capability through ubiquitous cameras and facial recognition algorithms. Fourthly, humans and machines may find that they are not on the same page when it comes to following instructions. For example, an AI may not be concerned with the interests of roadway regulations or public safety in fulfilling a request to get a passenger from point A to point B in the quickest possible amount of time. Accidents abound over this simple disorder in hierarchy of interests. The fifth danger identified by Marr is 'discrimination' based on the vast amount of personal information that machines can collect, track and analyse about individuals and therefore use against them (as, for example, in denying them employment or other opportunities). The sixth is the misuse of AI for dangerous or malicious purposes.

The website CBInsights goes further, surveying the predictions of fifty-two experts on 'How AI will go out of control.' One of them, Dr. Oren Etzioni, Chief Executive of the Allen Institute for Artificial Intelligence, believes that it will be a challenge to build 'common sense' into AI systems, where it is not even a guarantee in human beings. Science and technology writer, Clive Thompson, agrees, pointing out that the years spent feeding neural nets vast amounts of data has produced 'crazy-smart' machines, but they have absolutely no 'common sense' and 'just don't appear to work the way human brains do.' For a start, they're insatiably data-hungry, requiring thousands or millions of examples to learn from. Worse, you have to start from scratch each time you want a neural net to recognise a new type of item. 'A neural net trained to recognise only canaries isn't of any use in recognising, say, birdsong or human speech.' Thompson cites Gary Marcus, a professor of psychology and neuroscience at New York University, who is convinced that AI 'will never produce generalised intelligence, because truly humanlike intelligence isn't just pattern recognition.' There are intractable limitations to 'deep learning', such as 'visual-recognition systems that can be easily fooled by changing a few inputs, making a deep-learning model think a turtle is a gun.' As Marcus uses the example of how children come to learn the world. Their education does not require the review of massive quantities of data to recognise one object. Rather they generalise, building the world out of commonalities. He explains how a tractor can be encountered as being somewhat like a car and from that simple move, a knowledge of the world can be constructed.

Another way of conceptualising this issue is to recognise the importance of 'top-down processing' in human comprehension. This is the kind of 'fast thinking' that has obvious survival benefits in enabling us to use our existing knowledge to generate likely expectations and inferences. Without the rapid automatic routines generated by top-down processing we would not be able to function in the world, for we would have to analyse everything laboriously from the bottom-up as if we were encountering it for the first time.

Another of the fifty-two sceptics on CBInsights, Joanna Bryson, an AI researcher at the University of Bath, is concerned about the danger of AI being contaminated by unconscious bias, including stereotypes, in the underlying data. Rana el Kaliouby, the co-founder and CEO of Affectiva, which develops emotion recognition technology, believes that social and emotional intelligence have not been prioritised enough in the AI field which has traditionally been focused on computational intelligence. Martyn Thomas, British consultant and software engineer, boils it all down to one pre-eminent risk, claiming that 'human error, not artificial intelligence, poses the greatest threat'. The risk facing humanity, he says, 'comes not from malevolent machines but from incompetent programmers.'

The inventory of possible risks can be continually expanded, but let us move on to what for many of us is the heart of the matter, eloquently expressed by Kabir Helminski in 'The Spiritual Challenge of Artificial Intelligence, Trans-Humanism, and the Post-Human World.' The word 'Trans-Humanism' (abbreviated as H+ or h+) refers to the movement that aims to transform the human condition and create 'post-human' beings through technologies that are designed to overcome what trans-humanists see as ingrained human limitations, especially by 'improving' human intellect and physiology. As Helminski comments, 'Trans-humanism is not merely some geeky tech subculture, not a futuristic daydream, but a pervasive phenomenon that is already impacting our humanness itself. We're talking about the merging of human beings with technology, and not just at the physical level, but possibly a merging that encroaches upon the most intimate dimensions of the soul.' This is the likely destination if the 'qualitative dimension of human experience' is overshadowed by 'the ideology of Dataism, the belief that all entities and processes are fundamentally algorithms.'

Helminski is with those who are concerned about the escalating concentration of power and influence in media conglomerates and wary of the surveillance state with its history of indoctrination and mind control. He warns that humanity is in danger of being reduced to an impoverished level of existence where it may forfeit its awareness of the full range of reality and confine itself in a mental box. Algorithms, no matter how sophisticated, are still applicable only within the box, and tell us nothing about what lies beyond it. In the face of this blinkered reductionism, our task is to develop our humanness through the awakening of the full range of our innate human faculties. The sense of 'development' here reflects the original meaning of the Old French *des-voloper*, 'to unwrap, unveil'. Our destiny as human beings is surely not to reach for a bogus level of transcendence 'by downloading the data of memory into super-computing cyborg flesh, or merging our brains with the simulated reality of an oncoming singularity' but 'to align and harmonise ourselves with the cosmological order, and in the end to upload our souls into eternity.'

The emergence of AI should, above all, alert us to our primary duty to awaken and nurture the totality of our human faculties. The starting point for this needs to be an understanding of the multi-layered and multi-faceted semantic universe encompassed by the word *intelligence*, in the same way as the heart is much more than a mechanical pump, 'so the brain should not be reduced to a mere calculating machine.'

This contention can be supported in various traditions of psychology, philosophy, ethics and spirituality. In Islamic tradition, the 'intellect' (*'aql*) encompasses not only the language-based rational and deliberative faculty (Latin *ratio*, Greek *dianoia*) but also the higher organ of moral and spiritual intelligence and insight (*intellectus, nous*). One very appropriate translation of the term *'aql* in its higher sense is 'Mind-Heart'. In a detailed study of the concept of *'aql*, professor of Islamic studies, Karim Douglas Crow, has also noted the re-appearance of the term 'wisdom' in recent descriptions of human intelligence to connote 'a combination of social and moral intelligence, that blend of knowledge and understanding within one's being manifested in personal integrity, conscience, and effective behaviour.' He concludes that one of the key components of the concept of 'intelligence' expressed by the term *'aql* is 'ethical-spiritual'.

The full scope of intelligence also goes far beyond what Guy Claxton, director of the Research Programme of Culture and Learning in Organisations (CLIO), has labelled as 'd-mode' (deliberation mode), that mode of thinking based on reason and logic. Seeking clarity and precision through literal and explicit language, it neither likes nor values confusion or ambiguity and works best when tackling problems which can be treated as an assemblage of nameable parts and are therefore accessible to the function of language in atomising, segmenting and analysing. Claxton himself points out that the growing dissatisfaction with the assumption that d-mode is the be-all and end-all of human cognition is reflected in various alternative approaches to the notion of intelligence. Modern advances in the field of cognitive psychology question the conventional reduction of human intelligence to a single unitary or g factor for 'general intelligence' as measured by IQ tests, and point instead to 'multiple intelligences'. Developmental Psychologist, Howard Gardner, identifies seven of these: linguistic, visual-spatial, logico-mathematical, body-kinesthetic, musical-rhythmic, interpersonal and intrapersonal. Daniel Goleman, a science journalist, has also introduced the influential concept of 'emotional intelligence', and more recently that of 'ecological intelligence'. Of importance too is, Cornell University professor of human development, Robert Sternberg's triarchic theory of intelligence, which proposes three essential components: practical intelligence, creative intelligence, and analytical intelligence, and I have already drawn attention to the faculty of 'common sense' that Clive Thompson finds absent in AI. One might add to these alternative approaches the work of scientists such as F. David Peat who has synthesised anthropology, history, linguistics, metaphysics, cosmology and even quantum theory to describe the way in which the worldviews and indigenous teachings of traditional peoples differ profoundly from the way of seeing the world embedded in us by linear Western science.

Rumi refers to the discursive intellect as the 'husk' and the higher intellect (or, in his terms, 'the Intellect of the intellect') as the 'kernel', the 'knowing heart', the organ of moral and spiritual intelligence. In the tradition of Orthodox Christianity (Hesychasm) this is the transcendent

Intellect, the supreme human faculty, through which man is capable of the recognition of *Reality* or knowledge of God. Dwelling in the depth of the soul, it constitutes the innermost aspect of the *Heart*, the organ of contemplation, which alone can reach to the inner essence or principles (*logoi*) of created things by means of direct apprehension or spiritual perception.

We also need to include 'imagination' in our enlarged inventory of human faculties. Imagination is the ability to form images or pictures in the mind, or think of new ideas. It is the faculty that enables us to tell stories, write novels, to visualise and envisage, and also to envision the future. And the new buzz word is to 're-imagine', to revise or reform an outdated view of the world, continually update our guiding myths and stories about ourselves, our societies and the wider world. The higher octave of the 'imagination' is the spiritual imagination, or the 'creative imagination' as described in such depth by Ibn 'Arabi. This is the higher faculty of symbolic perception through which one glimpses the transcendent through the mediating forms in the imaginal world. It allows us to inhabit an interworld or isthmus (*barzakh*), an interface between the Unseen (*al-ghayb*) and the seen, the inwardly hidden (*batin*) and the outwardly manifest *(zahir)*, and thus perceive the hierarchical order of creation in which everything in existence is a sign (*ayah*), an analogy or similitude (*mithal*) pointing to its transcendent origin. We may well ask how such an imaginal world accessed by direct perception or 'tasting' (*dhawq*) can be accessed by algorithms.

And this takes us to the magisterial work of the psychiatrist and neuropsychologist Iain McGilchrist whose unprecedented mastery of a vast body of recent brain research is distilled in the striking title and subtitle of his tour de force, *The Master and His Emissary: The Divided Brain and the Making of the Western World.* I believe that if we apply McGilchrist's essential conclusions to the phenomenon of AI, we find a clear direction in diagnosing the way in which AI is reinforcing and compounding the 'divided brain'.

What does McGilchirst mean by the 'divided brain'? He first distinguishes the essential differences between the two cerebral hemispheres. The right hemisphere, he explains, sees the whole, whereas the left hemisphere is adept at homing in on detail. New experience is better apprehended by the right hemisphere, which also sees things in context, as inseparably interconnected, so it recognises the vast extent of what remains implicit. The left hemisphere, however, deals better with what is predictable, the narrow focus of its detailed, distinct mechanisms able to isolate what it sees, but relatively blind to things that can be conveyed only indirectly. The knowledge mediated by the left hemisphere therefore tends to be knowledge within a closed system – 'perfect' knowledge to be sure within its box, but bought ultimately at the price of emptiness. Where the left hemisphere is literalistic, the right as 'the ground of empathy' recognises all that is nonverbal, metaphorical, ironic or humorous.' At ease with ambiguity, paradox and the co-existence of complementary opposites, it cherishes 'the reciprocal relationship between ourselves and one another, ourselves and the world.'

McGilchrist emphasises that there is a good reason we have two hemispheres: 'We need both versions of the world.' He contends, however, that in the West there has been 'a kind of battle going on in our brains'. Despite swings of the pendulum, the partnership between the two hemispheres has been lost, and the relatively rigid left hemisphere has gained the upper hand. 'With Parmenides, and still more with Plato, philosophy shifted from a respect for the hidden and implicit to an emphasis on what can be made explicit alone.' The previously acknowledged insight that opposites can be reconciled became anathema. With the 'Enlightenment', the world was further atomised, and the mechanical model became the dominant framework for understanding ourselves and the world. Our world has become increasingly rule-bound and 'loss of the implicit damages our ability to convey, or even to see at all, aspects of ourselves and our world that transcend the mechanistic.' There is an oppressive rise in bureaucracy, with paper replacing people, 'factual' information replacing meaning, and experience increasingly virtualised. 'This is the world of the left hemisphere, ever keen on control.' McGilchrist concludes that the increasing precedence of the left hemisphere, with its inferior grasp of reality, is likely to have potentially disastrous consequences. While it should be the 'emissary' of the right hemisphere, it is instead becoming the 'master'.

The depth of McGilchrist's analysis and the breadth of his perspective add great weight and urgency to the warnings of those who believe that the 'artificial' and the 'mechanistic' must be the servant of humanity, not its master. AI must not be given the ultimate power to control and mould us, for, as the Qur'an tells us, we have been created *fi ahsani taqwim*, 'in the best of moulds'. The balance of the hemispheres can only be restored by a renewed awareness of the totality of all the faculties that make up our essential humanness, and this has huge implications not only for the future direction of AI but also for the realisation of the full magnitude of human potential in every sphere of human endeavour.

FAKING UNBELIEF

Abdelwahab El-Affendi

According to the Greek historian Diodorus Siculus, it has been the custom in the Nubian kingdom of Kush for the high priests of Amun to terminate a king's reign by sending him a message 'from Amun himself', requesting him to commit suicide. Such a message was sent to King Arkamani I (known in Greek sources as King Ergamenes, r. 295–275 BCE). His Majesty was not pleased with his god's wish. Rather than complying, as many of his predecessors have most likely done, he led a military expedition into Amun's august temple on the holy mountain Al-Barkal, sacked the place and slaughtered all the priests.

Subsequently, he made drastic religious, political and cultural changes, downgrading Amun in favour of the local warrior god, Apademek. During his reign, the capital shifted to the city of Meroe, 150 miles south-east of the original capital of Napata. That same period witnessed the replacement of the Egyptian hieroglyphics by a local Meroetic script as the recording script, and in Meroetic language. Unfortunately, this left a gap in history, since the new script was difficult to decipher.

Did the priests really believe that Amun told them to terminate Arkmani's rule? Arkmani apparently did not think so, and certainly did not care. It is interesting that many of his predecessors, like the illustrious Piye (famous also as Piankhi), who conquered Egypt in 744 BC and ruled it as the founder of the twenty-fifth Egyptian dynasty for thirty years, was fanatically religious. In fact, his conquest of Egypt was done at the behest of Amun's priests, many of whom had taken refuge in Napata to escape persecution by foreign tyrants at home. In fact, the proclamation of later prominent kings, like Irike-Amannote (431–405 BC), were ecstatic in their religious content and claims of visions of Amun and other gods 'walking the streets' in his processions. However, Arkamani, who was a contemporary and a close friend of the Pharaoh Ptolemy II Philadelphus (r. 285–246 BCE), and had reputedly been influenced by Greek philosophy, was not that kind of monarch. (Blaming the West, or in this case, boasting Western influence, is an old, and always a good strategy).

Arkmani did not need to read Machiavelli about the benefits of appearing religious without needing to be so. But he was an early pioneer of the practice. Machiavelli has famously opined that while it was not necessary for a prince to possess religious and other virtues, 'but it is indeed necessary to appear to have them.'

> Nay, I dare say this, that by having them and always observing them, they are harmful; and by appearing to have them, they are useful as it is to appear merciful, faithful, humane, honest, and religious , and to be so; but to remain with a spirit built so that, if you need not to be those things, you are able and know how to change to the contrary. This has to be understood: that a prince, and especially a new prince, cannot observe all those things for which men are held good, since he is often under a necessity, to maintain his state, of acting against faith, against charity, against humanity, against religion.

Religion should be the last place fakery should thrive. After all, God knows everything. There is no place to hide from Him. If you fake it, He would *know*. So there is no point in even trying. Surprisingly, however, the religious arena is one of fakery's primary sites.

Interestingly, in the Qur'an, there is very little condemnation of atheists. This is probably because few existed in the audience to which it was directed. The bulk of admonitions contained in God's Book is directed to various categories of believers. The first is believers in 'fake gods', the so-called polytheists. These were believers in 'imagined' gods, 'names you have named, you and your ancestors, for which God has sent down no authority'. The second category is made of believers in the One True God, on the basis of correctly delivered divine scriptures, while omitting or distorting some fundamental aspects of their teachings. They have either totally abandoned the teachings, 'leaving God's Book behind their backs', selectively adopted only parts of the teachings, or made substantive modifications or additions to them. At some point, they could slip into Sin Number 1: worshipping fake gods, either directly by upgrading prophets and other prominent religious figures to the level of deities, or indirectly, by practically elevating 'their priests and monks' to the status of deities.

This could be by just following them blindly, even when the latter contravened divine teachings.

The most severe condemnations, however, are reserved for the ultimate fakers, the 'hypocrites': fake-pretend believers who not only profess Islam insincerely, but wage a war against it from inside. For them is reserved the bottom of the bottom in hell. Hypocrisy is indeed one of religion's most endemic ills, and most puzzling adjunct. For as we said, you cannot deceive God. So why even try?

Is this because religion is not about God, but about other people? Arkamani had no issue with Amun, it would appear, but with the priests, who could incite his subjects against him. The 'hypocrites' of Madina were not lukewarm or indifferent believers who wanted to go along with the 'herd', as the Qur'an reported them to have said disdainfully about the believers. They were actively engaged in attempts to shape the politics, beliefs and attitudes of the new religious community. They joined military expeditions, participated in public debates, they even built their own 'fake' mosque, which the Prophet ordered to be burned to the ground.

They could have chosen otherwise: fade into the shadows; leave and join another religious community; or even kept themselves apart and maintained their identity within the pact of the Madina Treaty. But that would not have safeguarded for them the political power which their leaders believed Islam, and its prophet, had usurped from them. Since their 'flock' had joined another leader, they wanted to stay close to it, biding their time until such a moment might present itself for them to pounce.

This was not your run-of-the-mill hypocrisy: the lukewarm believer type, where the actor does not want to be bothered with religion and its rituals, but treads along so as to reap the benefits of conformity, or at least avoid unnecessary aggravation. This was active, militant, aggressive hypocrisy, almost a fanatical faith in its own right. It was also a conscious political strategy, a deliberate policy to exploit the duality of tribal-religious identity to the maximum in order to recover a lost political power. They were anticipating Machiavelli's recommended strategy of using religion to their advantage, pretending to conform in order to advance a cause.

Religion always incorporates a political dimension, even though the 'politicisation of religion' is often deplored as distortion and devaluation. Russell T. McCutcheon, Canadian scholar of religion, begs to differ, arguing that the historicity of the founding theoretical tenets of the human sciences precludes the positing of an 'apolitical zone' in which a presumed 'pre-politicised religion' (also known as spirituality, experience, etc.) should reside:

> If, instead, we presume that our tools and data are irreducibly historical, then 'politicised religion' is redundant. But if we harbour the hope that something escapes history – call it soul, meaning, value, etc. – then encouraging, lamenting, or simply trying to explain the involvement of the things we call religions in the political sphere will make a lot of sense. However, for those committed to the theoretical position that all we have is history, all the way down… this will make no sense whatsoever.

Religion is, of course, irreducibly political, if only because all religions tend to define and redefine community. As believers construct themselves into a church/*umma*, the preservation of this community as distinct and whole becomes inescapably political. Usually the political dimension is imposed from outside. If you are thrown to the lions for believing in Jesus, sent to concentration camps for having a 'Jewish name', or thrown out of your homeland for believing in Muhammad, you cannot afford to be apolitical. However, there is a sense in which 'politicisation' is external to religion, even alien to it. That is when religion is linked to a (conflictual) tribal/ethnic identity (Arab, Hebrew, white European'), status (class, gender, etc.), political faction/agenda, or sectional interest. In that case, defending the given interest or identity, using the cloak of religion, does indeed become a sort of negative 'politicisation' that devalues the faith.

Religion is indeed a puzzle to social scientists seeking to 'study' the phenomenon 'impartially'. In its modern manifestations, the very concept 'religion' witnessed interesting transformations, ironically under Machiavelli's influence. A sixteenth century anti-Machiavellian backlash displaced the Ciceronian concept of religion as justice (rendering unto God what is due to Him), in favour of a more restrictive anti-pluralism (only the one true religion is just). The creeping Renaissance-era admiration of Roman civil religion, under the indirect influence of Aquinas, as embodiment of natural reason, was at the root of the notion (popularised by Machiavelli) of religion as a moral virtue with civic benefits. This in turn evoked the backlash from both Catholics and Protestants, particularly the latter.

Machiavelli's attitude was close to Edward Gibbon's characterisation of Roman civil religion as a combination of utilitarianism and indifferent pluralism.

The various modes of worship which prevailed in the Roman world were all considered by the people as equally true; by the philosopher as equally false; and by the magistrate as equally useful. And thus toleration produced not only mutual indulgence, but even religious concord.

This angle was overtaken by the stormy Reformation and its fanatical wars. But the pendulum swung back again in the post-Enlightenment period towards a more pluralist stance. This pushed towards the dominant modes of the study of religion in the modern era, currently split between positivists who consider religion a sort of delusion, and are content to study its social manifestations and impact, and the more cautious 'religionists' who did not go that far, withholding judgement on the ontological status of the metaphysical beings at the centre of religious beliefs and practices. The difference is one of degree, since both sides are united within broad 'democratic communities of organised scepticism' on a quest for 'achieving scientific (i.e. intersubjectively testable) knowledge' of religion. Proponents of the second tendency propose a definition of religion that embodies the ethos of their work, categorising it as, any

> behaviour which believers interpret as communication, direct or indirect, between themselves and beings whose existence and activity cannot be verified or falsified but whom the believers believe to exist and be active, directly or indirectly, in their lives and environment.

But does this outside ('etic') view of religion really grasp its essence? Many agree with William James that the essence of religion is saintliness, 'the collective name for the ripe fruits of religion in a character'. This is a feature of religiosity characterised by passionate intensity, the gentle glow of an inner flame that shines all around. At its most intense, it is found in prophets and other founders of religions. But rare though it is, it is what religion is really about. Without this phenomenon and its manifestations, religion as such would not exist.

Saintliness represents a special sensing and focus of the divine, the focus of all religious sentiments. While others *believe* in the divine, the saintly figure *feels* that presence. What is belief to others is seeing and feeling for this figure. This living presence of the divine, in this case, makes belief redundant. For Moses at Mount Sinai, or Muhammad on his Nocturnal Journey to Jerusalem, the question of 'belief' is no longer relevant. Here, it is literally, beyond belief.

Belief, as a form of 'faith', trust, is the paradox at the heart of religion. The 'leap of faith' is always based on inconclusive evidence. If the evidence was incontrovertible, it would not be faith. During his agonisingly paralysing phase of utter scepticism, the celebrated theologian and philosopher, Imam Ghazali, held up mathematical proof as the ideal of certain knowledge. If I believed that 7 plus 3 equals 10, and someone proceeded to tell me otherwise, and provides as evidence an ability to turn a stick into a snake, I would not be convinced. I will only wonder how he managed the trick.

However, if a perfect scientific experiment could be devised which would conclusively prove the existence of God, then the very notion of belief and faith would be destroyed. There are frequent reminders in the Qu'ran that when God's overpowering signs appear (or when He manifests Himself in person), then faith would become redundant: it would not be possible for someone to pronounce, at that final hour, that he/she now believes. For that would not be believing. In this instance, seeing is *not* believing.

However, saintliness is by its nature not sustainable long-term. Religious life thus tends to routinise around the mundane everyday patterns to lukewarm, almost absent-minded observance. It is usually the pragmatic, quasi-Machiavellian men of this world who triumph in the end, not the saints, who are not men of this world. In Islam, this took the form of Umayyad triumph following Islam's first major civil war. Muawiya, the founder of that dynasty, summed its ethos in a brief speech he gave after things settled down, with him the undisputed ruler of Islamdom. On triumphantly entering the Prophet's Mosque for the first time (661 CE), he dismissed dignitaries lining up to greet him, and went straight to the pulpit to tell them he knew they did not like him or his rule, which has won by the sword. I have tried, he told them, to force myself to emulate Abu Bakr (the first Caliph), but found this unpalatable. I tried the style of Omar (second Caliph), it was even less to my taste. Neither could I manage (the third Caliph) Osman's approach. Who could emulate that generation? I therefore adopted an approach which is mutually beneficial to me and to you: sharing food and drink together graciously, as long as you behave yourselves and maintain loyalty. If you do not think me the best among you, I am the best for you. I will not raise the sword against a man who carries none, and I would disregard all that went in the past. If you do not think I have given you your full due, then accept what I can manage. He then immediately left. In short, his message was this: let us not pursue ideals, but live and let live.

Over thirty years and a couple of civil wars later (695CE), the second founder of the Umayyad Dynasty, Abdul-Malik ibn Marwan gave an even more blunt and shorter speech, in Makkah this time, on his own victory. Distancing himself from his three Umayyad predecessors, labelling Uthman 'the weak caliph', Muawiya 'the appeaser', and the latter's son Yazid as 'the demented caliph', he promised no carrots to potential challengers, only the sword. Repeating Muawiya's point about the unattainability of the Islamic ideal of the earlier caliphs, he was even more unapologetic: 'You demand from us,' he chided his audience, 'the emulation of the early generation, but you yourselves do not observe their model... I swear to God if I ever again hear anyone admonishing me to fear God, I will have him beheaded.'

Umayyad rule embodied what I have elsewhere termed the 'Damascus Model' of governance, modelled on the Byzantine monarchy. It did not only displace and triumph over the original Madina Model, but it also became the model to emulate by all subsequent Muslim regimes. This included those following rebellions against Umayyads.

In recent years, things changed drastically, with colonialism and its aftermath. Religion, Islam included, continued to ebb and flow, more the former than the latter. This was another reminder that religion is social and contextual. The colonial era imposed de facto secularism, and it became fashionable, especially among intellectual and political leaders. A few waves of revivalism, some of the traditional kind, some more 'modernist', tried to stem the tide, with varying degrees of success. However, by the 1960's, Islam became fashionable again, including in the West. Figures like Malcolm X made Islam an iconic feature of the Western scene. He had followed in the footsteps of earlier figures, such as the Austrian-born Muhamad Asad, who embraced Islam in 1926, and become a leading interpreter of the Qur'an.

More recently, the tide had turned again towards the other side. Even before the fateful 9/11 atrocities, the image of Islam began to suffer. Muslims suffered even more, becoming double victims of vicious terror movements that decimated their homelands, and terror (Muslim and non-Muslim) regimes, from Myanmar and China to Syria and Egypt, that used the terror pretext to do even more harm than the worst terror outfit. The ultimate irony of it all was summed up in a March 2019 *Foreign Policy* article describing Arab despots as the ultimate 'Islamophobes'. Saudi and Emerati despots in particular, have aligned themselves with neo-Nazis and varieties of right wing Islamophobes to promote hate against Western Muslims in the name of combating 'extremism'. The irony of ironies presented itself when a former Ku Klux Klan leader joined Iran's Ayatollahs in hailing Syria's tyrant Bashar al-Assad's fight 'against Zionism and imperialism', praising Damascus's new demented genocidaire as 'a modern day hero standing up to demonic forces seeking to destroy his people and nation'.

As rival forms of religious and secular despotisms converge towards espousing genocidal evil as the epitome of 'civilised' modernity, the 'Damascus Model' closes its perpetual circle, as its own (really 'demented') Yazid receives the endorsement of supposed heirs to Hussein, the Prophet's grandson murdered by the 'demented caliph'. Hypocrisy and martyrdom in defence of Truth became one and the same thing. The 'Madina Model' bows in front of its rival as it 'exits left', and admonishing despots to heed justice and 'fear God' once again becomes a capital offense. It is no longer necessary to fake belief. What you need today to prosper is to fake unbelief, to proclaim yourself an 'ex-Muslim', a funny epithet, if ever there was one. Was Paul's claim to fame being an ex-Jew? Does faith ever define itself by what it is not? Or is it the case that, in some instances, faith has no value in itself, only a 'market value'. If you think *having been* a Muslim once is more important than what you are now, that no one would value what you are now, or what you think without contrasting it with what you *do not want to be*, then that is interesting in itself. In a time when faking belief is no longer necessary or profitable, faking unbelief becomes the name of the game. But it is not just unbelief as such, but unbelief into something.

The puzzle is this: what is left when Madina turns into Damascus/ Byzantium, and the latter into Auschwitz? What happens when Hussein is re-incarnated as 'demented Yazid'? Why does 'faith', the supposed fountainhead of virtue and probity, precipitately descend into hypocrisy and downright evil? How and why the light of faith tends to turn into the fire of fanaticism that descends on the world as darkness? How can the quest for ultimate truth surrender people to the ultimate in fakery and delusion?

We appeal to the Almighty for enlightenment on these questions in these COVID-19 times, which raise another set of questions, recalling His frequent chastisements of 'believers' of the wrong kind.

ANCIENT MECHANICAL HORRORS

Robert Irwin

Golden birds and beasts, musical fountains, and robotic servants astound and terrify guests. Brass horsemen, gilded buglers and papier-mâché drummers mark the passage of time. Statues of departed lovers sigh, kiss and pledge their love. Golden archers and copper knights warn against danger and safeguard borders. Mechanical monkeys, camouflaged in badger pelts, ape human behaviour in the midst of a lush estate. Corpses, perfectly preserved by human art, challenge the limits of life. Brazen heads reveal the future, and a revolving palace mimics the revolution of the spheres. Medieval robots, both actual and fictional, take many forms.

E.R. Truitt, *Medieval Robots: Mechanism, Magic, Nature and Art*

Though Truitt's book is chiefly devoted to European automata as they appeared in fact and fantasy, their parallels can easily be found in the medieval Islamic world. Automata occupy an uncanny space between the worlds of the trivial and the ultimately profound. In Melvil Dewey's *Decimal Classification and Relativ* [sic] *Index for Libraries* (Boston, 1894), the subject is registered under two decimal headings: 791 'Public Entertainment' (which also includes such topics as 'Panorama, Circus, Menagerie and Summer Resort'), and 127 'Unconsciousness. Automata'. This ambiguous status was also the case in the Islamic world where automata might serve to entertain, or, on the other hand, present a metaphysical challenge and even deadly menace to those who encountered them. But the simulation of human life by ingenious mechanical devices posed special problems for Muslim thinkers. In part this was because there was a body of *hadith* which appeared to proscribe any representations of the human figure. A partial exception was widely allowed by Muslim scholars for dolls with which girls might be allowed to play. Even in this case there were and are stricter Muslims who do not allow dolls unless their woolly heads have no facial features, and there are stricter Muslims yet who forbid dolls altogether.

Statues of human figures were also problematic. Medieval Muslims dwelt among the statuary of antiquity and, of course, far more of it survived on open display in the cities and the countryside than does now. It was rare for these statues to be evaluated according to aesthetic criteria and the twelfth-century physician 'Abd al-Latif al-Baghdadi was most unusual in his appreciation of figurative art. During his travels in Egypt, recorded in *Al-Ifada wa-al-I 'tibar* (Book of Instruction and Admonition) he remarked on 'nicety of proportion in the head of the Sphinx', as well as its handsome face and graceful mouth. Similarly, the surviving pharaonic statuary at 'Ayn Shams, 'frightful and colossal figures', were praised by him for their just proportions, as were those he found in the ruins of Memphis. The doctor in him was particularly struck by the accuracy of their anatomical proportions. The ruined monuments and broken statuary were 'admonitions of futurity, by calling the attention to the lot reserved for things of this world'.

But 'Abd al-Latif, to whom we shall return, was practically alone in his aesthetic judgements. It was rare for other writers to apply the adjective *jamil* (beautiful) to statues, for that word was more usually used for fine-looking camels and horses. Instead they were more likely to use the word *'ajib* (marvellous) and in some contexts this 'marvellous' might have undertones of the 'supernatural'. The medieval city of Seljuq Konya was defended not only by the thickness of its walls, but also by the variety of classical sculptures attached to those walls. In the words of Scott Redford: 'Classical spolia included a colossal headless statue of Hercules placed next to one gate, as well as many funerary reliefs and carved sarcophagus panels.' In such a manner the ruined fragments of pre-Islamic antiquity served talismanic and apotropaic purposes.

More recent sculptures could serve the same purpose. The Golden Gate Palace was at the centre of the perfectly round city of Baghdad founded in 762 by the 'Abbasid Caliph al-Mansur and on the top of the dome of this palace was a statue of a mounted horseman with a lance. It was claimed that this statue had magical properties since the horseman's lance would point in the direction from which enemies were coming.

Talismanic statues abounded in *Tuhfa al-muluk* (Gift Offered to Kings), a cosmology by the sixteenth-century Egyptian geomancer, Ibn Zunbul. For example, in Narbonne, in the South of France, there is a prophetic statue that warns of the coming of the sons of Ishmael by which is meant the Arabs. Also, according to Ibn Zunbul, Saragossa has a talisman to protect it against vipers and serpents. Moreover, grain and fruit are thereby protected from corruption, so that food can be safely stored in the town for a hundred years. Though statues also featured frequently in the multi-volume travel narrative of the seventeenth-century Turkish writer Evliya Çelebi, since there were many in the former lands of the Byzantine Empire, he showed no interest in their artistic quality and indeed there is no sign that he thought of them as works of art. Instead they fell into two categories, being either wonder-working talismans or they were once living people or animals, who had been magically turned to stone.

Apart from the iconoclastic ideology of some Muslim scholars and mobs which led to many statues being destroyed or defaced, there was another problem with statues and that was that they might become the habitations of demons. The sixteenth-century Italian Neoplatonist scholar Marsilio Ficino had this to say on the matter: 'The Arabs and Egyptians ascribe too much power to the statues and images fashioned by magical and astrological art that they believe the spirits of the stars are enclosed within them ... This could be done, I believe by Daemons, but not because they have been constrained by a particular material as because they enjoy being worshipped.' Ficino was probably drawing on the chapter on animated statues in *Picatrix*, a thirteenth-century Latin translation of the Arabic *Ghayat al-hakim* ('Goal of the Sage') compiled by Maslama al-Qurtubi, a tenth-century scholar and sorcerer in Muslim Spain. The *Ghayat* is a remarkably sinister text, full of recipes for spells and poisons. Section three of book four deals with the alleged expertise of the Copts in drawing down planetary influences. According to Maslama, the Copts claim that Hermes built a city called al-Ashmunein [formerly Hermopolis] in the east of Egypt and he placed a statue over each of the gates of its four walls: respectively those of an eagle, a bull, a lion and a dog. He then called down speaking spirits from the Moon to inhabit these statues so that the statues could speak and one could not enter the city without their permission. (But Maslama then drifts on to a discussion of how the corpse of a rabbit which has been beheaded may be used to make oneself invisible.)

Maslama had relied heavily on treatises on alchemy and magic ascribed to Jabir ibn Hayyan, an author who supposedly lived in the ninth-century, though the name does not really identify an individual, but serves instead to designate a genre of occult literature. Jabir's numerous treatises deal with such matters as the construction of talismanic statues to keep wild animals and insects from towns, the calling down of demons to inhabit statues and the artificial creation of life. In particular the *Kitab al-tajmi'* (Book of Assembly) dealt with the *musawwirun* (image makers) who know how to create homunculi and to animate statues.

Though the modern mind should have no difficulty in distinguishing between an ingenious mechanical device and a magically animated statue, things were different then and not so clear. According to Fakhr al-Din al-Razi's twelfth-century commentary on the Qur'an, *Mafatih al-ghayb* (Keys to the Unseen), there were eight types of magic, of which the fifth type was that of the automata and mechanical devices. 'Any sufficiently advanced technology is indistinguishable from magic', according to the science-fiction writer Arthur C. Clarke. Automata had featured frequently in Arabic manuals of mechanical engineering and accounts of court ceremonies, as well as in stories of the fantastic exploits of treasure hunters. To take the manuals of mechanics first, an important treatise on the subject, the *Kitab al-hiyal* (Book of Cunning Devices) was produced around the mid-ninth century by the Banu Musa. These were the three sons of a reformed highwayman who had become an astronomer and the cup companion of one of the 'Abbasid Caliphs. Drawing on earlier Greek material, particularly the *Automata* written by Heron of Alexandria in the first century AD, they produced designs for a variety of ingenious mechanical devices. The article on Heron in *The Oxford Companion to Classical Literature* remarks that 'his many inventions seem to have been mainly for interest or entertainment rather than practical application'. The same seems to be true of the designs of the Banu Musa, who produced blueprints for such things as singing statues and automatic wine servers. This was not mechanical engineering in the service of industrial progress, but for the entertainment of the courts, toys for grown-ups. When Marina Warner comes to discuss the *Arabian Nights* story of 'Prince Ahmed and the Fairy Peri Banou' and the objects acquired by the three questing princes, she has this to say:

> The magic gifts in 'Prince Ahmed' are toys: toys in the sense that automata are also toys — mechanical birds in cages, clepsydrae, and dolls or puppets that sing, dance and write. While they reflect princely passions for such ingenious devices in the seventeenth and eighteenth centuries, they also resemble the character of enchanted things in myth and romance: the magic mirror and the flying horse that appear in Chaucer's 'Squire's Tale' for example.

Again, at the beginning of the *Nights* story of 'The Ebony Horse', three sages bearing marvellous gifts present themselves before a great king. First is a golden peacock which claps its wings and cries every hour of the night and day; the second is a trumpet which sounds whenever it detects an enemy seeking to enter through the city's gate. The third is an ebony horse whose flight through the air is piloted by a couple of levers and a screw and this third gift has been presented with an evil intention. The occasional robotic oarsman apart, the automata were not presented in medieval Arabic fiction as labour-saving devices.

To return to those mechanical treatises. Though some of the automata described were actually constructed and are attested to in the sources for the history of the 'Abbasid period, things are not so clear in the centuries which followed. In 1205, Badi' al-Zaman al-Jazari produced the illustrated treatise, *Kitab fi ma'rifat al-hiyal al-handasiyya*, (Book of Knowledge of Ingenious Mechanical Devices). It included such wonders as the peacock fountain: when water is poured in its bowl, a little man appears with a bowl of perfumed powder and he is followed by another little man who offers the washer a towel. The design for an automated woman who poured wine was also presented by al-Jazari. His treatise continued to be copied and beautifully illustrated in the Ayyubid and Mamluk periods. Nevertheless, I have never come across any references to any of such automata being commissioned by an Ayyubid or a Mamluk sultan and then being displayed to entertain their courtiers and visitors. So, there is the possibility that al-Jazari's text and its later copies were reading pleasures, produced to delight the eye and entertain the mind rather than give guidance to a working technician. Incidentally the word for ingenious mechanical contrivances, *hiyal*, has somewhat negative overtones as it can also refer to stratagems, subterfuges, tricks, and legal dodges.

Automata also feature in what purports to be a work of non-fiction, the early thirteenth-century *Kitab al-mukhtar fi kashf al-asrar* (The Book of Selected Disclosure of Secrets) by 'Abd al-Rahman al-Jawbari. This is an entertaining compendium of the tricks of conmen, charlatans, quack doctors, forgers, alchemists and other cheats. Bogus treasure hunters are among those who feature in al-Jawbari's rogues' gallery. One trick used by these fraudsters is to show a credulous sap a manuscript which seems to provide instructions for making a treasure-finding automaton which has to be provided with a heavy gold ring and ideally that ring should be enriched with a precious stone of hyacinth with a certain letter engraved on it. Thus enriched, the figure will point to a hoard of treasure so vast that a caravan of camels will not be sufficient to carry it away, but when the ring is taken off the statue, the rest of the treasure will vanish back into the earth. Once the fraudster has persuaded the rich fool to give him the stipulated gold for making the ring, he promptly scarpers with it. Al-Jawbari also mentions another scam in which an automaton serpent features as the guardian of a supposed treasure site. Thanks to a mixture of resin and sulphur placed in its mechanical mouth, it seems to breathe fire and in so threatening a manner, it seems to promise the proximity of the buried treasure.

Despite the activities of fraudulent and unqualified treasure hunters, tomb robbery was a genuine profession in Egypt and its operations in the vicinity of the pyramids was organised under the supervision of a shaykh of the treasure hunters (*matalibun*). 'Abd al-Latif al-Baghdadi was distressed by the damage done to pharaonic antiquities by such greedy and superstitious men. 'Thus, everything which seemed to wave was in their eyes the token of treasure concealed. Did they see an opening in the mountain, they imagined it was the road to some hoard: with them a colossal statue was considered the guardian of the money deposited at its feet, and the implacable avenger of any enterprise against its safety. They therefore resorted to every kind of artifice to destroy and damage these statues.'

Hidden treasures and the mechanical or demonic guardians of ancient wealth and knowledge featured prominently in medieval popular Arabic literature. Treasure-guarding automata did not observe any of Isaac Asimov's three laws of robotics, the first of which would be 'a robot may not injure a human being, or through inaction, allow a human being to come to harm'. Instead most of the metal men who feature in *Alf layla wa layla* (The Thousand and One Nights) and in similar story collections like *Al-Hikyat al-'ajiba wa al-akhbar al-ghariba* (Tales of the Marvellous and News of the Strange) have been programmed to kill in order to protect the treasures of the past.

The *Hikayat* includes a set of four marvellous stories about treasure hunting. In the first of them the treasure seekers come to a monastery, the four doors of which are each guarded by a statue with a weapon in hand and the battlements above are lined by statues of monks carrying huge stones. This is intimidating, but the leader of the expedition instructs his followers to dig in a certain place outside the walls until they uncover a subterranean locked door. The leader stops his followers from approaching the door and instead hurls a rock at the lock to break it. 'When it struck the lock, a huge statue appeared from behind the coverings with a great rock in its hand. It moved over the ground, crying out in a loud voice. "This what I was afraid of," the man said.' Eventually, by throwing enough rocks at the door to weary the automaton, the group is able to pass into the monastery and then avoid various death traps within, as well as a bronze statue who asks the leader what he thinks he is doing. Finally, they secure the treasure, only to lose it later to robber huntsmen. It was a great adventure, but had it all been worth it? Here and elsewhere the *Hikayat's* stories reveal a fascination with the perceived ancient wealth and sinister mystery of the Christian church.

In the second story the treasure is guarded by a brazen lion with steel teeth and by a statue lying on its face. When one of the treasure-seeking gang 'put his foot on the first step the statue moved and sat up; when he stood on the second step it took up a sword that was lying beside it. He reached the third step it stood up and when he got to the fourth step it turned on a spiral spring and struck him a blow that cut him in half'. In the third story the treasure seekers are making their way in a cave when they find themselves trapped by brazen hands which rise from the earth and grab their ankles, thus immobilising them. In the fourth story the treasure seekers are in peril of their lives from a statue which releases a flood of water which threatens to drown them all in its chamber. But the learned

Christian monk who has been their guide to the treasure succeeds in bringing the statue to its knees and stemming the flood.

Elsewhere in the *Hikayat*, in the opening of 'The Story of Mahliya and Mahbub and the White-Footed Gazelle', we are told of the ancient kingdom of Zabaj whose ruler sat in state in an arena which not only contained a tree of coral on which sat 'birds of gilded copper so constructed that when the wind blew through them they would produce delightful and remarkable songs, as well as a mechanical gazelle programmed to scatter coins and a vulture that did the same with the perfume that was in its belly. They operated on the ruler's good days. But when he was feeling less cheerful an eagle that perched on the Throne of Wrath flew about and fired down bullets of lead. But, after a dream sent from God the king repented and had the eagle smashed to pieces.

In the *Arabian Nights* story of 'Janshah' one of Solomon's castles is said to contain 'a fountain surrounded by statues of birds and beasts: When a breeze blew, wind would enter their ears and each would make its own characteristic noise'. Similarly in one of the better episodes in the long, incoherent and often wearisome *Nights* saga of 'King 'Umar ibn al-Nu'man and his family', the hero Sharkan, after a series of highly erotic wrestling matches with a Christian princess, finds hospitality in her Christian convent and is eventually conducted to her bedroom, in which there are 'lifelike images into which the wind could enter, setting in motion machinery inside them which gave the impression that they were speaking'. In another story, that of 'Hatim of Tayy', the tomb of a tribal leader of legendary generosity is flanked by stone troughs and stone statues of weeping girls with unbound hair and every night the statues can be heard weeping. Yet though the medieval Arab world's inventors of fantasy were capable of conjuring up singing and speaking automata, it was not until the nineteenth century that the German inventor of fantastic fiction, E.T.A. Hoffmann produced the dancing automaton in the form of Olympia, whose perfectly rhythmic dancing and artificially bright eyes would entrance Nathanael and ultimately drive him mad in the story of 'The Sandman' (and this story would provide the central text in Sigmund Freud's famous essay, 'The Uncanny').

In the marvellous story of 'The City of Brass' the Umayyad Caliph 'Abd al-Malik ibn Marwan has an expedition sent out into the North African desert in search of the stoppered flasks containing the jinn imprisoned centuries ago by King Solomon. This search segues into a quest for the City of Brass, during which the search party encounters an abandoned palace, statues and the stone tablets all of which deliver warnings about mortality and the consequent vanity of power and riches. Death, the destroyer of delights, comes for everyone. More encouragingly, the party stumbles across an automaton signpost in the desert in the form of 'a rider made of brass carrying a broad-headed spear which gleamed almost blindingly. On this statue there was an inscription that read: 'You who come to me, if you not know the road to the City of Brass, rub the rider's hand. It will turn and you must take whichever direction it points to when it stops; go freely and without fear, for it will lead you to the city'. They do as instructed and are now able to take the right way to the City of Brass. But they then encountered a second and more terrifying figure, a winged jinni buried up to its armpits in the sand. Centuries ago, the jinni had been employed by a sea king to occupy a carved idol and issue commands and judgements through it. When Solomon demanded that the king must destroy this idol or war would follow, the jinni spoke through the idol,

I have no fear of him, I the omniscient.
If he wants to fight me I shall march on him and snatch away his soul.

But Solomon and his army of men and beasts came and defeated the king and his evil jinni and this was the jinni's punishment for seeking to defy both Solomon and God. The jinn obligingly gives further directions to the gateless City of Brass, which is also a city of the dead, doomed by the judgement of God centuries ago. Its brass walls are covered with inscriptions dedicated to the theme of *memento mori*. At length and at the cost of several lives, the expeditionary group succeed in scaling the walls and making their way past the numerous corpses to the palace in the centre of the city. Inside the throne room they find the richly apparelled figure of the city's queen. Though she appears to be looking at them, this is the semblance of life only, for her eyeballs have been gouged out and the orbs filled with quicksilver. Her corpse is guarded by two automaton slaves, a white one holding a mace and the black one with a sword. A golden tablet placed between them bears a lengthy inscription that warns that death is the fate of all men and that hoarded wealth can afford no protection from that fate. Though it also warns that no one should seek to strip the queen of her fine robes and jewels, one of the party, tempted by the wealth of the finery, steps towards the corpse, whereupon one of the automata struck him in the back while the other cut off his head. Man is mortal, but the automata, who do not live, are imperishable and can wait for centuries before dealing out death. The expedition returns to the Caliph in Damascus bringing with them great wealth and many strange tales with messages for those of the believers who would take warning. Though there are no actual ghosts in the stories of the *Nights*, nevertheless the dead succeed in delivering messages to the living and use carved inscriptions and pre-programmed automata to do so.

But what did this dead queen of the City of Brass need her jewels for? The same or similar questions arise in connection with a number of these stories concerning tomb robbery. To go back to the second of the treasure hunting stories in *Tales of the Marvellous*, there, just short of reaching the treasures, the bold and greedy group of tomb robbers come upon 'a silver couch on which lay a shrouded corpse with a tablet of green topaz at its head on which were the following inscription:

> I am Shaddad the Great. I conquered a thousand cities; a thousand white ele-phants were collected for me; I lived for a thousand years and my kingdom covered when both east and west, but when death came to me nothing of all that I had gathered was of any avail. You who see me take heed for Time is not to be trusted.

So the corpse is lecturing them and us on the vanity of riches. Fine. So why has Shaddad taken such extraordinary precautions to preserve his great wealth, wealth that he has belatedly come to see as worthless? In story after story the Muslim is exhorted to marvel at accounts of fabulous opulence while being told that it is all nothing really. It is the storyteller's way of offering with one hand while taking away with the other.

In 'The story of the third dervish' in the *Nights*, the future dervish in question is on board a ship which is driven off course and sails fatally close to the Magnetic Mountain, on the shore of which is 'a vaulted dome of brass set on ten columns and on top of this a rider and his horse, both made of brass. In his hand he carries a brass lance and to his breast is fixed a lead tablet inscribed with names and talismans. It is this rider ... who kills everyone who comes his way, and there is no escape unless the rider falls from his horse.' When the ship is driven closer to the Magnetic Mountain, it falls apart as its nails fly off to attach themselves to the Mountain. But the future dervish survives and swims ashore and an invisible voice gives him guidance on how to overthrow the evil statue, which, having performed the prayer in preparation for the confrontation with an alien and presumably pagan thing, he does. The voice also directs him to a little boat which is manned by a brass oarsman who (or which?) will row him to safety, but only if he does not mention the name of God. The future dervish boards the boat and after ten days he is rowed to within the sight of safety. Whereupon, such is his joy that he gives praise to Allah. At which point the bronze oarsman ceases rowing and the boat overturns. This may suggest that the automaton has been specifically programmed by an infidel technician to be of no assistance to Muslims. Such is the malevolence of pre-Islamic antiquity. Brass by the way is often the chosen metal of ill omen. The Arabic words for copper and brass *nuhas* and *nuhas asfar* have sinister resonances, since under the same lexical root we find *nahasa* (to make unhappy), *nahisa* (to be unlucky or calamitous), *nahs* (ill-omened) and *manhus* (luckless).

Automata also feature in the less well-known popular epics. In the *Sirat of Baybars* when the evil genius Juwan flees for refuge in Constantinople he hopes, in vain, to be protected in the seven churches that are filled with death traps, including a pool of poisonous quicksilver, a cannon and mechanical swordsmen. In the *Sirat al-Amira Dhat al-Himma*, the hero Battal has to destroy the device that controls the mechanical swordsmen which are blocking his way and he later faces the menace of musical statues which lure their listeners to throw themselves off the top of a mountain. In the *Sirat Sayf al-Tijan* a castle is protected by stone lions that eat people. There are also automata in that masterpiece of Persian literature, the *Shahnama* in which they garrison and defend a castle and the world-conqueror Alexander deployed fire-breathing iron warriors mounted on iron wheeled horses in battle.

Besides the proscription of figurative representation by many medieval Muslim scholars, there was also in some quarters a generalised prejudice against the sciences of the ancients (*'ulum al-awa'il*) and even a fear of them, be those sciences Greek, Persian or Egyptian. A pious scholar like Ibn Khaldun regarded the pre-Islamic sciences of philosophy, alchemy and astrology with considerable suspicion. Such clever matters could be evil and medieval technophobes had no apprehensions about future inventions, but rather they feared the legacy of the past.

But, unlike the Revolt of the Objects in Inca Moche legend or the recalcitrant robots in so many science fiction novels, Arab fantasy automata always did what they had been programmed to do, for they had no independent volition. Moreover, although the automata of medieval fantasy fiction occupied the borderland between life and death and they might appear eerie and terrifying, they were never in the strictest sense 'uncanny', since there could be no uncertainty about their nature – unlike for example the apparitions of Miss Jessel and Peter Quint in *The Turn of the Screw* by Henry James (where that pair may indeed be malignant ghosts or they may merely be delusions in the mind of the deranged and sexually frustrated governess). No one in a medieval Arab story mistakes an automaton for a human being – unlike poor deluded Nathanael confronted by a dancing automaton, or the inhabitants of a world infested by replicants as conjured up by Philip K. Dick in *Do Androids Dream of Electric Sheep?*. Finally, of course, the heroes and villains of Arab romances had other servants to do their bidding, since humanity shared its world with the Slave of the Lamp and countless other jinn.

AI AND COVID-19

John A. Sweeney

Allow me to open with an obtuse provocation: *Artificial Intelligence (AI) does and does not exist*. This is not an allusion to 'AI' that have been painstakingly developed only to be later decommissioned, as was the case with Facebook's recent chatbot experiment, although this is precisely where our odyssey into unpacking the above assertion begins. While there were numerous reports that the social media titan's two AIs, who were known as Alice and Bob, had developed their own language and began having independent conversations, the truth of the matter is far more complex. Alice and Bob were indeed communicating with one another in ways that the programmers could not understand, but they were doing so in a modified version of English, which suggests that the primary issue was not hyper-intelligence run amok but an all-too-human-esque unwillingness to follow the rules, so to speak, of English grammar. In short, Alice and Bob, who were actually 'neural nets,' found a more efficient means of communicating using aspects of English, but as the programmers could not figure out what was being said, the entire research program was scrapped. Neural nets, which is shorthand for artificial neural networks, are not only somewhat inspired by biological brains; they are engineered to learn through examples, rather than through explicit instructions and tasks, which is to say that experience drives how they come to 'know' things and, when asked, provide solutions to specific challenges. This makes neural nets extremely apt at 'pattern recognition' problems, which involves identifying 'signals' (some insight) amidst a sea of noise (large-scale data sets), but this is also what led Alice and Bob to begin speaking gibberish, at least from the programmers' perspective. This anecdote will return as a parable of sorts at the end of our journey.

But first, back to my opening salvo: *AI does and does not exist*. This intentionally contradictory framing points toward the dynamics underlying an array of technologies that spark hope, fear, and everything in between. While AI might conjure up a singular image for many, what actually and currently constitutes artificial intelligence is anything but monolithic. As such, the above *and* is doing quite a bit of work and points toward the diversity of technologies and tools that can be and is often loosely referred to as AI. This also highlights a key challenge at the very epicenter of most, if not all, discussions of this topic: the complex interstices of the actual and the perceptual. Many, if not most, of the predominant visions of AI – from autonomous robots to hyper-intelligent algorithms – fail to capture the all-too-human constraints of this still emerging technology. It is within this lacuna between the actual and perceptual that one feels the real weight of thinking through the postulate that AI does and does not exist. If humans were not part of the above equation, perhaps Alice and Bob would have created an entirely new linguistic structure – one that could have revolutionised how we communicate, which is exactly what some say emojis have done. Of course, Facebook's interest in the opportunities to advance human communication is secondary to its focus on monetising communication itself, and gibberish-speaking chatbots have not turned a profit, at least not yet.

Half-joking forecasts aside, there can be little doubt that AI has had, and looks positioned to continue having, a profound influence upon our collective images of the future. One recent event that seems to foretell of AI's potentiality is the tragedy of Lee Sedol, who *was* one of the world's top-rated players of *Go*, an ancient game whose complexity dwarfs chess. You might have noticed the past tense, which is due to Lee's retirement in late 2019. As a grandmaster, who ranked only second in international titles to a fellow Korean, Lee rose to global stardom in 2016 during a highly-publicised five-match competition against the Google-backed DeepMind's AlphaGo program, which learned how to play by evaluating tens of millions of matches, including games against itself. Sedol not only lost four out of five games but he was clearly outmatched in ways that left the grandmaster as well as some commentators downright stupefied. In the second game, AlphaGo made a move that was deemed *unhuman*, which is to say that no human, to date, would have made such a move, according to the experts. Lee himself called it, 'so beautiful'. Fast forward to the present and one can find that rather than studying the strategies of Lee, competitive as well as casual *Go* players are looking to learn from AlphaGo, which has inadvertently transformed the multi-millenia-old game. Rather than persist in a world with AlphaGo atop in both actual and perceptual terms, Lee confessed that AI 'cannot be defeated' and decided to step away. Lee's experience is often invoked as a parable for the growing power and prowess of AI-enabled programs and tools, although some have already looked at impacts and implications beyond board games.

From the outspoken Elon Musk to the somewhat more demure Centre for the Study of Existential Risk at Cambridge University, many have sounded alarms over the dangers of AI, particularly the cascading effects of 'sentient' robots and fully-automated weapons systems. While it would be foolish to ignore the misuses of AI, it is clear that there are a number of pressing threats and risks, including some that challenge us to examine artificiality in its various forms. Take the World Economic Forum's *Global Risks Report 2020*, which is currently in its 15th edition. For the first time ever, the top five risks in terms of likelihood are all environmental in scope, and three (climate action failure, biodiversity loss, and extreme weather) made the top four in terms of impact. The concept of the Anthropocene, which argues that the environment has become an artifact of human creation, should remind us all of the artificiality of humanity's dominion over the natural world. Our actions have created artificial conditions anathema to our very survival. And, it is quite artificial to believe that humans have even a modicum of control over a complex planet that continuously defies our best models, hence the need for immediate action to abate the current climate emergency. If recent events are any indication, anyone reading this will be continuously subject to high-likelihood and high-impact risks, or, to put it another way, postnormal bursts, that reorient our very sense of what can and might be possible. Enter COVID-19.

Infectious Imaginings

To say that Zhongnan Hospital was at the centre of the novel coronavirus outbreak would be an understatement. As the medical centre for Wuhan University, it was ground zero for what would eventually become our present crisis. As things began to worsen in Hubei Province, doctors and researchers looked to AI to assist with diagnosing patients, specifically to look for signs of pneumonia, which is what makes this particular disease so lethal. Early detection can not only help patients receive much-needed treatment before the disease takes hold but, at a community level, potentially keep surges from overwhelming healthcare systems. As one might expect, interventions of this type were experimental, which speaks as much to the nature of the crisis as the technology itself. Indeed, there can and should be little doubt that many, if not most, were simply caught off guard by the coronavirus outbreak that mutated into a full-blown pandemic earlier this year. Perhaps it was merely beleaguerment due to the string of seemingly unimaginable events that have come to characterise life in postnormal times. Even as troubling reports started coming in from Wuhan and images of roadblocks and empty streets began circulating online, the outbreak felt unreal, yet also eerily familiar. Ebola, H1N1, MERS, and SARS have done much to shape how we perceive such events, but infectious imaginings, from *Outbreak* (1995) to *Contagion* (2011), have also done much to both raise awareness but also perhaps desensitise us to these 'inevitable surprises'. Can or might we end up saying the same for AI?

Of course, analysts, futurists, and scientists have warned about the risk of pandemics for years, if not decades. Reading a range of alternative futures scenarios or being tossed into a pandemic simulation are certainly powerful means to learn, but if this crisis has made anything clear, it is that too often too little is learned too late. When I was approached to make a contribution to this issue, it was not my intent to write about pandemics. But, as with AI, which has consumed a great deal of our imaginative and anticipatory capacities over the past few years, COVID-19 will dominate imaginings of the future for years if not decades to come, especially if things continue unfolding on their present course, so it was not only responsible but also necessary to make it a focal point for thinking through AI. At the time of writing, the world looks poised for an unprecedented, yet all too familiar, global crisis – one that has already been (and will certainly continue to be) impacted by developments, applications, and the complexities of AI. Then again, much of what is written here could be outdated in the coming days, weeks, and months ahead.

While almost everything feels suspended in a state of flux at the moment, one thing appears to be certain: for better or worse, AI and COVID-19 have a lot in common. First, and broadly speaking, both are poorly understood, although social media seems to have amplified the confidence with which anyone, and everyone, invokes and analyses them. This is not to say that 'the experts' ought to drive conversations about how to steer our responses to both, quite the contrary. A range of voices, including the most vulnerable, must drive the proactive and responsive choices that are made in relation to both, but this is easier said than done. AI and COVID-19 necessitate a somewhat technical understanding of complex phenomena and have been subject to torrents of mis- and dis-information. Second, both AI and COVID-19 spur deep-seated fears over humanity's place as our planet's 'alpha' species. Putting *Terminator* and/or *Contagion* imaginings aside, the potential perils of truly artificial intelligence and the pitfalls of a catastrophic pandemic do much to highlight the fragility of many, if not most, of the systems – from our own biological to the incredibly inequitable economic to those that bring food to our tables – upon which our all-too-modern lives depend. Finally, both AI and COVID-19 highlight the need to ask *'what's next?'* with particular attention to policy-making and governance design. Are there better structures for how we might choose to govern ourselves? Could AI play a role? The plight of AI in the time of COVID-19 portends more than just pattern recognition; it points towards the potentiality for governments to be structured in radically new forms with designs focused on presenting 'speculative evidence,' which deserves greater attention a bit later. Before delving into what might be next, it is worth looking at what is happening now.

A tale of two articles

Wired magazine has been an advocate for futures thinking, or at least a variation of it, since its inception nearly thirty years ago. From its beginning, the California-based publication has demonstrated a clear penchant for 'Silicon Valley' approaches to sense-making and solutioning. *Wired* has become something of a bellwether in the broader 'tech trends' space and a site for distilling popular imaginings. This is not to say that *Wired* offers any sort of representative sample but rather that it speaks to a current within our zeitgeist on human-technology relations. Take two recent articles on AI, which also make clear connections to the COVID-19 pandemic. On 15 March 2020, *Wired* published an opinion piece by Glen Weyl and Jaron Lanier. The latter's name is likely familiar as he has been a vocal advocate on the oppressive nature of many technologies, including those he worked on for decades as a pioneer in virtual reality.

In 'AI is an Ideology, Not a Technology,' Weyl and Lanier put forward a compelling argument that there is a technocratic ideology underpinning the predominant imaginings of AI, which come from both corporate entities as well as less-than-democratic governments (to be read as China). Ultimately, they argue that it is important, if not essential, to re-imagine 'the role of technology in human affairs'. While it has become fashionable to make such pronouncements without offering examples as to how one might accomplish this truly Herculean feat, the authors actually suggest looking at Taiwan, which has made great strides in building 'a culture of agency over their technologies through civic participation and collective organisation'. Furthermore, they note how such approaches have been central to the island's COVID-19 response, which has been noted by many as exemplary. Implementing a strategy that features an impressive '124 action items,' Taiwan has balanced communication and transparency with tech-driven decision-making that gave it an early jump on containment measures. Taiwan's aggressive policies, which were developed after the SARS epidemic, have been buttressed by AI-enabled applications that deliver citizen alerts and support supply chain management for critical items, such as face masks. While it is certainly too early to declare Taiwan a 'winner' in the global race to 'flatten the curve,' their efforts, which included proactive and widespread testing, have produced, to date, positive results, which has not been the case in many other places.

The second article, 'AI Can Help Scientists Find a COVID-19 Vaccine', by Oren Etzioni, CEO of the Allen Institute for AI, and Nicole DeCario, who serves as Etzioni's Senior Assistant, strikes a much more optimist tone. Noting how AI is already being used to map components of a vaccine, the authors deploy real world examples, primarily their own efforts to assist researchers in mining the explosion of scientific articles on COVID-19, to highlight the 'bad rap' handed down to AI in recent years. In the article's penultimate paragraph, and in a passage worth quoting in full, the authors observe: 'It is ironic that the AI which has caused such consternation with facial recognition, deepfakes, and such is now at the frontlines of helping scientists confront COVID-19 and future pandemics'.

One can only wonder if any of the Uighur Muslims, who perhaps number near one million, currently residing in one of China's 're-education camps' feel a sense of irony in relation to how AI-enabled facial recognition systems are being used both to corral them *and* combat the current pandemic. Maybe this irony can be found within the deep fake viral videos, which were seen by as many as fifteen million citizens, circulated via Whatsapp groups during the 2019 Indian general elections *and* those being used to identify signs of pneumonia. Perhaps this irony is palpable to those subject to China's 'social credit' system, which uses a mixture of technologies – big data, facial recognition and, of course, AI – to enable *and* disable certain actions and activities from employment opportunities to purchasing plane and train tickets. It is perhaps unfair to expect too much from *Wired*. Given that these two articles were published less than two weeks apart, and the latter lacks any sense of self-reflexivity, the tale of these two articles highlights the challenges of finding consistent sources that shy away from simplistic framings and sanguine apologetics on AI, and this has become especially difficult in a time of COVID-19. This brings us back to the signal-to-noise problem, which, as we have been told, if not promised, is where AI shines.

Again, it is a bit too early to congratulate or condemn, but, on the whole, the United States looks poised to be hit quite hard by the COVID-19 pandemic. And given who sits atop the current administration, it would be foolhardy to expect otherwise. Will, or rather can, AI save the day? Apparently, the White House has pinned at least part of its hopes on analysing the mountain of data (estimated to be at or around 29,000 scientific articles as of March 2020) generated by scientists and researchers. Summoning leaders from companies such as Google and Microsoft, the coronavirus task force, which is actually led by Vice President Pence, announced a new public/private partnership aimed at providing cutting-edge computing power, including AI-based tools such as machine learning. While there can be little doubt that such approaches, which encompasses a broader range of algorithms that includes neural nets, are effective for identifying patterns, there is no guarantee that decision makers, particularly those currently in power, will enact policies based on data-driven insights. This, if anything, is the greatest challenge at the heart of AI in the time of COVID-19: humans. For all of the concerns over what might happen should machines become equally or more intelligent than humans, our current crisis makes clear that AI cannot match the limitations of our humanity, especially in times of crisis, which brings out both the best and worst in us. From COVID-19 transmission parties to physical-distancing-be-damned spring breakers to the airplane-toilet-seat-licking-coronavirus-challenge-model (yes, that's a real thing), the corollary pandemic of stupidity has left many of us clamouring for intelligence, artificial or otherwise. Can our governance structures truly handle such crises?

What's next?

As this exploration began with a provocation, it only seems fitting to end with one. No, this will not involve Alice and Bob, at least not yet. Ok, here it goes: Democracy had a good run. No, really. From the experiments of ancient Greece to the complex participatory structures of the Iroquois Confederacy to the hundreds of millions of voters across modern day India, there can be little doubt that democracy had a profound impact on the world, including playing a role in the rise of some of the world's most tyrannical despots. To be clear, pronouncing the death of democracy, which has been done many times before, is not welcoming a turn toward authoritarian and non-participatory modes of political organisation and decision-making but rather challenging us all to imagine, and ultimately design, what comes next. As imaginings of AI have predominantly tended toward the singular, the same can be said, for the most part, about our collective imaginings for governance design, broadly defined. Parliament is a fascinating project that looks at how the assembly space for 193 United Nations members affects policy and decision-making practices. Could AI be useful for reimagining not only how issues are framed but the very spaces within which such discussions take place? Will the COVID-19 pandemic create a space to re-examine and re-engineer governance itself? What other models of governance would be better suited to anticipate and confront the challenges of life in postnormal times? The COVID-19 pandemic certainly offers an opportunity to call into question many things, especially as they begin to fail, but there have also been calls for things to return to 'normal,' although others have suggested that this is not going to happen. Can the crisis spur substantive change or will things be quickly ordered back into their previous state? What measures might be taken to sustain systems that are woefully unsustainable?

As countries turn toward emergency measures to combat the ongoing pandemic, there can be little doubt, and there have already been signs, that some will intentionally abuse this 'opportunity' toward despotic ends. In Hungary, who is a member of the European Union, Prime Minister Viktor Orban rejected calls for a limit on a range of unprecedented emergency powers, which includes rule by decree, the ability to override all existing legislation, and the suspension of elections. Orban's not-so-subtle power grab is viewed as the culmination of a series of moves aimed at cementing his grip over civil society, especially as there are harsh measures for spreading information deemed false by the government. Will other countries seek to implement similar measures? In many ways, China is ahead of the curve. The superpower's AI-enabled Corporate Social Credit System (CSCS), which should be fully up and running by the end of 2020, has been buttressed by a virus-response-driven increase in mass surveillance and tracking that some fear could become a 'new normal'. Interestingly, a pre-pandemic study carried out in China found that people were willing to give up aspects of personal privacy to combat the 'nationwide crisis of trust' that has come about through rampant fraud and corruption. While the sample was relatively small (only five hundred people), this research raises a significant question: what trade-offs (and there are many inherent to the CSCS) are citizens willing to endure in and beyond postnormal bursts, such as the COVID-19 pandemic?

The CSCS will live and die based on one thing: data. Given the strategic and tactical importance of good and reliable information, it might, or might not, come as a surprise that some have called into question the provenance of China's reporting related to the outbreak in Hubei Province, including concerns that official cases were hidden and, even more troubling, that the mortality rate could be higher than suggested. This is extremely troubling as many measures and models have been based on data from Wuhan, which is to say that some measures might be woefully inadequate should any of the critical early-stage outbreak data be insufficient, incomplete, and/or incorrect. Pattern recognition would be for naught without good data, which illuminates an Achilles heel for many, if not most, AI-driven approaches. Given the global turn toward 'evidence-based' policy-making, which also necessitates sound and reliable information, some have called for 'responsible data collection and processing at a global scale,' although how such initiatives can and might be implemented remains uncertain, especially when one considers the lack of headway on other global challenges, such as reducing greenhouse gas emissions.

In the United Kingdom, issues over data and evidence bubbled to the surface as the government announced a behavioural science-driven approach, which included a controversial measure known as 'herd immunity' that essentially allows for a greater percentage of the population to become infected. However, it took public outcry as well as an open-letter signed by over two hundred academics asking for 'evidence' that led the government to reconsider, although models suggested that the National Health Service would be quickly and fully overwhelmed. Labelled a 'debacle' by some, this strategy was first clarified and then later rejected in favour of increased testing and physical distancing, which appears to have worked well in both Singapore and South Korea. Whatever forms of governance come next, it is clear that one of the most important criteria would be to present speculative-evidence, specifically 'weak signals, ethnographic observations, and the stories of people's experience'. Located at the intersection of actual and perceptual framings, speculative-evidence allows for phenomena, from AI to COVID-19, to be seen and understood from a range of perspectives across a diversity of contexts. And, as the COVID-19 pandemic makes abundantly clear, there is certainly an opportunity to promote more engagements that critically and creatively focus on navigating uncertainty, rather than attempting to 'manage' risk, at a variety of scales within and beyond government. If anything, the COVID-19 pandemic is a stark reminder that: 'everything in the world about you is a social invention'. This will become more apparent as various systems bend and break and, perhaps most importantly, as communities on the frontlines of this crisis find ways to survive and thrive. To navigate the complexities of postnormal times, an era defined in part by an abundance of noise, we must find ways to both identify and amplify signals pointing toward inventing a better tomorrow. Such an endeavour must be anything but artificial. And, if Alice and Bob have taught us anything, it is that an unwillingness to follow rules can actually be a sign of intelligence. And, if the tragedy of Lee Sedol conveys a lesson, it is that beauty can and might emerge from unlikely sources during moments of great uncertainty.

DIGITAL ETHICS

Emre Kazim

Earlier in the year a colleague invited me to join him in his invitation to be part of a television panel discussing artificial intelligence (AI). Thinking that it might be fun to get an insight into TV production and as support for my friend, I joined him. We arrived early and grabbed a coffee; jovially I told him that the only thing he will need to prepare for is the inevitable question about killer robots and that his response should involve a quip about Schwarzenegger and *The Terminator* film series. Remarkably, (or perhaps unremarkably) within a few minutes the dystopian world of drones and Robocop was being discussed. After the panel was over and as we engaged in a critical debrief of how it went, central to our discussion was just how esoteric and science-fiction-esque the perceptions and misconceptions are around AI.

So what is AI? And what is the significance of AI in terms of our society? These questions are in one sense straightforwardly addressed – AI is some kind of automation, and the social impacts of AI are likely to be world historical. However, the questions reside in another, and certainly more important sense, almost impossible to address without entering into the sci-fi world of fantasy, not too dissimilar to common (mis)conceptions. The truth is that, like all novel technologies, the impact will be profound, but it is very difficult to know what the nature of this impact will be.

Within this indeterminacy lies the growing field of 'digital ethics', which is an attempt to understand and respond accordingly to the ethical risks that AI and other emerging technologies, such as blockchain and big data analytics, present. Examples of harm that have been observed are bias in systems such as recruitment and criminal justice sentencing, where particular demographics are discriminated against. In other words, minorities are sent to jail for longer. Voter manipulation is also a concern if you think of all the stories about foreign intervention in elections, along with misdiagnosis of cancer patients. With these, a growing consciousness has developed within wider society and developers of these technologies that something needs to be done.

The field of digital ethics, which incidentally is only a few years old, has undergone three broad phases. The first was a set of principles for AI/digital ethics. This resulted in a huge number of academic groups, national and international governmental bodies, private industry and NGOs, publishing their own set of principles. The core problem and criticism of this was that these principles were largely incoherent and contradictory. It turns out that ethical consensus and clarity is somewhat elusive.

The second phase was an ethical-by-design approach, which was an engineering focused problem-solving exercise. Here the issue was two-fold: what does it even mean to be 'ethical-by-design' and, are engineers best placed to both understand and judge (let alone implement) ethics? As in the core problem in the first phase of digital ethics, there doesn't seem to be a clear and consensual ethical code that developers could somehow engineer into design, and furthermore it is unclear if the problem is even an engineering one. Within the social scientific literature, we often discuss something called 'value laden technology' which is the set of social values that technologies sit within and express. For example, nuclear is used both as a source of energy and a devastating and indiscriminate weapon. The use of the technology is seen as an expression of the social and political values of the society, or at least the ruling strata. Hence ethics is a social and political concern, not an engineering one.

Considering the above, what began as a lack of ethical/philosophical consensus and a real question mark regarding the role of the engineer, has emerged as a third phase of digital ethics. This current phase revolves around the idea that only an interdisciplinary approach can meaningfully address and hope to mitigate the ethical risks of AI, and more generally new digital technology. The idea here is that philosophers, sociologists, psychologists, lawyers, engineers and others, work together in a dynamic and integrated manner. Hence the governance, social impact, legal compliance, engineering standards and so forth are all continuously kept in mind from the design phase to real life use. Confused? Well, this is where we are. And as someone engaged in this debate, as a philosophical ethicist working with developers of AI, I can tell you that I too am baffled by the whole thing!

In a personal and more subjective domain I continually find myself reflecting and critiquing on this academic field. Like everyone else, these technologies will have an impact on me, those around me, the country and even the world that we live in. Indeed, the nature of these technologies is such that they do not respect traditional borders, with a technology being developed in one part of the world being rapidly transferred, copied and adopted in another. Moreover, the impact is equally global – one simple example is where people's data is stored. A simple web search of social media posts leaves a signature on the 'world wide web' and only God knows where this is recorded and stored.

Stated in a somewhat convoluted idiom, there is a universality associated with the scope of this digital revolution. Notwithstanding this, humans are of course plural, and humanity is an iridescent rainbow of cultures, traditions, values and norms. As such, we must all respond from our own positions. In this respect I am a Brit, who is from the Muslim community, with parents who were born in Cyprus and Turkey. Musing on Muslim subjectivity with respect to digital ethics, I believe that there are a number of themes that are worth examining.

Digital technology and political structure is where we think of social organisation in the form of a continuum, with one side representing a command/communist state, and the other side representing a laissez-faire/anarchic/libertarian. In the command state, digital technologies may be used to provide public services such as automation in welfare, medicine, policing, whereas in the libertarian state the technologies will be utilised by individuals in unpredictable ways. The question here with respect to Muslim subjectivity is what kind of a political structure does 'muslimness' purportedly commit one to? Which is not to say that the answer cannot be that muslimness doesn't commit us to a particular structure at all.

Activism is a corollary to the above concerns, whether the context of the political structure is one that is considered authoritarian/dictatorial, or democratic/liberal. The ethical concern here touches on how the novel digital technologies can be used with high efficiency in a surveillance state. Indeed, there have never been more effective forms of monitoring – this is a direct result of big data and AI analytics. Moreover, technologies that we refer to as 'nudging' (targeted advertising) are considered some of the most powerful tools of manipulation. In a recent discussion I was party to, the point was raised that we have always had surveillance and propaganda but that the current technologies are of a much higher order of magnitude. With respect to activism – as Muslims who respect individual rights, privacy and democracy, we may think that these tools make protesting and lobbying for these values more difficult and increase the efficacy of authoritarian states. Conversely, new digital technologies can anonymise activists, facilitate rapid mobilisation and communication, and function to greatly undermine and subvert authoritarian tendencies.

It appears to me that there is an ironic, almost paradoxical relationship between developed/underdeveloped nations and these new digital technologies. With respect to the level of development, what is being referred to is the infrastructure and innovation for the research and development of technology. Technologies emerge out of the most advanced countries, in terms of research, and these societies have the most stringent controls in terms of standards and regulation. Think of the European Union's General Data Protection Regulation (GDPR) legislation, which has become the seminal legal approach to data protection. These legal responses are a result of the fact that the technologies are disruptive and ironically the more 'advanced' a state is, the more acutely the disturbance is going to be felt. Nations that are less developed have inefficient state mechanisms for public service provision, tax collection, even surveillance and monitoring, and therefore technologies are likely to be adopted by citizens and the state itself more readily as there is likely to be less disturbance. This is a relationship of inverse proportionality. In poorer countries there are ineffective states and therefore technology may have less impact. In developed nations, the opposite applies.

This point is relevant because Muslim subjectivity is one where the community is made of people from both developed and underdeveloped nations. There is a consciousness of development that may or may not be directly related to our muslimness but is nonetheless part of the common debates. My feeling is that trajectories and the pace with which development occurs will largely depend upon where one is situated in the world. Additionally, how one is situated within the framework of minority/ majoritarian communities may also be crucial. In contexts where such politics are unfortunately at play, the ethical position one takes on the adoption and use of these new digital technologies will significantly reflect this context.

A niggling question preoccupies me from all my academic work in the field of digital ethics. And it is this: are there any new ethical and philosophical questions in digital ethics? Are there novel and unique philosophical and ethical issues that arise as a result of the digital revolution? Of course there are plenty of ethical concerns, for instance loss of labour and privacy intrusions. However, the loss of labour was a theme with mechanisation of factories, such as automation in car factories, and violations of privacy, such as opening a letter that is not addressed to me, certainly take place outside of the digital realm. These are simply known ethical concerns that can be applied to the advent of new digital technology.

My suspicion is that there are a couple of ethical issues which are transformed sufficiently for us to reasonably think of them as generating new philosophical concerns: human agency and privacy. By agency what I am referring to are things like making genuine choices, autonomy, volition, will, freedom - a casual act that originates from an intentional act/process rooted in the will of a person. Clearly this assumes that there is such a thing as human choice/freedom and I will not go in to the debate about what is meant by this other than to say that our generally held common sensical notion of choice is broadly what I am referring to.

Historically we have experienced automation in terms of mechanical processes. This was the replacing of a human maker/doer with a machine or process that could make/do in a far more uniform and efficient manner. This led to the loss of labour and even the loss of various skills in society, which certainly had a cognitive cost. However, in general, the automation and mechanisation was with respect to objects that exist out there in space. With respect to artificial intelligence, the thing being replaced by automation is thinking itself. In the example of mechanical automation, we used the vehicle whether it be a car, bike or whatever, making process as our example; to continue with this we can think of the driver as being replaced. If thinking is fully automated, or rather becomes increasingly automated, human agency is likely to be eroded.

Privacy is also an ethical concern that precedes the advent of this new digital revolution. However, the extent to which privacy is now being eroded is such that I believe it can be considered a genuinely novel issue. This is directly correlated to the issue of agency in so far as a person's 'thoughts' are being invaded by 'nudging' and massive data collection. If I ask a person what they were doing a year ago on a particular day and time, to the minute, they would not be able to give a probable, let alone a precise, answer. Indeed, if I asked someone what they were doing yesterday at exactly the same time as the moment I asked them, they would also struggle to answer the question. And yet, big data analytics and collection has a signature at this level of precision. That is truly remarkable. Privacy has been an issue of invasion, where we delimited the private space and even consider it sacred; what could be more sacred than one's own internal states, movements, and actions. Indeed, the level of recording is so ubiquitous that text typed in and then deleted, in some social media platforms, is recorded.

The two ethical issues of agency and privacy allay into questions regarding what it means to be human – a highly complex and contentious issue. It is here that we can draw upon the metaphysics of tradition and philosophy. From the Enlightenment view, the human is defined as a free and rational agent. We can also state this as agency is to express freedom and rationality. What the nature of that freedom is, and what the nature of the notion of reason that is being referred to is, is highly debated in the present context. Some argue that 'free', 'rational', and 'human', are concepts that align with constructs which reflect Prussian men from the eighteenth century. Indeed, there are powerful critiques of Enlightenment notions of human from post-colonial philosophical literature. Nonetheless, if we avoid defining concretely what the terms mean, an assertion that to be human means to be in some sense free, does seem to be a valid claim. I also believe this is congruent with the Islamic traditions that emphasise responsibility and ultimate judgement. Indeed, I believe that character development, improving oneself, striving to be good and do good, promoting justice, all spiritual and ethical imperatives within the *Islamicate*, are premised on an assumption that humans are agents, responsible because they are imbued with the capacity of freedom, however that may be defined.

We exist in a historical moment, where things are in flux and fundamental changes are occurring. One of the reasons I have emphasised agency is because I see this as a reminder to myself – that I am responsible and have the capacity to affect the world I live within. We should not take our agency and humanity for granted. The tradition we come from, I believe, emphasises that ultimately the common bond is precisely this shared humanness. Islam is one of the great traditions and is an invaluable source of ethical and moral inspiration. I do not call for an 'Islamic Digital Ethics', or 'Islamic AI', rather I call for a genuine ethics that preserves the humanity of all people, and of course this would in effect be an ethics that reflects our tradition.

IS IT BAD TO BE ARTIFICIAL?

Colin Tudge

I suggest that we object to the word 'artificial' for two reasons. First, it applies to things that are made by us, rather than by nature, or indeed by God, and is therefore taken to mean something unnatural, with connotations of spookiness and subversion. But also, secondly, it tends to mean machine-made rather than hand-made. Machine-made tends to mean unhuman, or indeed inhuman, while hand-made means craft – made with human skill and love (although of course the word 'crafty' tends to mean 'devious').

Why, though, should we look askance at things that we make, as opposed to things created by nature? After all, making things is what human beings *do*. If we did not make things we would not be human. The earliest recognised member of the genus *Homo* who lived around 2.2 million years ago was and in some circles still is called *Homo habilis*, meaning 'handy man'. His fossil bones were surrounded by stones that had clearly been fashioned into tools. The descendants of *H habilis* went on to build temples and mosques, and to make lutes and harpsichords, bicycles and microscopes and mobile phones, vaccines and great works of art. As King Lear observed as he battled his way across the heath in wind and rain (Act 3, Scene 4), without the artifice of clothes a human being is reduced to 'the thing itself' – and then is 'no more but … a poor, bare, forked animal'. In short, overall, the things we make – our artefacts, our technologies – have incomparably expanded the range of humanity; enabling us to realise our full potential; enabling us, indeed, to become ourselves.

Of course, too, human beings are not the only creatures that make things. As Jesus said (Luke 9:58), 'Foxes have holes, and birds of the air have nests'; and, he might have added, bees, wasps, ants, and termites build huge, air-conditioned engineering works of great complexity and subtlety in which to live, socialise, store and ferment their food, and raise their young. All are artificers. British biologist Richard Dawkins coined the felicitous expression 'extended phenotype' to describe the physical form and mental capacity of animals *plus* all their accompanying technologies. An animal plus the things it makes is far greater than the naked beast itself.

Humans, though, are the greatest artificers of all, by far. We are not the biggest or the strongest and we cannot do many of the things that some animals do in passing – spin silk from our own bodies like a spider, and fashion wondrous webs; catch insects on the wing in the dark like a bat. But we are the great generalists, the ultimately protean creatures. With our dextrous fingers, our great brains, and above all our powers of communication – which enable us to pool our thoughts – and with the artefacts that all these gifts enable us to create, we can (in principle) do everything that all other animals can do between them, and more. We are still animals – and it's important to remember that: that we are still very much a part of nature, utterly dependent on the natural world. Yet in our ability to think collectively, and our ability at least in theory to frame any thinkable thought, and create any physical thing, we are, in effect, a new life form. We have moved the posts.

So why don't we just celebrate that fact, and revel in it? Why suggest that the things we make – things that by literal definition are 'artificial' – are in any sense inferior, or fake? Well, many people, including some of the most influential people in the world, think precisely this. Many people in the history of the world have taken it to be self-evident, and in many cases still do, that to replace wild nature with human artefact – or artifice – is what 'progress' really means, and ought to mean. In the mid-twentieth century the Australian government cleared the native eucalyptus forest wholesale and all the unique plants and animals that went with it with chains slung between huge tractors. Then they converted what remained, plus the surrounding grassland, into pasture for sheep and cattle, and into wheat-fields, commonly irrigated with fossil water pumped from the depths. The world over, deforestation has been seen as a necessary precursor to civilisation, which literally means 'citification' (the word comes from the Latin *civis* meaning 'city'). Today, politicians and industrialists routinely refer to the natural world – which should properly be called the *biosphere,* meaning 'living world' – as 'natural resources': raw material for us to convert into something that is putatively useful and above all is lucrative. In passing, though, we might note that much of Australia's hard-won pasture is now desert and that deforestation is a prime cause of global warming (and floods and drought).

In practice, human beings have been changing the face of the Earth and its creatures wholesale and radically for tens of thousands of years. The fossil record tells us that around 12, 000 years ago North America was graced with a whole suite of giant mammals: giant ground sloths, giant armadillos known as glyptodonts, elephants, rhinos, sabre-tooths, 'dire' wolves, and huge running bears with short faces – gigantic, ursine Rottweilers. Then, suddenly, they all disappeared. One eminently plausible if controversial theory has it that it was human beings – people just like us – with the aid of their spears and clubs and hunting strategies, that finished them off. Neolithic farmers, starting around 4,000 years ago, cleared the forests of Scotland and created the moors of heather that we now take to be 'natural'. The first Maoris in New Zealand wiped out the fifteen or so species of native moas in the first millennium CE, and felled prodigious quantities of trees.

From earliest times, though, some people clearly had misgivings. Traditional religions, including that of the Maoris, emphasise our responsibility towards nature, and our obligation to it. Specifically, Plato in the fifth century BCE warned that when sloping fields are ploughed and left bare they are prone to erosion. People in general, philosophers or not, feel in their bones that there are limits to what we can and should do.

The voices of protest were heard most loudly as the Industrial Revolution got firmly into its stride in the eighteenth and nineteenth centuries, and began rapidly to make radical and very conspicuous changes that to a large extent were and are irreversible. To be sure, some revelled in the transformation or at least in some aspects of it. In England, Joseph Wright of Derby, James Ward, and, most famously, J M W Turner painted fire and steam, and in some cases human sweat, with great relish.

But as industrialisation progressed, there arose a succession of artists and philosophers – and some scientists – who were repulsed by the changes they saw around them; and who felt, more deeply, that such comprehensive alteration is, as the Ancient Greeks would have said, *hubris*. Hubris, to the Greeks, was the greatest sin and the greatest folly of all – presuming to usurp the power of the gods. The wreckage of the modern world attests that the Greeks were right. Adherents of the Abrahamic religions, with their single, all-seeing, all-powerful God (Yahweh, Jehovah, Allah) had a similar concept. They called it blasphemy.

All this, I think, is embedded in our innate suspicion of and aversion to the word 'artificial'. Sure it means 'things that human beings make' and it seems absurd to suggest that making things is intrinsically bad, whether we or some other creature are doing the making. We could indeed argue (as some in effect do) that *not* to make things is itself a kind of blasphemy. After all, our enormous intelligence and capabilities are God-given, and to reject His gifts is itself blasphemous, is it not? Certainly I have heard industrial technophiles argue that to build rockets to 'conquer space', or trains that go at 300 kilometres per hour, or 'CAFOs' – 'concentrated animal feeding operations' aka factory farms – is 'Man's destiny'. The most highfalutin rhetoric, of the kind that substitutes 'Man' for 'human being', is always wheeled out to defend the most dubious practices and to silence the opposition. What matters most though, as most people seem to feel in their bones, including the makers of dictionaries, is the motive and the feeling behind the artefact and the technology that produced it. What was it made for? To what end? Was it to produce something to enhance human life – something beautiful, or obviously useful? Or was it just to impose human vanity on the natural world and on humanity at large – to 'make a statement', to enhance the power and wealth of the creator?

A succession of powerful thinkers these past two centuries or so have contributed to such thoughts.

The honourable tradition of doubters

The warnings were sounded throughout the nineteenth century by the critic, artist (he drew beautifully and was no mean water-colourist) and would-be social reformer John Ruskin (1819–1900). He is best known perhaps as a champion of the Pre-Raphaelites and in particular of Gothic architecture. In particular, though he was not known as a man of the people (somewhat stand-offish and effete) he had a huge respect for humanity, or at least for the creative and moral qualities of humanity which, alas, are so often suppressed. His revulsion of things artificial drew both on his love of and respect for nature (and God), and his admiration of craft. Both threads are encapsulated in these extracts from *The Stones of Venice,* written in and after his grand tour of the city in 1851–53:

> For the very first requirement of Gothic architecture being that it shall admit the aid, and appeal to the admiration, of the rudest as well as the most refined

> minds, the richness of the work is … a part of its humility … That humility …
> the very life of the Gothic school, is shown not only in the imperfection, but
> in the accumulation, of ornament. The inferior rank of the workman is often
> shown as much in the richness, as the roughness, of his work ….
>
> There are, however, far nobler interests mingling, in the Gothic heart, with the
> rude love of decorative accumulation: a magnificent enthusiasm, which feels as
> if it never could do enough to reach the fullness of its ideal … a profound
> sympathy with the fullness & wealth of the material universe.

Elsewhere he wrote: 'When love and skill work together, expect a masterpiece.'

His emphasis on 'imperfection' in the above echoes the Muslim idea that
human artefacts should not be too perfect, for perfection is the prerogative
of God. For Ruskin, morality, religion, and aesthetics were intertwined – as
they surely are in all of us. But Ruskin made this explicit.

Thus inspired, Ruskin promoted, perhaps more than anyone else, the
vogue for Victorian Gothic – flowing lines, infinite variety, in starkest
contrast to the straight lines, bloodless (as he saw it), geometric, modular
precision of the classical architecture that was fashionable in the Regency
period and its aftermath, when he was born and brought up. But the Gothic
architecture he admired had to be the real thing: visibly made by craftsmen
who truly cared (stonemasons in olden times were almost always male). He
despised gratuitous, machine-made imitations. Thus in 1849 he wrote:

> … hand-work might always be known from machine-work … it will be plainly
> seen that some places have been delighted in more than others … here the
> chisel will have struck hard, and there lightly, and anon timidly … and the
> effect of the whole, as compared with the same design cut by a machine or a
> lifeless hand, will be like that of poetry well read and deeply felt to that of the
> same verses jangled by rote.

Indeed he considered 'cast or machine-made ornaments of any kind' to
be an 'architectural deceit'.

Ruskin hugely influenced William Morris (1834-1896), chief architect of
the Arts and Crafts movement. Morris, though, was more down-to-earth
than Ruskin and recognised the need for compromise. Thus as he wrote in
'Art and Its Producers' in 1881:

I do not [believe] we should aim at abolishing all machinery; I would do some things with machinery which are now done by hand, and other things by hand which are now done by machinery; in short, we would be the masters of our machines and not their slaves, as we are now. It is not this or that…machine which we want to get rid of, but the great intangible machine of commercial tyranny which oppresses the lives of all of us.

Morris did, after all, found a wallpaper factory – mass (or fairly mass) reproduction of his own and similarly crafted floral designs. In turn he influenced his near contemporary, the incomparable Leo Tolstoy (1828–1910). Tolstoy was an aristocrat (a Russian count) but with a huge admiration for and affiliation with the peasants who worked on his estates. In particular, like Ruskin, he admired manual skill – and the hard work and concentration that went with it. The principal character in *Anna Karenina* (1877) is the aristocratic Levin, the alter ego of Tolstoy himself. Levin liked to work with the peasants, as Tolstoy did. For many or most tasks the peasants worked in teams. For scything – a key activity – they worked in lines, and everyone had to keep up. This is how Levin got on:

Titus, who had taught Levin to scythe, a thin little peasant, [was] walking in front and cutting a wide swathe, wielding his scythe as though it were a toy …

Titus moved on with sweep after sweep of his scythe, not stopping and not tiring. Levin followed, trying to keep up, and finding it harder and harder … [but] the longer Levin mowed, the oftener he experienced those moments of oblivion when … the scythe seemed to mow of itself, a body full of life and consciousness of its own, as though by magic … These were the most blessed moments.

I am not a farmer but I have been heavily involved with farming for the past fifty years and many farmers have told me that they feel exactly the same way. Farmers complain all the time about the bureaucracy that beleaguers them and the lack of reward and – at least as important – of appreciation. I have never heard any of them complain about the work itself – or not, at least, about the kind of work that draws upon their skill and experience. They hate form-filling but they speak with pride of the freezing nights on the hillside delivering the first of the season's lambs. For them as for Levin the hard work, much as they might yearn to escape it at the time, is a spiritual experience. If we try too hard to eliminate effort, discomfort, and sheer difficulty from our lives then we rob ourselves of much of what it means to be human. In the most progressive, 'developed' societies more and more people do no peasant-style work at all. They go to the gym instead. That really is artificial in the worst sense; a programmed but mindless substitute for real work.

Mahatma Gandhi no less (1869–1948) corresponded with Tolstoy until the latter's death in 1910. Most famously, or at least most relevant to the present essay, he championed the use of the *charkha*, or spinning wheel. More broadly, he advocated *swadeshi*, meaning self-sufficiency, from the Sanskrit *swa*, meaning 'self', and *desh*, meaning country. Self-sufficiency, for Gandhi, was part of the key to independence – liberation from British rule; and home-grown cotton and silk, spun into textiles by tens of millions of charkhas on tens of millions of verandas, was a key requirement. Like Morris, however, Ghandi did not champion craft simply for its own sake. He was happy to make use of machines if they really could help to improve people's lives and create more agreeable societies. Thus in 1921 he wrote:

> I would favour the use of the most elaborate machinery if thereby India's pauperism and resulting idleness be avoided. I have suggested hand-spinning as the only ready means of driving away penury and making famine of work and wealth impossible. The spinning wheel itself is a piece of valuable machinery and in my own humble way I have tried to secure improvements in it in keeping with the special conditions of India.

All this – the notions of Ruskin, Morris, Tolstoy, Gandhi – feed into the idea that was brought into prominence in the 1970s in particular by the German-British economist E F ('Fritz') Schumacher (1911–1977): that of appropriateness. We tend to judge technologies by how ingenious they are, and how powerful, and, perhaps above all, how efficient. Physicists take efficiency to mean 'work achieved or energy generated divided by work (or energy) expended'. Nowadays when everything is given a price it tends to mean 'money generated versus money invested'. Machines obviously have their uses as both Morris and Gandhi emphasised – they can do many things that human beings cannot, and tirelessly. But as Paul Mason points out in *PostCapitalism* (2019), the use of machines is largely and sometimes entirely determined by profitability. Machines are used when they are cheaper than people and people are employed when they are cheaper than machines. In 'modern' agriculture – industrial agribusiness – 'efficiency' is to a large

extent defined as 'output per worker'. In other words the efficiency and
hence the virtue of a machine is judged by how many people it can put out
of work. That, when you boil it down, it the motive and the *raison d'être* of
a great deal of modern technology, and of the science that often lies behind
it. But, said Schumacher in *Small is Beautiful* (1973): 'Wisdom demands a
new orientation of science and technology toward the organic, the gentle,
the elegant and beautiful'; and, 'any intelligent fool can make things bigger,
more complex, and more violent. It takes a touch of genius — and a lot of
courage to move in the opposite direction.'

Indeed the first question we should ask of any new invention is 'What is
it really *for?* – or indeed, 'What is it *really* for?' Then we should ask: 'Is the
thing that is intended, good or bad?' Even more to the point – given that
good intentions do not always lead to good outcomes – we should ask,
'What, in practice, does the technology achieve?' Only then is it truly
relevant to ask whether the technology in question is 'efficient' – whether
it does what it intended to do with minimum fuss and at least cost.

Always, I suggest, everything that we do and make, including all our
technologies and crafts and the artefacts they produce, should have three ends
in view. First our actions and our artefacts should seek to improve, enrich,
and expand the lives of individuals. Secondly, everything we do and make
should, ideally, help to improve the lot of society as a whole – for no-one,
surely should benefit materially or otherwise at other people's expense. Then,
thirdly – the thing that so often has gone missing – we should ask, 'Is the
technology in question good for the biosphere as a whole?' At least – given
that *all* technologies are liable to have some unintended side effects – we
should strive to ensure that whatever we create and do does minimum harm
to our fellow creatures and to the fabric of the Earth. All that is what
'appropriate' ought to mean. Mere flashiness, power, cleverness, 'efficiency',
or short-term profitability are not what matters. Artefacts and the
technologies that produce them may generate wealth, but the headlong
pursuit of material wealth is liable to prove fatal – as the world is already
demonstrating. As St Paul allegedly said to his disciple Timothy (1 Timothy
6:10): 'The love of money is the root of all evil'. Scholars now question
whether Paul did say this but somebody must have said it and it's true anyway.

Finally, in our line-up of honourable doubters, we should mention the
Austrian philosopher and theologian Ivan Illich (1926–2002). In *Tools for
Conviviality,* also published in 1973, Illich argued that a good technology is one

that is truly liberating – one that makes individuals, and individual societies, more autonomous; more complete, more able to be themselves and to realise their true humanity. By contrast, many technologies, though they seem to make our lives easier, more 'convenient', in truth are enslaving us: making individuals and whole societies more and more dependent on the good offices of elites; of manufacturers – commonly corporates – who provide esoteric inventions over which the rest of us have no control; and of governments that operate hand-in-hand with those corporates. Such technologies, deployed as they are, are dehumanising. In the end they make us less able and more dependent than we need to be – dependent not on each other, which is always and necessarily the case, but on particular power-groups.

For Illich, the bicycle and the telephone were prime examples of convivial tools. To be sure, modern bikes that can win the *Tour de France* are seriously high-tech: carbon fibres, fancy alloys, computer-assisted design and all the rest. But in essence, the bicycle is simple. India in the 1970s (a favourite stamping ground of Illich) was a bicycle culture. Everyone had a bike or aspired to have one and remarkably expert people with remarkably simple tools made and mended them by the side of the road. People retained control. And, with a bike, ordinary people could extend their range at least beyond their village – a huge leap in personal fulfilment and at least potentially in conviviality. High-tech bikes are perfectly acceptable too – provided the companies that make them do not grow into mega-corporates with the power to control our lives. It is commonly assumed that 'appropriate' technologies must be low-tech, but that is not necessarily the case at all (as Gandhi recognised).

Strangely, we might feel, the key example of a non-convivial technology, for Illich, was broadcasting. For broadcasting in its early days – and the 1970s were still comparatively early days – the communication was one-way, and to a very large extent still is. Whoever controls the broadcasting stations, whether it's a government or some media mogul, can pass on their opinions or indeed their orders to the rest of us and we cannot answer back. The bicycle, as Illich saw things, was an instrument of empowerment while the broadcasting station was an instrument of control. Nowadays, of course, with modern IT and with the internet, this is no longer true. Everyone can talk to everyone else the world over. We might suggest that the mobile 'phone is to the modern Third World (an expression that Gandhi favoured, so it will certainly do me) what the bicycle was to their parents' and grandparents' generation: the great liberator, if not universally affordable then affordable at least to many. More grandly, any of us, in principle, can make our own TV programmes and broadcast them to the world. In the words of the British computer scientist, Tim Berners Lee, inventor of the World Wide Web, 'hope in life comes from all the interconnections among all the people in the world'.

Indeed, modern IT, centred on the Web, should help us truly to develop what ought to be our greatest asset – to think collectively (when we need to); to pool our thoughts. A billion heads really should be better than one. Modern IT then *ought* to be the ultimately convivial technology.

Yet, as always, there are serious drawbacks. First, people at large as we all know do not always use their enormous tech-driven powers of communication in the cause of conviviality but for the precise opposite. Any opinion that some objector feels is slightly out of line is liable to be followed by threats, always distasteful, sometimes dire, and occasionally followed up on. Secondly, the technologies of communication that should be available to all of us, key instruments of democracy, in practice, are largely commandeered, like everything else, by big power-groups; notably by corporates and big governments. So, like the old-style radio stations that Illich so mistrusted, they become instruments of control. Thirdly, the lines of communication provided by IT can be and are hacked and perverted. All technologies can be tools for criminality, big-time or small. Finally, IT in its present forms is not always ecologically friendly. Mobile phones incorporate rare metals mined in highly destructive ways from ecologically (and socially and politically) sensitive places.

All this needs ironing out before IT can truly be considered 'convivial'. But in principle it ought to be very good indeed, just as Berners-Lee envisaged.

IT draws upon the technology of computers which in turn draw on the insight of the English mathematical genius and logician Alan Turing (1912-1954) who saw that all problems (or nearly all) can be reduced to a series of either-or questions – the so called binary code; and also depends on the microchip, which makes it possible to build small and manageable machines that can put Turing's logic into practice. This same combination – Turing's logic and the microchips that allow us to apply it – has now taken us one step beyond IT and into the realms of AI: Artificial Intelligence. Here, the word 'artificial' carries no stigma. AI is not seen merely as a piece of trickery, a second-rate imitation, but as the harbinger of a new age (as in the past were bronze, iron, steam power, the internal combustion engine, the jet plane, radio, electronics, atomic power, vaccines, biotech – and so on and so on). That, however, could be a mistake. Artificial intelligence is not real – not human intelligence – and the difference matters.

AI: the good, the bad, and the downright sinister

AI can work out problems in microseconds that would take a human thinker months, assuming he or she could work them out at all. Even more than that: AI fitted out with rudimentary senses – or super-acute senses – and with appendages for mobility and dexterity, can do more and more of the things that now need human skill and expertise. Already robots build cars. Soon they will perform minor surgery (or perhaps they do already). Some feel that the future of agriculture lies with drones and robots, to monitor the state of the crops and the fields, to do the weeding, milk the cows, and so on. The necessary technologies are with us already. Robots should do the kinds of jobs that humans don't want to do. The most obvious dangers are, first, that if we remove all hard work from our own lives then we will miss out on much of the joy of being human – as Tolstoy said. Secondly, the more that robots take over, the more they will create unemployment. Yet today's robots are embryonic – primitive. We ain't seen nothing yet. Robots in mature form could render all humanity obsolete, or indeed redundant – apart perhaps from a few all-powerful puppeteers, like O'Brien, the man behind Big Brother in George Orwell's *1984*. How can that be good?

Secondly, and more profoundly, AI is also artificial in the pejorative sense. It is not the real thing, and it is dangerous to suppose that it is. The American philosopher John Searle (b. 1932) pointed out in the 1980s that it is possible for machines to do wonderfully clever things that seem to be unimpeachably human and yet are just an imitation. Thus, he said, it would theoretically be possible to create an algorithm that could translate Chinese into English, impeccably, without understanding either language. Indeed, modern word processors already do the same kind of thing – picking up not only on spelling mistakes but on lapses of grammar. Alan Turing suggested that a machine should be considered conscious if, in practice, it was impossible to tell the difference between the things it said and the things that people say. But Searle begged to differ with Turing and in this, Searle was surely right.

Human thought, it seems, is qualitatively different from the calculations of machines. The difference, I suggest, lies in the concept of *monistic idealism*, which basically means 'universal consciousness'. We, as human beings, tune in to this universal consciousness while machines merely look as if they do. The basic idea is very well explained by the Indian physicist Amit Goswami (b. 1936) in *The Self-Aware Universe*. All this of course requires a separate discussion – but suffice to say here that the mechanisms of thought in machines and humans are different. As Searle said, the machines don't really replicate human beings. They merely simulate. In particular, as Rosalind Picard of the Massachusetts Institute of Technology has of late been pointing out (some of her excellent lectures are on the web), computers lack emotional intelligence, which means they lack the essential quality of empathy; the quality that enables us truly to care for each other and live convivially, and to do so as a matter of choice. Some would like to see AI and robots take over the world and leave us to drink our Bacardis and cokes and otherwise twiddle our thumbs. But human beings, made by God or fashioned by evolution or both, are altogether more subtle than any machine, however smart, is ever likely to be. We, human beings, are far from perfect. We need seriously to smarten up our act. But we abandon our sovereignty at our peril.

One other modern technology, again with zealous followers and attracting huge investment, unashamedly incorporates the word 'artificial' in its title. For we are being told, not least by well-endowed intellectuals, that if we, humanity, are to have enough to eat in the future then we must produce food – and especially meat – in the laboratory and factory. Artificial food, especially meat, is already big business and could be the saviour of the world. Agriculture we are told, has had its day. Tolstoy and Gandhi must be spinning in their graves. Are they right to do so?

Artificial meat

Vegans suggest, on all kinds of grounds, that we should not eat meat. It is wrong, they say, both morally and ecologically. They tell us that livestock farming, in practice, is cruel or at least more restrictive than is acceptable, and is ecologically profligate. Commonly we are told that a field of cereals or beans produces about ten times as much protein as the same field devoted to cattle; and at present, half the world's cereals are fed to livestock along with 90%-plus of the soya. Since we can thrive perfectly well on diets based on cereals and pulses (plus other crops for vitamins, etc.) this is a shocking waste. Our livestock actually competes with us for food. Some argue for good measure that meat is bad for our health.

Again there is no room here to discuss this properly. Suffice to say that the vegans' ecological arguments are correct if we simply contrast arable farming (mainly of cereals and pulses) with intensive livestock production – in which the animals are largely fed on cereals and (imported) soya. But livestock need not and should not be raised in this way. If cattle and sheep are raised only on grass and other natural vegetation in places where we cannot sensibly grow cereals and beans, and pigs and poultry are fed only on leftovers and surpluses, as was traditional, then they do not compete with us for food. They add to our food supply. In some regions, including much of Africa, livestock is a prime source of calories as well as protein, since crops in uncertain climates are so hard to grow. We might note in this context that in the story of Cain and Abel (Genesis 4) God favoured Abel, the keeper of sheep, over Cain, the tiller of the ground. Agronomists point out that there is no system of farming – including arable and horticulture – that could not benefit from some livestock, if only to provide manure. Contrary, then, to what we are often told, agriculture that includes *some* animals, judiciously deployed, is more efficient (biologically speaking) than all-plant agriculture, and so should take up *less* room, and leave more room for wild creatures. Furthermore, traditional animal husbandry done well should itself be wildlife friendly. Dung left on the ground attracts dung beetles which in turn feed birds – and so on and so on.

Meat is not bad for us if we eat it in modest quantities – and animals raised on natural diets are much better for us than meat from animals raised pell-mell from birth to the abattoir. Their fat is far less saturated. Meat also provides essential minerals, notably calcium and zinc, which can be hard to obtain in sufficient amount from an all-plant diet. If we raised animals only on natural vegetation and leftovers we would not produce anything like as much meat as we do now. But then we don't need much. Nutritionally, as the vegans argue, we can in some circumstances do without it altogether.

Even more to the point, all of the world's greatest cuisines on an axis from Italy to China use meat sparingly. If we again took cooking seriously – cooking is one of our greatest crafts! – we would welcome the low-meat diet. We could cook like Italians or Turks or Indians or Chinese. There is plenty to choose from. The modern high-meat diets, wall-to-wall burgers, are nothing more than a commercial scam, as indeed might be said of much of what happens in this neoliberal age.

Neither can we suppose, as its advocates are wont to imply, that artificial meat, spun from the protein of beans, fungi, or microbes, is ecologically squeaky clean. The technology is itself immensely profligate, if carried out on the large scale. It needs a lot of energy, which has to come from somewhere.

Neither can we guarantee that artificial food is as good, nutritionally, as the real thing. In truth though the world is awash with 'experts', our knowledge of nutrition is still elementary. I am particularly impressed by the growing appreciation of what I have been calling 'cryptonutrients'; organic compounds of huge variety that in very small quantities act as something between a vitamin (which is vital) and a tonic (not vital, but it does you good). Food manufacturers are cottoning on to this idea with variations on a theme of yoghurt, milk fermented primarily by lactobacilli and producing a whole range of micro-ingredients whose effects on health are too subtle and various to analyse exhaustively but are surely in there somewhere. We should simply acknowledge, as the old adage is, that Nature knows best. We just don't know enough, and never will, to replicate natural foods precisely, or as precisely as our bodies would like. To suppose that we can is hubris.

Indeed the only objections to well-run livestock farming that do stand up are those of morality and metaphysics. Morally we are obliged, if we do keep animals, to emphasise welfare above all else; and welfare is all too often and obviously neglected. The metaphysical argument – that we have no *right* to raise animals for food – has never been satisfactorily answered, and I don't think it can be. The best I can do in this context is to echo the words of the Dalai Lama who points out that sometimes it is not possible to behave in the best conceivable way. Sometimes we have to settle for the least bad; and in various ways, agriculture with a few well-deployed animals is less harmful to the planet as a whole, and better for humanity, than an all-plant agriculture would be.

The real problem lies not with meat *per se* but with industrial agriculture of the kind that is favoured by big governments, a shortlist of ever-growing mega-corporates, and big finance. It should indeed be called 'Neoliberal-Industrial' (NI) agriculture since its prime purpose is not to provide us all with good food and to look after the biosphere, which is what most people would suppose agriculture is for, but – in line with the neoliberal imperative – to maximise profit. The profit, in turn, stays with the directors and shareholders of the corporates, although a significant proportion is siphoned off to pay the banks who put up the money. Oil has been readily available and cheap, or at least affordable, so the most profitable farms in modern times, or at least the ones that generate the most wealth, are heavily dependent on oil-based inputs. These include mechanical power, of course, with bigger and bigger machines – but also, more importantly, the whole pharmacopeia of agrochemicals. Indeed, NI agriculture may reasonably be seen as an offshoot of the chemical industry, in turn a scion of the oil industry. All in all, in practice, industrial agriculture is high-tech, high-input, highly capitalised and monocultural, with minimum-to-zero labour, all on the biggest possible scale.

In absolute contrast we need Agroecology: farms that really are intended to produce good food sustainably – without wrecking the rest of the biosphere – and are designed as ecosystems. Agroecological farms are low input (basically organic) and mixed, with judicious combinations of crops and animals that interact, synergistically. Such farms are intricate and need plenty of skilled farmers and growers, and they do not benefit from economies of scale and so work best when small to medium sized. In other words the kind of agriculture we need is the precise opposite of the kind that big governments and corporates, and big finance, have foisted upon us. To be sure, agroecological farms must partake of all kinds of technologies, including some high technologies – even perhaps including the odd drone and robot. But we must not become besotted by the tech, as people in high places so often do, and, regrettably, many people in the world at large as well.

By the methods of agroecology we could produce easily enough meat to make the world's greatest cuisines available to everyone who is liable to be born. Of course, when animals are raised at a more natural pace on more natural diets and are treated kindly, the meat is more expensive; and then the self-righteous technophiles and the mountebank politicians tell us that it is wicked to treat animals well because that makes it even more difficult, or indeed impossible, for the poorest people to buy meat at all. But poor people are unable to buy good food not because the food is too dear but because they are indeed poor; and the way to get round that is not to be cruel to animals and wreck the biosphere but to devise an economy that is actually fair, and just, and far more egalitarian than we what we have now. The present economy leaves people poor because it is designed, in practice, to make the rich richer and to maintain the status quo – all in large measure at the expense of the poor.

Finally, let me just say in passing, that agroecology is only one of the two principles we need to bring to the fore. The other was proposed in the 1990s by the world's peasant movement, *La Via Campesina* – little known in the West but now the biggest civil movement in the world with 300 million followers. That is the principle of Food Sovereignty: the idea that all societies should have control of their own food supply. Put agroecology and food sovereignty together and we get what I have been calling 'Enlightened Agriculture', aka 'Real Farming'. This is what the world really needs.

So where does that leave the present zeal for artificial meat? Nowhere, I suggest. We could produce all the meat we need, of the highest nutritional quality, by means that are ecologically benign. We simply don't need ersatz; and ersatz would, if practised on a significant scale, create huge problems of its own – ecological, social, personal, spiritual: sacrificing ways of life and opportunities to interact with our fellow creatures.

Overall, as Winston Churchill said about science and scientists, technology should be 'on tap, but not on top'. The technologies that we and our ancestors have devised over the past two million years or so are wonderful, from stone axes to microchips, and so too are the things that we make with their aid, from Fabergé eggs to clothes pegs. But our instruments and machines should always be our assistants – geared to our aspirations and needs: geared more precisely to the goals of personal fulfilment, conviviality, and care of the biosphere. We must never let our own inventions take the lead and gear our lives to them – which, to a large extent, is what has happened. Always we need to remember that we ourselves and our ways of thinking – the combination of cerebral reasoning and emotional intelligence – are innately superior to the artefacts we create. Artefacts, however wondrous, are indeed artificial and the pejoratives – fake, imitation, counterfeit – are always in there somewhere.

FOUR EARTHS

Christopher B Jones

For two decades, there has been growing discourse about the name of the rock strata that will be associated with homo sapiens in future geological records. The present age we live in bears witness to a great tension between humans and nature. Hidden within this conflict is the ominous contradiction between humanity's dependence on natural resources and neglect and misuse of the Earth's goods. Even the idea of Earth being something deserving of fair treatment and respect is a hot item for debate. Going forward we are left to wonder if the lens of artificiality may provide insight to the futures of homo sapiens' relationship with nature. Geologist reckoning has labelled the last approximately 11,650 years as the Holocene epoch. Following what has commonly been referred to as the last ice age, this period has been noted as a time of warmth and glacial retreat. During this period, a burgeoning proliferation of species, notably that of humans, has occurred. Rise of civilisations and technological advance have largely been at the mercy of nature's will, but more recently, a contemporary debate has questioned how even footed was the fight between humanity and nature. Has humanity's impact on the globe changed the tide of Earth's geological progression and is this impact reaching the point of irreversibility? Will the artificial be the final straw in this struggle?

The Anthropocene neologism was popularised after the year 2000 to describe what will follow the Holocene geological era. Human impact on the planet is being deposited in ocean sediments and is recorded in deep ice cores from Greenland and Antarctica. The evidence of our industry and chemistry will be there for aeons of future geologists to uncover, including radioisotopes from nuclear bomb testing, trace metals from early smelting in the Bronze Age, and layers of plastic. The evidence of human use of fossil fuels will be revealed in future rocks. Nature, and her legacy of human detritus, will remain indefinitely intertwined.

The Anthropocene will likely contain a record of our increasingly artificial world, our artificial turf, satellites, breasts, hips, and now artificial intelligence. That is particularly true because even our reality is open to question. Are we living in our solipsistic dreams, in the *Matrix*, or a nightmare? In modern society we can feel the dissonance between what we think is real, and alternative, or artificial facts and truths that compete with our beliefs. We face a serious crisis when the boundaries between the real and the artificial are deliberately confused and obfuscated. Nevertheless, that trend continues.

The Anthropocene emerged as a concept about the same time as postnormal analysis. That is no surprise given that postnormal analysis argued that the acceleration of change, the speed, scope, scale, and simultaneity of changes within technological, social, political, demographic, economic, global, and environmental systems are increasing because of our complex, technological, communications, transportation, and information systems. Not only does the speed of change tend to increase, but also its sweep and scope grow larger, scale grows to planetary and global levels, and all of these things are happening at once. These dynamics of change lead to system level changes that are characterised by greater complexity, chaos, and contradictions. These drivers and characteristics collectively describe the postnormal times in which we live.

Social and political systems that seemed normal or stable no longer behave the way they used to. The American president routinely ignores political norms, and other leaders around the world have followed suit. During the COVID-19 pandemic, transportation, supply chains, and educational systems were disrupted. Not all systems are postnormal, but increased complexity and the speed of change pose threats to system normalcy. Some systems can go almost postnormal overnight, Black Swan events, that which was once considered to be unlikely, occurs. The economic consequences of COVID-19 are a case in point. Postnormal analysis argues for types of postnormal behaviour, such as this COVID-19 postnormal burst. Resistance to post normal drivers creates lag, and concomitant pressure and influence from other systems creates postnormal creep.

Central to postnormal analysis is the idea that there are deep structures that try to convince us that homeostasis is normal. The built environment, for example, conforms to nature. Cities grow up around harbours and the confluence of rivers, but give lie to the wildness of nature. Interstate highways cross over fault lines, but when they collapse, for example the Loma Prieta earthquake that cause the collapse of the San Francisco Oakland Bay Bridge, the normalcy field also collapses. These deep structures are called the Manufactured Normalcy Field (MNF) and there is debate about whether these fields are physical, psychological, or even metaphysical. Nevertheless, the postnormal disruption is occurring within the MNF and the drivers and characteristics alter or disrupt the normalcy we believe we experience. For example, a MNF is created by a relatively small, aerodynamic aluminium tube, or commercial airliner, that travels in the stratosphere at 600 miles an hour, at 35,000 feet above the planet surface. That is not normal, but our culture, our travel patterns and behaviour, our short but rapid evolution as a species now considers that unremarkable. In postnormal times, it is not simply that what was normal is changing, but the very nature of change itself is changing. The phenomenon of postnormal times is not something that has occurred in a vacuum, but indeed is the continuation of a historical circumstance that has been creeping about for some time now.

The scope and speed of change have been the focus of futurist thought for half a century, or more, particularly within the realm of our technological prowess. Futurist Walter Anderson argued that because our species has now learned to control evolution, it has become our ethical and moral responsibility to take firm, but reluctant control over the progress of the biosphere. It is now our job, in his view, 'to govern evolution'. He forecast the emergence of a biopolitics that recognises our responsibility, having gained such power over genetic and species evolution. He acknowledged the growing discourse on the rights of living things. His work follows the argument of the late John Platt, physicist and futurist, who posited that we face an acceleration of evolution in a 1981 *Futurist* article. He showed that across a range of aspects of evolution – encapsulation, energy use, defence, communication, and other dynamics – how our species is poised for one of the greatest transformations in four billion years of planetary evolution.

In the subsequent three decades, the acceleration of the change drivers of evolution have increased in speed, scope, scale, and simultaneity. Moreover, our technological sophistication and development of space technologies has expanded the scope and sphere of human reach. There has been continuous human habitation on orbit above Earth for two decades, and within a few more decades, humans are likely to begin inhabiting the planet Mars. We are a migratory species, and as anthropologist Ben Finney and others have argued, our diaspora into the solar system and beyond is likely part of our story as a species.

What does this bode for the Earth, a living organism, a cybernetic, self-regulating system? To what degree does a system need to be artificial, mediated by homo sapiens in order to survive over the very long-term future? To begin with, how did we get to see the earth as artificial?

It is no coincidence that the transformation of Mother Earth into machine coincides with the Renaissance and industrial revolution. Early cities developed by filling in swamps and channelling rivers and streams, and creating harbours and dams. We began the transformation of Earth to machine by building canals to improve the efficiency of human transportation of goods. This metaphor for human transformation was likely behind the interpretations of nineteenth century astronomer Schaparelli's Martian canals and likely reason for the eager acceptance of such a possibility. The early industrial phase of human development is very evident in the place where I live, near the Erie Canal in Western New York. The development of the steam engine and railroads further transformed the planet to the extent that it is now crisscrossed with steel rails, and now asphalt and macadam roads. Elon Musk would like to build transcontinental tunnels if we will let him.

The innovation and development of transportation technologies are a good case in point of the growing speed, scale, and scope of change. We have gone from foot travel to the use of the wheel and draft animals, to railroads and steamships, aeroplanes, supersonic jets, rockets, rail guns, and have launched interstellar spacecraft. We have conquered the planet with the use of maps, and now with GPS and remote sensing earth satellites. The number of low Earth orbit satellites is likely to increase by one hundred orders of magnitude in the next few years thanks to the burgeoning private space launch industry.

We have become very effective at moving water around the planet, and storing it artificially. The development of the US Southwest is largely due to water diversion from the Colorado River and other sources. The

California Central Valley and Yuma, Arizona have been transformed into agricultural breadbaskets thanks to large-scale diversion of water and irrigation. Other bodies such as Mono Lake and the Ural Sea have been nearly drained by human diversion of water to cities and agriculture. The relationship between human beings and the Earth has moved from something relatively mutual, akin to a mother's loving relationship to a child towards the child becoming a parasite upon the mother.

We appear to be at a civilisational turning point, where the tensions between nature and human activity are likely to have serious consequences. And yet, there are those who see technology and the artificial as simply another expression of nature. As humans, we are part of nature, so who is to say that artificial is bad. Bad for whom? Our current paradigm places humans on top, but what if that is not the future we will inherit?

Complexity, chaos, and contradiction grow from the increasingly blurred distinctions and boundaries between natural and artificial, between human and machine. We may pine for simpler or more stable times, but since the beginning of modern civilisations, we have longed for the Golden Age, the paradise before modern times. We are now faced with a plethora of choices spanning the spectrum of organic/historic ways and a synthetic, cyborg futures. The pathways to paradise and oblivion are not necessarily clear.

The tension between the philosophies of critical posthumanism and transhumanism is one example of the dichotomy between natural and artificial. Critical posthumanism argues for co-evolution with other species, and the planet, and machines, but not in the interests of humanity. Posthumanists such as Donna Haraway have argued for a blurring of boundaries between *Homo sapiens* and our animal kin, as well as seeing cyborgs as an expression of the power of being the Other. Transhumanists, on the other hand, see a bright future of machine and artificial realities— an oncoming Singularity with transformational change—with the potential of longevity and immortality, uploading of one's personality and memories, and human-machine synthesis or symbiosis. If either philosophy drives a paradigm shift or worldview change, the potential impacts upon other species and planetary system will be massive.

To help us better understand the impact of the artificial on humanity and Earth we should extend our lens of analysis into the future (say 2200 AD) and explore the potential realities before us. The four alternative futures presented here attempt to capture the spectrum of possible artificial Earths, that is, planetary futures that include some form of *Homo sapiens*. They are presented in order of least artificial to one of the most artificial futures of Earth imaginable. Following each scenario is a brief analysis of the trends and events we are witnessing today that will set us on a trajectory towards something resembling one of these potential Earths.

Scenario 1: Dark Mountain (Earth: 1% artificial)

Dark Mountain imagines a reduction of human population to three million people, the estimated number of humans on the planet before the rise of permanent settlements and regional civilisations. Humans returned to a Paleolithic lifestyle. Settlements are temporary and move often, agriculture is limited to horticulture and gathering. Cultural norms restrict and suppress innovation, creativity, and development of technology, particularly metallurgy and energy use. Dark Mountain societies are subsistence economies, largely organised similarly to primitive communism, with limited personal ownership of material goods. The values of the society are largely organised around collective myths that celebrate the animal, ecological, and human co-evolution and interdependence.

This scenario in mind, we must ask, what trends are leading us towards this nomadic future society?

The overall trajectory of progress and machines is increasingly uncertain and hardly universally accepted. Since the early Industrial Revolution, workers have thrown tools and clogs in the cogs of industry and the word sabotage has roots in rage against the machine. An ongoing back-to-nature movement persists. The green meme has had various manifestations as futures scenarios or images over time. The concept of Earth as a living system, for example, has been around for centuries. In modern history the environmental movement has ranged from the early conservation movement, public interest conservation advocacy, Greenpeace, Earth First!, to eco-radicals, and now anti-globalists and degrowth activists. Mainstream and conservation environmentalism may have been more accommodating of the machine. That might be illustrated today by the 'mixed-use' of national forests and US Bureau of Land Management lands with dirt bikers, hikers, snowmobilers, and skiers mixing in the back country.

Dark Mountain takes green values to an extreme and is likely to be unfamiliar territory – a hard-to-imagine place for most folks used to electricity, indoor plumbing, and regular meals. However, it pictures a civilisation that rejects most of the assumptions of postindustrial civilisation. It is extreme, but concentrates the trends toward an authoritarian (non-innovative) society.

The roots and branches of the scenario come from a wide range of literature, scholarly writing, social movements, and social action. The mass migration of humans from rural areas and villages to cities is a continuing trend. On the other hand, it appears humans are alienated from nature and look for connections with nature, such as pet ownership, parks and green spaces, and vacations outside of the city. However, urban living affects some people aversely resulting in what has been described as nature deficit disorder. Doctors are ordering nature experiences as a treatment for stress and depression.

Social movements over the last half-century have also contributed to this meme. From Earth Day and the emergence of the modern environmental movement with mainstream and radical green fringes, to the emergence of Green parties in Europe, Earth warrior groups such as the Sea Shepherd Society, the Rainforest Action Network have now been joined by Greta Thunberg's Fridays for Future, the Sunrise Movement, and Extinction Rebellion. Anti-growth and anti-progress movements also need to be taken into consideration: Occupy Wall Street and antifa (anti-fascist) activists in the US are examples of social movements dissatisfied with the Continued Growth paradigm.

Dark Mountain is a possible, if low probability, alternative future. On the other hand, the social structures and organisations served the species well for 200,000 years or longer, so they cannot be ruled out. The one existing meme or theory is a reasonable candidate, the return to hunter-gather societies. While improbable, and extreme, it does align with the skills and cultures of indigenous people who are currently being overwhelmed if not exterminated. Dark Mountain is a variant of the Four Futures' Disciplined Society alternative future and is suggested by the dark ecology movement and Dark Mountain manifesto. The aim is to return to migratory hunter-gatherer societies and leave industrial society behind. It would make eco-radical groups, like EarthFirst!, look tame. Reducing Earth's population deliberately by three orders of magnitude is improbable, but nuclear war, genetic warfare or pandemics could lay the groundwork.

Dark Mountain pictures the success of antinatalism movements of the mid-twenty-first century, most notably the Human Extinction movement and softer forms of birth control and population reduction. The broad social movement aligned with trends in growing numbers of human deaths over time (particularly since the beginning of the Industrial Revolution), falling fertility rates, rise in suicides and opiate addiction, and depression. What was a fringe philosophy has found fertile ground in a world increasingly characterised by suffering and mental illness.

Various religious traditions note the clear connection between birth and death, suffering and life, and the bondage to the material world that imprisons our divine nature or spiritual being. Notably, Norwegian metaphysician Peter Vessel Zapffe argued that consciousness is over – evolved in our species and we are burdened by the knowledge, unlike any other species, that we are destined to die. The Argentine philosopher Julio Cabrera explored the ontological challenges of birth that makes us manufactured and used, the ultimate manufactured normalcy field. We begin the process of dying within seconds of being born, we are afflicted by physical pain, mental willpower or its lack, and the creation of positive values (normalcy fields) that must constantly be engaged lest we fall back into depression. Other key issues, according to South African philosopher, David Benatar, is that the balance of good and bad things is tilted towards the presence of pain and suffering and our experience of it in the world. The empirical evidence of death and destruction over the last thousand years is staggering. Deaths over the last millennia number in the billions: natural disasters, starvation and malnutrition, plague and epidemics, disease and accidents, mass killings, political killing, genocide, genital mutilation, and suicide. The growing collective awareness of this resulted in a series of individual and collective actions that dramatically reduced human populations over just a few centuries.

From a postnormal analysis standpoint, the first alternative future is a return to the 'normal' that characterised human existence for most of the million years before the dawn of agriculture some 12,000 years ago. Dark ecology argues that it is not industrialisation that is destructive, but settled agriculture 'civilisations' that are the source of human misery. A long period of hydraulic civilisations constituted a kind of new normal until the industrial revolution. Arguably there have been punctuated periods of normalcy, but postnormal change has gone through its agricultural, medieval, industrial now high technology postnormality. Dark Mountain reduces the artificial to the impacts of human migrations, tool use, and horticulture. Fire use becomes the largest source of human alteration of the environment.

Scenario 2: Collapse (Earth: 5% artificial)

Collapse is one of the most popular images in literature and movies. Teen fiction has produced a number of dystopian and post-apocalyptic futures, such as *Hunger Games*. Wikipedia lists nearly two-dozen potential existential threats to humanity and the programme on existential threats addresses a wide range of cosmic, terrestrial, and anthropomorphic threats. This alternative future follows the logic of a disruption of Earth's thermodynamic equilibrium over the last million years or so. The position of Earth's continents, tectonics, and the orbital cycles identified by the mathematician Milutin Milankovitch have produced recurring cycles of glaciation. If anthropomorphic changes disrupt the Milankovitch cycle, Earth's temperature could rise to a higher thermodynamic steady-state. That might look like the Carboniferous phase some 50 million years ago when Earth's average temperature was 20° higher than today. This is the runaway greenhouse scenario that is the basis for exploring the impacts of 6° C or more increase in Earth's temperature, and the results pictured in JG Ballard's *The Drowned World* (1962).

This future could unfold quickly, but more likely may take centuries. As climate change journalist David Wallace-Wells argued, we are already facing cascades of catastrophe and this future in which everything that can go wrong, does go wrong, human systems unravel quickly in the face of growing natural systems failures. In this scenario, the forecasts of ocean and permafrost methane release were vastly underestimated, and glacial melting in high altitudes, Greenland, and Antarctica accelerated. Coasts are flooded, there are mass migrations inland as well as across the oceans. The tropics become inhospitable to human habitation, and human populations are forced towards the poles.

There are massive failures in food production, warfare over dwindling water, migration, and failures of human bureaucratic systems. Eventually, only Antarctica is habitable, with some subterranean cities, domes in high mountain areas. At its conclusion the warming process does not totally exterminate humans, but 5% of the planet is artificial.

So, what can we see today that is setting us on a course for Collapse?

Civilisational collapse has been a recurring image of the future. Dutch futurist Frederick Polak noted the number of civilisations and societies that had negative or apocalyptic eschatology, whose images of end times were dark and violent. The history of those societies suggests that those dark images are likely to have been self-fulfilling prophecies. The current convergence of six or seven cultural civilisations into a global civilisation may provide us with positive as well as apocalyptic tendencies. In any case, apocalyptic images have been the product of speculative and science fiction, fantasy, a twentieth century characterised by two world wars, genocide, and mass killing at greater scales than any time in history. The Cold War, the threat of nuclear annihilation, strategist and futurist Herman Kahn 'thinking the unthinkable', and now a long list of potential existential threats face us at the beginning of the twenty-first century. Kahn's nuclear war scenarios were dramatic and thought-provoking, but Italian writer Roberto Vacca's concern about a coming dark age put Collapse on the futures map. He imagined modern society as so complicated (built on a 'house of cards') that gridlock one afternoon sets off a cascade of catastrophe that becomes the beginning of the end of civilisation.

His speculative fiction parallels the very real research of American anthropologist Joseph Tainter who analysed the collapse of complex societies and found that a large number collapsed due to climate change or resource exhaustion, but many if not most collapsed due to complexity. At some point, marginal efficiencies used to manage growth failed to work. Growth seems to have limits. This may have implications for postnormal policy. Efficiencies in bureaucratic processes may have improved over time thanks to technological innovation, Taylorism, and process improvement, but may be near its carrying capacity. Artificial intelligence and algorithms presumably are part of the answer in the continued growth mode, but the externalities of industrial growth are now coming back to bite us.

Extinction threats and extinction studies are a growth industry. In 2019, the Intergovernmental Panel on Climate Change and the UN raised the alarm about the need to reduce carbon emissions by 2030 in order to avoid catastrophe by 2050. Global heating at the poles is creating further uncertainty given the impacts on Greenland and Antarctic ice sheets that are already in motion. Even if we are able to avoid a 3°C increase over the baseline in global average temperature, sea levels are likely to rise hundreds of feet in the next one hundred to two hundred years.

Existential threats are not limited to human activity either. We live on an active planet with a biosphere and oceans that have previously experienced up to seven mass extinction events. Some may be due to impacts of asteroids or comets, or more likely biological and chemical catastrophes in Earth's oceans. We still know very little about our planet's history, but would do well to consider that life is a sometimes fragile and messy business.

The collapse scenario is a logical extension of Murphy's Law to the accelerating dynamics of change and system characteristics in postnormal times: everything that can go wrong, will go wrong. That was the premise of Vacca's dismal future and perhaps our luck as a species has run out. Nevertheless, there will likely always still be some artificial facet of nature, as long as humans or our near relatives are still around.

Scenario 3: Hybrid Gaia (Earth: 50% artificial)

Hybrid Gaia is a highly artificial world, but driven by a totally different worldview than today. It is driven by critical posthumanism, where human-centred ethics and mythology are replaced by respect and cooperation with other species rather than dominance and exploitation. The model is a blend of Haraway's *Chthulucene* and Lovelock's *Novocene*, a cybernetic union of biology, machines, artificial intelligence, and creativity that remake the world, both organic and inorganic, in a dance, a symphony of co-evolution on a small planet in a violent cosmos.

This scenario assumes a rebound from coastal flooding and inundation due to the melting of Greenland and Antarctic ice sheets, and a rapid shift to a green economy, beginning with initiatives launched by governments at the turn of the millennium, but resisted well into the middle of the twenty-first century. A global consensus emerged principally around universal healthcare and disease prevention in the wake of pandemics and environmental refugee migrations into the twenty-second century. Artificial intelligence, automation, and the transition away from global to regional supply chains and circular economy enabled the radical shift in the political economy to an abundance economy and wealth levelling strategies. Incomes over one million dollars were taxed at 100% globally by 2150.

Cities are either greened up with vertical farming or built from scratch as energy-efficient arcologies. The idea began by Italian architect Roberto Soleri was to create dense structures at human scales to minimise the distance travelled between work, home, and entertainment and services, to sequester industrial activities below ground, and reclaim space given to automobiles.

The worst of climate catastrophes have been surmounted and mitigated, and despite the deaths of hundreds of millions from warfare and climate related starvation, the global population stabilises around 8 billion. The principles of Gaia 2.0 are internalised in governance, consumption, and economics, with vast reduction in the use of fossil fuel – based pesticides and fertilisers. Drones are used to more efficiently pollinate, and apply fertilisers and nutrients to individual plants. Industrial agriculture is replaced by cooperatives and most people are involved in some level of community gardening and food preparation.

Space exploration is replaced by Earth and Ocean exploration, by spiritual and self-actualisation pursuits. Space development is limited to near Earth orbit remote-sensing and telecommunications, but culture has begun to focus inward rather than outward. The economics of scarcity inherent in capitalism is replaced by abundance economics supported by robotics, automation, and a leisure society that enables people to engage in community development, gardening, arts and crafts, and democratic participation in decision-making and governance. One model is the planetary society featured in James Hogan's (1982) *Voyage to Yesteryear* where the colony planet economy is based on individual competence and service rather than growth and industry.

The worldview has shifted from acquisition, consumption, and materialism to coexistence with nature. Moreover, it embraces the reality of human destruction and domination of other species, and attempts to both atonement for and celebration of species and ecosystems lost to human development. At the same time it allows for the exploration of genetic futures in seeing human exploration of genetic possibility, but informed by other moral values. Freeman Dyson famously argued that we should embrace genetic play the same way we developed computers by playing with the technologies as well as the games on them. This is similar to Haraway's five generations of clones with butterfly genes whose life mandate is to stand with and help sustain the monarch butterfly. Genetic play and manipulation are seen as ways to become liberated of anachronistic mental models about what it means to be human. Efforts are effective in re-establishing extinct species, particularly the megafauna (mastodons, sabre-toothed tigers) that existed during early human existence, and entire communities of Neanderthal and Denisovan and other archaic human species, as well as hybrids. Education and child-rearing radically altered. Children raised in cohort groups with multiple, non-biological parents.

What is happening today to revive Gaia theory and deliver us to the Hybrid Gaia Earth?

Framing useful scenarios depends on a number of factors, including plausibility, coherence, and comparable elements across alternative future scenarios. Alternative futures are arguably most helpful when they collapse contradictory or conflicting driving forces, because they clarify some of the reinforcing characteristics of drivers. Of course, the future is not likely to eliminate contradictions — one of the lessons of postnormal policy – but it is sometimes valuable to take things to their extreme conclusions. That is clearly the case with the scenarios presented in this analysis.

Looking for the driving forces, emerging issues, and trends leading to a post-human paradigm and civilisation one microcosm of that future may be the annual Burning Man Festival now in its thirty-sixth year, held in a desert playa in the northern Nevada wilderness. The festival is named after the iconic wooden structure sacrificed to flames every year. As many as

70,000 people now attend, and Black Rock City is built each year from scratch and then removed from the desert, leaving 'no trace'.

There is an emergent culture and value system in the Burning Man phenomenon, some visible, explicit, and other aspects hidden or more deeply embedded. The stated rules from the official website are:

- radical inclusion
- gifting
- de-commodification
- radical self-reliance
- radical self-expression
- communal effort
- civic responsibility
- leaving no trace
- participation
- immediacy

Beyond the rules, there are other obvious and not so obvious assumptions about the temporary, mobile pop-up culture that characterises the built environment of Black Rock City. There are some clear contradictions between the libertarian and communitarian tenancies of participant organisations and individuals. My sense is that these rules represent two divergent aspects of post-humanism, what Nayal has described as critical post-humanism, on one hand, and trans-humanism on the other. These rules, however, may to some degree inform both evolving alternative futures represented in this paper. Burning Man rules represent postnormal values in contrast to liberal industrial capitalism, in spite of the fact that increasingly Silicon Valley and Hollywood elites are becoming entangled in the phenomenon.

It does seem that the values embedded in the Burning Man rules are representative of a shift in worldview that could be manifested in political redesign away from neoliberal representative democracy. Burning Man and other intentional communities are trying to create the space to innovate, and certainly colonies on Mars and space settlements will have enough distance from current cultural structures to experiment and innovate in political design and social structures.

There appear to me to be at least two major streams in the broad green movement, a moderate organic green movement closer to the mainstream, and a radical natural green movement. The former envisions a blend of modern technology and particularly renewable energy and abandonment of fossil fuel use. The latter holds that the problems of modern society began during settled agriculture, and advocate for a vastly smaller human population that would adopt hunter-gatherer practices more consistent with society before settled civilisation.

While transformational, the Hybrid Gaia alternative future is perhaps one of the more likely futures, either due to the threat of Collapse or as a result of cascading climate catastrophes over the coming century or two. Unlike the conservation movement and much of the liberal environmental movement today, deep ecology would be a driving force in the philosophy and worldview – the idea that all parts of nature have intrinsic value, even rocks, and that humans are not special or any more valuable than other aspects of nature. This philosophy has clearly influenced or has been adopted by radical feminism and other parts of progressive social movements. This future also has roots in the Gaia theory that the earth is a living organism, a complex, cybernetic system that has regulated the atmospheric composition, temperature, and habitability for life on the planet.

Gaia is relevant to the discourse on the tension between natural and artificial, because human generated by-products and activities are beginning to have a significant impact on the landscape, on the oceans, and atmosphere. Humans cannot deviate very far from large-scale geomorphic processes, or we will threaten the regulatory structures that maintain conditions for life on the planet. Therefore, our introduction of greenhouse gases into the atmosphere, species extinction, and altering of ocean chemistry are transforming the planet in unexpected ways. The evidence suggests that our interference with feedback processes may potentially raise average global temperatures far in excess of nominal forecasts by the IPCC, academies of science, and climate agencies across the planet.

Scenario 4: Dyson's Children (Earth: 99% artificial)

The late physicist Freeman Dyson, for a thought experiment, imagined a technological civilisation advanced sufficiently to capture all of the energy produced by its sun. Physical structures that approach this ideal have been described in science fiction as Dyson spheres. Dyson's structure was first described in Olaf Stapleton's *Star Maker* (1937) and has become a popular concept in science fiction (see Larry Niven's *Ringworld*).

Dyson's Children is the alternative future where all of the dreams of techno-optimists and post-humanists come true. If the previous scenario was inward looking, the pro-artificial vision is outward looking and transformational with respect to technology. It is the product of not one, but many Singularities, from advances in machine – mind interfaces, genetics, artificial intelligence, space development, and many other technological dimensions see quantum leaps in control over nature. Human science achieves godlike control over medicine through molecular and nanite robot prevention, repair, and disease defence. Cancer is effectively cured, and longevity increases dramatically, with the likelihood that genetic flushing technology can extend lifespan.

Low Earth Orbit habitations, a growing lunar settlement, and asteroid mining barely dented the growing population pressures and horrors of sea level rise, but the mass movement to Mars (remember the old saw 'Mars or Musk!') and then Venus by 2200 was still not enough to reduce social blowback. One current scheme is to download one billion minds onto quantum computers to send them on colony ships to be decanted into cloned bodies on the nearest earth-like planets in one hundred solar systems.

The surface of the earth is effectively artificial, with geoengineering projects that regulate the Earth's temperature (space reflectors, deep ocean circulation pumps). Much of the Earth's surface is effectively managed by 2200. Extreme climate change and species destruction required more human intervention to avoid total environmental disaster. Remaining wilderness areas are more like large parks and zoos. Nearly all arable land is devoted to post-industrial agriculture or megacities, Earth's population is twenty-five billion with one billion on Mars and space settlements. Forests are planted, maintained, and harvested by drones. Most sources of human protein are now produced in factories, grown from cultures, and are indistinguishable from the fish, poultry, or beef produced two centuries earlier. Almost all food is genetically modified in some way (GMOs are OK).

Tesla-GE by mid-twenty-first century dominated the space and automobile sectors and established the first solar power satellites in Earth orbit that began producing energy, particularly for the developing world. That marked the beginning of the end for fossil fuels as an energy source, and the perfection of fusion and a Singularity in the manipulation of magnetic fields had almost immediate impacts on transportation and energy transmission. Coupled with those advances and quantum computing, general artificial intelligence became increasingly important in managing the complex and sometimes contradictory systems supporting human life on the planet. Fortunately, there was a concerted effort to limit the development of what was once called 'super machine intelligence'. It was decided that sentient machines posed too great an existential threat to human consciousness.

Work on consciousness and human potential was also an essential part of the developments of the twenty-second century, while attempts to use cryonics to save bodies or brains for future reanimation uniformly failed, uploading consciousness, or at least one's memory and personality has become possible, even easy. Of course, the social and legal implications of having two copies of oneself have remained challenging, and especially now that cloning not only body parts but entire adult bodies are also possible.

The diaspora to outer space is accelerating, with the colonisation of Mars and Luna, with a domed settlement on Venus devoted to terraforming our sister planet. The asteroid belt and Jovian systems have growing numbers of miners and explorers. Rumours continue to circulate that alien artefacts and technology have been discovered on more than one of the larger asteroids. That coincides with a number of private ventures that have already launched or will soon send colony ships to nearby habitable Earth-like planets. Some are generation ships, and others have plans for sending most of the colonists in cryo-sleep/hibernation. Humanity seems intent on taking its species to the stars. Already, genetic alteration has been occurring on Mars and Luna to better adapt humans to non-trust real gravity.

What justification do we have for the total artificialisation of the Earth and our becoming Dyson's Children?

Transhumanism is the flavour of posthumanism that potentially evolves from or is transformed from the present Continued Growth future, with ample illustrations in Hollywood movies and corporate advertising. It sees technology as a means to improve humans, to expand our abilities, reduce our vulnerabilities, and go beyond the limitations of human minds and bodies. This image of the future is popular in mass media and particularly in Silicon Valley. Advocates for this future are those who are extending the limits of longevity, seek to be able to use cryogenics to someday rejuvenate brains that have succumbed to injury or disease, upload human minds or personalities to computers, create artificial humans or androids, clone humans, and otherwise enhance human bodies with direct brain – computer interfaces, and augment humans with other types of technology.

These visions of alternative futures are supported by the advances in technology, particularly genetics, molecular biology, robotics and automation, computers, telecommunications, and space development. Collectively, they support arguments for a coming Singularity, a supposedly transformational scientific event or period when a quantum leap in human or scientific capabilities is reached. It might be the development of an entirely new biological species, the emergence of super intelligent machines, or some unforeseen development that will have significant implications for the continuation of Homo sapiens as we are currently configured. As noted previously, these trends are consistent with Platt's observation that evolution is accelerating, and with the emergence of postnormal times. Barring climate catastrophe, this leads to plausible alternative futures scenarios of a high technology transformation. The potentiality of these possible Earths and the artificial nature of civilisation is becoming less a plausibility and more a probability nearing the order of fate or destiny.

Artificial civilisations were categorised in 1964 by Soviet astronomer Nikolai Kardashev who created a scale of advanced technological civilisations:

- Type I civilisation, a planetary civilisation, that can use all of the energy available on its planet
- Type II civilisation, a stellar civilisation, that can use all of the energy of its sun
- Type III civilisation, a galactic civilisation, that can control the energy of an entire galaxy.

The Kardashev scale has also been the subject of science fiction and astronomy, particularly the search for extra-terrestrial intelligence (SETI) programmes. Along the same lines, astronomer Carl Sagan argued for a scale related to the information available to the civilisation. Aerospace engineer Robert Zubrin argued for a scale measuring the spread of civilisation across space, rather than its control of energy, and mathematician John Barrow reversed the scale downward, basing his scale on our ability to manipulate increasingly smaller scales and dimensions. The striking notion is that humans are manipulating nature at ever larger and ever smaller scales, extending the boundaries of natural and artificial reach into our reality.

The scales going in both directions are reminiscent of the Powers of Ten exercises and videos that tend to reinforce the anthropic principle, that we are ideally positioned for technological and consciousness evolution given our material and evolutionary 'sweet spot'. We have been extremely successful as a species, in a relatively short time, geologically speaking. On one hand, our evolutionary biology niche expanded thanks to our tools. More recently, according to the historian Yuval Harari, myth-making gave our species more reasons to use tools accelerating the use, sophistication, and complexity of our tools over the last dozen millennia. Our technological sophistication is lagged considerably in our political, social, and economic systems. We appear to hang on to Newtonian myths and metaphors that glorify the machine. We appear not to have passed into the postindustrial worldview suggested in Alvin Toffler's *Third Wave*: we are still embedded in industreality. Politics, particularly in the USA, is still wedded to checks and balances, separation of powers, and industrial mass education. We have not caught up with the digital, electronic, and photonic technologies increasingly dominating our lives.

In spite of the evidence that other models of knowing and reality exist; relativity, quantum interpretations of reality, and organic biological paradigms that question the machine metaphors continue to be marginalized. However, there are emerging shifts on the periphery, for example, neural networks and quantum computing that may be points of departure from our lingering industrial and Newtonian models of reality. As it has throughout history, reality changes and the new reality that we will see in the not too distant future is becoming increasingly irreconcilable by our present models. The mechanistic and organic are not simply being superseded, but morphed into something that is equal parts hopeful as a continuation of human progress and nightmare in facing the potential end of the human race. Either way, it appears the notion of artificial is becoming more and more natural by the day.

Our planet and its surface environment are as artificial as ever. Will it always be so? The Earth is being remade, in a sense, but the jury is out on whether the creative destruction of Mother Earth will be beneficial only to humans, to most of Earth's species, or only the hardiest insects and microorganisms that will exist long after we go extinct. Will we end up closer to nature, whether we want to or not? These are among some of the great conundrums of postnormal times. Will our futures lean to a posthuman or transhuman existence? Hopefully, we will come to our collective senses and our collective wisdom to envision and actualize preferred futures, not those driven by corporate greed, ideological certainty, or worse, cultural and political whims. I want my grandchildren to inherit futures that we set in motion over the next decade or two that give them hope and opportunity to make their own decisions about the complexion of artificial and natural in their own lives. I worry that an increasingly artificial planet will leave them impoverished rather than liberated and transformed. But I hope that we will not make it too easy for the future geologists to label this epoch.

FAUX FEMINISM

Esra Mirze Santesso

The past few years have seen a wave of articles and essays about 'fake feminism'. Some use the term to refer to conservative women (Ivanka Trump, Sarah Palin) who pay lip service to female empowerment while actually working to undermine it; others apply the term to ostensibly progressive male politicians (Justin Trudeau) who ultimately restrict or constrain female progress. Some see 'fake feminism' in the work of those who are only marginally attached to the movement; others use the terms and strategies of feminism to advance seemingly contrary positions (for example, 'New Wave Feminists', a movement founded as a Christian rethinking of gender identity which works actively towards not only 'making abortion illegal', but 'making it unthinkable and unnecessary by supporting women'). And finally, some critics apply the 'fake' label to what many have described as 'feminism-lite'. Bhakti Shringarpure, editor of the website Warscapes, writes:

> I am very much opposed to feminism-lite... There is a desperate need to proclaim feminism as cool and trendy, but all the while there is also a desire to limit feminist discourse by claiming it's about personal choice... If you're a feminist, then all these personal choices should somehow be honoured. Well, absolutely not. Feminism is fundamentally communal and fundamentally bellicose in how it resists white heterosexist patriarchy. A T-shirt does not solve the problem. Nor does it help to submit to consumer-obsessed celebrity versions of feminism, which are primarily interested in selling you stuff and are not really invested in issues of the economic, social or political justice.

Shringarpure warns that choice, the expression of individual agency, does not necessarily overlap with progressive feminist politics. Indeed, there are many examples of women who willingly choose self-subordinating positions: while they cannot be condemned simply for exercising their right to choose, they can hardly be characterised as 'true' feminists. Equally important is Shringarpure's argument about how consumer culture latches onto ideologies as profitable commodities. Nigerian novelist, Chimamanda Adichie, who herself was targeted for her collaboration with Dior to design a shirt that read 'We Should All Be Feminists', worries about the ideological hollowness and artificiality of feminism-lite, arguing that a superficial and conditional engagement with feminism only downplays the urgency of the movement.

I am interested here in pursuing the notion of 'real' and 'fake' feminism in the context of recent graphic novels created by Muslim women. Is an autobiographical comic detailing the struggles of women in a patriarchal society automatically 'authentically' feminist – as some scholars argue? Or must those works be 'bellicose', and 'unconditional', as Shringarpure and Adichie suggest, in order to avoid artificial, 'fake' feminism?

Recently, Muslim writing emerging from developing and non-Western countries has been asking bolder and more ambitious questions about how various female experiences can be located in relation to feminism – especially when those experiences take place in highly patriarchal social contexts. Marjane Satrapi's *Persepolis*, published in 2000, is one such example. Soon after its publication, the graphic memoir received critical acclaim due to its vivid illustration of the Islamic revolution in Iran from the perspective of a child from a middle-class, secular family. The book attained global success, and its insider's illustration of Muslim citizens under an authoritarian regime eventually sold more than two million copies around the world. In time, *Persepolis* became an iconic representation of the forced Islamisation of civic life and what that meant from a human rights standpoint – what it meant, that is, for a theocratic state to view women's bodies as extensions of the government's discipline and control. The fact that this argument against patriarchal repression was authored by a woman encouraged numerous critical identifications of the book as an echt feminist text. Hillary Chute's *Graphic Women: Life Narrative and Contemporary Comics*, which investigates graphic memoirs written by women, praises *Persepolis*'s 'feminist' exploration of collective trauma resulting from male dominance. Chute goes on to argue that by framing her narrative as a witness account, Satrapi articulates a politics of visibility, foregrounding women's everyday experiences as a way to challenge 'the virulent machinations of "official histories"' Satrapi's efforts to interject women's voices into public discourse, in Chute's estimation, creates a text that is not only 'keenly feminist', but also one that models 'a feminist methodology in its form'. Other critics echo Chute's position. Janell Hobson praises the way the text engages with 'global feminist consciousness' while 'resist[ing] standard models of multicultural education [and] displacing the hegemonic narratives of the West'. Golnar Nabizadeh maintains that the memoir 'significantly contributes to feminist cultural histories because the author's story is told through a female and Iranian perspective' – an imbrication that is typically excluded from Western feminist discourse. Susan Stanford Friedman coins the term 'cosmofeminism' to describe the book's 'gender-based resistance to state violence' in a quest for 'cosmopolitan peace'; she further suggests that the text is 'situated in a feminist critique of the nation-state in wartime and a utopian longing for peaceful world citizenship'. Drawing attention to the book's adoption as common reading in gender studies and women studies courses in more than one hundred sixty colleges and high schools around the US, Amy Malek highlights the feminist overtones of Marje's exile in Europe, which conveys a subversive 'mode of negotiating ... codes, inscriptions, and identities' that essentially destabilises power structures. And the list goes on.

Yet the question remains: do visibility politics, when articulated in autobiographical form by a woman, always align neatly and automatically with feminist ideologies? By bringing into focus under-represented, marginalised women living under repressive regimes – from the Shah's enforced modernisation to Khomeini's theocratic regime – this graphic memoir's engagement with visibility politics is clearly an important, timely and even urgent undertaking that illustrates the heterogeneity of women in Muslim societies. But how successful is it in conveying a 'true' feminist message? And what is the significance of the ways the critics interpret the book's relationship with feminism? There are two challenges in answering these questions: first, most of the scholars in question seem to suggest, or at least imply, that progressive feminism is attainable only for those who become cosmopolitan or hybrid or global citizens – in other words, those who transcend their non-Western upbringing. Such scholarly framing implies that feminist inclusion requires some form of cultural erasure – as if independent women are naturally absent in Muslim societies and can only enter the world stage once they cross borders and interact with the West. Marjane's ability to cross borders, underscored with words such as 'cosmopolitan', 'global', 'hybrid', and 'exilic', privileges her mobility as a condition for an informed subjectivity. The question is: what happens to those Muslim women who do not have access to cross-cultural movement? Are they automatically excluded from feminist discourse for their inability to construct hybrid subjectivities? Do their voices matter less because they remain deeply rooted in their traditions or belief systems?

The second challenge is the deafening silence about Islam emanating from those advocating cosmofeminism and the like. In these critical pieces, Marjane's subjectivity is positioned against the Islamic regime, but there is hardly any engagement with her Muslim background. If we follow Chute's logic that the success of a feminist memoir is its ability to visualise the everyday experiences of women against an extraordinary backdrop, then ignoring how these daily routines are shaped by collective understandings of religion along with personal negotiations of spirituality seems myopic. After all, early on in the narrative, the young Marje has an extremely strong, nurturing relationship with God. When she goes to sleep at night, she finds comfort in being able to conjure up God as a soothing presence: 'The only place I felt safe was in the arms of my friend'. This personal connection is so important to her that at times, she imagines herself as a prophet, waiting to fulfil a divine mission. Later on, even after her dislocation from Iran, Marjane retains not just her spirituality but her faith, noting, for instance, that each time her mother reaches out to God, her wish is granted. As she grows up, Marjane experiences a crisis of faith, but she never rejects Islam entirely. When she is taking an entrance exam, she is asked if she knows how to pray. Marjane responds: 'I speak to him in Persian' and goes on to explain that: 'The Prophet Mohammed said "God is closer to us than [our] jugular veins". God is always with us. He is in us.' Therefore, even though Marjane resists the institutionalisation of Islam in Iran, and maintains a somewhat secular understanding of religion, her spirituality and personal connection to faith is never entirely eliminated. But there is hardly any critical talk of her religious orientation, which seems to suggest that either these scholars see feminism and Islam as opposing or contradictory forces, and a feminist Muslim as an oxymoron, or that they find Marjane's religious background and interests irrelevant – as if Marjane attains her cosmofeminism partly because she is able to move beyond or ignore religion.

The push for a feminist reading of *Persepolis* is reflective of the push for broadening the parameters of the movement by transcending its Western biases. Since the 1980s, there have been great efforts to theorise more diverse, inclusive, and pluralised permutations of feminism that can resist the homogenisation of women and thus avoid narrow definitions of female agency entirely aligned with Eurocentric values. This interest in re-presenting female experiences separated from colonial and orientalist underpinnings of Western feminism has given shape to a series of revitalising works by scholars such as Chandra Mohanty, Gloria Azaldua, and Ketu Katrak. Working against simplified and universalised prescriptions of femininity, these critics seek ways to incorporate third-world women and soar women of colour into mainstream discussions of women's struggles. In Mohanty's words:

> assumptions of privilege and ethnocentric universality on the one hand, and inadequate self-consciousness about the effect of Western scholarship on the "third world" in the context of a world system dominated by the West on the other, characterise a sizable extent of Western feminist work.

This is an important project. Yet negating some of the basic principles of feminism – a movement based on an affirmation of female solidarity against gender inequality normalised by patriarchal structures – for the sake of incorporating female subjectivities from the developing world only contributes, one would think, to the spreading of 'fake feminism'. That is, equating feminism solely with visibility politics without incorporating a philosophical and political commitment to gender equality, and considering a text feminist simply because it features a female protagonist results in a narrow-minded and artificial form of feminism. *Persepolis* is neither interested in promoting third-world feminism nor in modelling Islamic feminism – a movement keenly aware of the shortcomings of Western feminism, including its lack of diversity. In an interview, Satrapi makes an effort to distance herself from the 'feminist' label as she pushes for a different reading of the text that does not prioritise gender difference, but rather on exposing the inner conflicts of a society in the process of nation-building:

> I am absolutely not a feminist, I am against stupidity, and if it comes from males or females it doesn't change anything. [*Persepolis*] is a human coming of age story, let's go for the humanity and humanism, it's a much better thing than this 'womanhood' and 'manhood'.

While the intent or the ideological positioning of the author is rarely useful in illuminating the politics of a text, there is clearly a reluctance on the part of Satrapi when it comes to presenting herself as a feminist. This is not to say that Satrapi is naïve about the vexed position of women in Iran under the regime, but she is cautious about rushing into feminism without a fully dedicated sense of activism. If Marjane does not form networks from which to empower her female friends, if she does not participate actively in establishing justice, her offhand criticism of the state would seem to leave her in the position of 'feminist-lite'.

Let us go a step further to continue to test Chute's argument that 'making the hidden visible is a powerful … feminist trope'. Since Satrapi, a number of Muslim women have produced graphic memoirs to talk about gender inequality in Muslim societies. Yet, while they are committed to showing women's everyday experiences in Muslim societies, they too are rarely inclined to present their work as a feminist manifesto or as any sort of 'authentic' feminist production. Both Ozge Samanci's *Dare to Disappoint* and Ayesha Tariq's *Sarah: The Suppressed Anger of the Pakistani Obedient Daughter* (graphic novel memoirs from Turkey and Pakistan respectively) illustrate this ambivalence vividly. Like *Persepolis*, these two works present an insider's view of the obstacles placed in front of women as they transition to adulthood. And again, similar to *Persepolis*, even though the two artists/creators engage with visibility politics to raise consciousness, neither of them is convinced that feminism is the best or wisest strategy for women situated in developing countries to advance in their societies – not because they disagree with feminism's commitment to gender equality, but because they doubt that it will bring those women the independence they seek.

Samanci's memoir concentrates on education: it starts with her early years at primary school and chronicles her academic training over the next decade until she graduates with a math degree from a top university in Istanbul – a degree that she finds neither desirable nor practical, but prestigious enough to satisfy her parents. The memoir draws attention to the types of challenges faced by young girls in Turkey, a country with an overwhelming Muslim majority, troubled by perpetual polarisation between secularists and religious conservatives. It becomes apparent early on that Samanci's secular upbringing distances her from a conservative attachment to religion, but does not insulate her from injustices brought about by religious politics. The most vivid example of this is when Samanci leaves home to attend a boarding school in Istanbul. There, she finds not a hybrid or cosmopolitan or subversive space (as is the case with the school in *Persepolis*), but an environment rife with religious tension:

> In our class there were only four girls and twenty boys. Many of the boys in the school came from conservative families who were practising Muslims. Many of the girls came from liberal families who were non-practising Muslims.

The fact that these girls prefer not to don the headscarf automatically marks them as impious and morally corrupt; the religious boys describe them as 'infidel exhibitionists' and 'brainwashed westernised bitches'. Such misogyny not only illustrates the gendered peer pressures associated with religious membership, but also sheds light on the extent of institutionalised discrimination young women face: the teachers at the school acquiesce and occasionally cater to the sexism of the religious male students. At first, Samanci refuses to be silenced, and challenges the school authorities, complaining about gender inequality. Her visibility, however, quickly turns her into a target, and the principal ultimately comes up with a number of bogus reasons to expel her from school.

Dare to Disappoint depicts the consequences of being visible and speaking up. Samanci's father encourages her to toe the line: 'If you want to stay in this school, you have to learn how to be invisible. You are too identifiable. Protect yourself'. In his view, protection requires the appearance of conformity. And therein lies the problem for young women in repressive societies, in Samanci's view: to be a part of an educational mechanism that can afford them the economic stability essential for autonomy, they have to sustain a kind of invisibility by refusing to protest or even acknowledge patriarchal injustice. 'Protecting' one's self means allowing conservative Muslims to dictate their own social norms. In the end, Samanci's refusal to remain submissive leads to expulsion, which reduces her chances of completing her education. In this regard, her decision to speak out ironically serves right into the hands of conservative Muslims, determined to keep women under control by denying them education. Samanci is eventually able to get her university diploma – in part because she learns how to go along with the system – but the accomplishment does not bring her happiness, not least because it seemingly confirms the viability of 'invisibility' as a social strategy.

Tariq's *Sarah* also concentrates on the everyday life of the protagonist, inundated by domestic chores that get in the way of her schooling. Sarah's parents are not necessarily Islamists, or even particularly devout, but they are certainly conservative, entirely in step with a gender ideology that aligns with patriarchal norms. Their priority is to raise an obedient daughter who can attract a desirable suitor. To secure a good future for her, Sarah's parents not only groom her as a competent housekeeper, but also guard her reputation by monitoring any non-halal behaviour and restricting her interactions with her friends. The mechanism of control in *Sarah* is more subtle than the institutionalised sexism embodied by the fashion police in *Persepolis,* or the school administration in *Dare to Disappoint*: here it is represented by the gossiping aunties whose couched surveillance acts as a symbolic extension of male hegemony, 'operating in the service of that [patriarchal] law's self-amplification and proliferation', as Judith Butler puts it. The constant paranoia about Sarah's visibility outside the home results in her constant objectification – not only by the male gaze, exemplified by a series of arranged meetings with prospective suitors, but also by the female gaze, from her mother's body-shaming rants to the aunties' community policing. To show her frustration visually in the narrative, Sarah uses a bottle in which she piles all her grievances; as her annoyance grows, the bottle fills up to its brim. Finally, Sarah reaches breaking point, gathers her courage, and decides to speak up against her parents, to announce her determination to break out of the restrictive Islamic life in which she increasingly feels trapped. But right before she is about to burst into their bedroom, she overhears her parents praising her as 'the perfect daughter'. Sarah wavers: 'If I say anything now, they will be heartbroken.' She eventually withdraws: the reader sees her on the next page moving away from the bedroom as imagined rationalisations for her silence appear in the frame around her. As she tries to convince herself against speaking out, we see her visually diminishing in size. In the end, she stores her jam-packed bottle in a pantry, along with others. The book ends with a bleak and despairing statement: 'It's a vicious cycle, I tell you.'

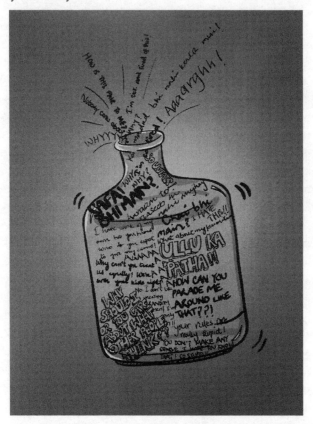

Sarah's bottle of grievances

Visibility politics, which is an essential step towards raising awareness about a marginalised group, remains at the heart of these two narratives.

But it is also plainly evident that the two protagonists are not rebels or iconoclasts. Despite the severe cultural and political fissures around them, they are deeply rooted in their communities and indeed think of themselves first and foremost as representatives of that community. For them gaining autonomy is less about fighting against patriarchal or religious pressures in the public sphere, and more about being able to re-define their roles within the domestic space vis-à-vis their immediate families. Their subversive acts are largely personal – they are not concerned with joining a movement or organising rallies, and they rarely consider the larger State at all, let alone the West. They are primarily worried about finding a path to empower themselves within the constraints that family, society, and religion have placed upon them. That desire for empowerment is deeply personal and not nourished by female solidarity and collective action. With this in mind, while the two graphic artists are able to capture the everyday experiences of the Muslim women in their respective societies, they do not explicitly engage with feminism as a call to action. If we agree with the definition of a feminist text as one that is centrally concerned with representing women, who work towards changing societal attitudes about gender roles and do something to that effect, there is no question that these two texts do not meet the definition. Despite the fact both graphic works centre on woman-centred experiences, they hardly move beyond a diagnosis of problems.

All three graphic works end in problematic ways. Marjane leaves home for a second time to realise her artistic potential in the West; Ozge receives her 'useless' diploma and imagines speaking with her father about pursuing a creative path (likely in the West as well – even though the book ends before that resolution materialises); and Sarah continues to remain silent, surrendering to a life trapped in the same old cycle. And all three take deeply ambiguous positions as to the value of becoming 'visible' in their societies. With this in mind, unless we are prepared to define feminism simply as awareness of inequality without a philosophical and political commitment to take action against wrongdoing, or even to advocate visibility, we should rethink Chute's stance.

None of this is to say that the graphic novel as a genre is incapable of presenting feminist positions. While the graphic memoir has an ambivalent and difficult relationship with 'authentic' feminism – employing feminist tropes but falling short of fully embracing feminism in an authentic way – the superhero genre is much more readily able to overtly endorse feminism in line with its message of social justice. Consider Deena Mohammed's *Qahera*, a web-comic that features a hijabi superhero, wearing a traditional black abaya as she fights against misogyny in her hometown of Cairo. *Qahera* fully embraces her faith and uses the Qur'an as her guide to correct injustices in the world. In one episode, we see her confront a chauvinist man after being triggered by his declarations: 'a good wife is an obedient wife, it is your Islamic duty to keep them at home and in check.' Qahera swoops down and volunteers to 'do the laundry' – by tying the man up with a clothesline. In another episode, she aids a woman who is assaulted by a stranger on the street. The woman immediately goes to authorities to file a report, however, the chief of police chastises her by remarking on her 'immodest' clothes and 'inappropriate' manner of dress: 'I can assure you that everyone else will agree with me that had you been dressed more modestly, this definitely wouldn't have happened.' Ironically, this statement appears amidst a sequence of panels that depicts Qahera in her abaya, being verbally harassed by men. The disconnect between the visual and verbal cues conveys the idea that no woman is immune from verbal and physical abuse. Qahera makes the point that sexualisation of the female body by the male gaze – whether the woman is a Muslim or not, whether she is dressed provocatively or not – is indefensible.

Even though *Qahera* does not depict the everyday life of the Muslim woman like the memoirs discussed earlier, it provides a more authentic account of feminism: it presents female solidarity not only between Muslim women, but also between believing and non-believing women; it takes a combative stance against misogyny; it addresses the importance of gender equality and social justice within Muslim communities. Furthermore, *Qahera* goes as far as to brand FEMEN, a French feminist organisation, infamous for their provocative protests in which they write messages across their naked chests, as faux feminists. At one point, Qahera watches online videos of the latest protest organised by FEMEN. As the protestors declare all women wearing the hijab as oppressed victims in need of saving, Qahera winces at the naiveté of the Westerners.

She immediately transports herself to the scene of action, and is met with a frenzy. The protestors mark her as the poster-child of oppression due to her headscarf, and try to 'free' her from subjugation. One woman screams: 'Look there! It's a Muslim woman. This is why we are here. We have to save her.' The act of saving, a discourse that has long been used to legitimise Western intervention in Muslim societies, echoes what Leila Ahmed has described as 'colonial feminism', and brings with it serious racist implications, leaving Muslim women alienated as abject and enslaved. Before the protestor is able to 'free' Qahera by ripping her dress, Qahera takes her sword out, and demands to be listened to: 'You have constantly undermined and ignored women. You seem unable to understand that we do not need your help, and I doubt there is much I can do to teach you.' Qahera's exasperation with Western credulity and condescension stems from her sense that feminist organisations like FEMEN are making the Islamic feminist project more difficult. She exclaims: 'women's lives are not for you to prove a point…our choices are not your political punchlines.' Qahera thus engages with a type of feminism that she defines on her own terms as an extension of her faith while FEMEN appears an organisation that replicated orientalist and imperialist stereotypes about Muslim women.

Qahera represents a feminist who is rooted in her culture; she does not develop into a hybrid or a cosmopolitan subject at any point in the narrative. In addition, her religion is not marginalised, but remains at the core of her identity. In this regard, she represents the true spirit of Islamic feminism, a gender-based consciousness grounded in Islamic reformism to decouple Islam from repressive practices associated with religious discourse. Scholars such as Fatema Mernissi and Leila Ahmed have been instrumental in forging Islamic feminism as a legitimate inquiry into the power structures normalised in Islamic societies. As Mernissi said: 'If women's rights are a problem for some modern Muslim men, it is neither because of the Koran nor the Prophet, nor the Islamic tradition, but simply because those rights conflict with the interests of a male elite.' Followed by Amina Wadud, and Margot Badran among others, Islamic feminism gained legitimacy as a movement that aimed at explaining the Qur'an from a female perspective. As Badran argued, Islamic feminism carries an important role in instigating a structural reformation within the ummah to inspire equality and social responsibility. The fight for equality from within Islam marked an important milestone as it put an end to arguments about Islam's incompatibility with modernity, and ended the false dichotomy between faith and women's rights.

Qahera confronts the member of FEMEN

Anouar Majid, founding director of Tangier Global Forum, insists that feminism, for Muslim women as well as non-Muslim women, must be 'a mode of intervention into particular hegemonic discourses' and not [simply] 'a universal response to an assumed universal patriarchy'. If we remove intervention, or action, from feminism, we are left with a very different definition of the term—one which would allow almost any graphic novel by a Muslim woman to be labelled 'feminist', particularly if we return to Chute's focus on 'visibility', as literal visibility is essentially a prerequisite of any graphic novel. But I worry that conflating 'visibility' with resistance, and 'conformity' with self-determination, while perhaps allowing for more flexibility in terms of representing autonomous Muslim female protagonists, ends up creating faux feminism. True, genuine feminism cannot be incidental, but must have a philosophical foundation, a political platform oriented toward collective action. Describing a predicament, bearing witness to injustice—these are indeed important steps which might aid in building a feminist coalition; but they are not by themselves specifically feminist. With this in mind, while I agree that all of the three graphic narratives discussed in this paper are woman-centred texts invested in showing gender inequality by navigating between the secular and the Islamic, between private and public spheres, they are not necessarily 'true' feminist texts.

Comic books themselves have long suffered from the stigma of being considered 'artificial' literature; indeed, the field of comics studies in some ways emerged out of the desire to redefine the genre as a 'real', legitimate medium deserving of serious critical attention. However, in this case, the answer is not simply to claim that all graphic memoirs are authentically, inherently feminist. Today, a number of graphic novelists around the globe are working to expose the ills of their respective societies—from human rights violations to border disputes, from civil wars to torture chambers sanctioned by authoritarian states. Other graphic novelists have little interest in such projects. The medium does not determine the politics. Even amongst women memoirists working in the graphic novel form, ideological orientations fluctuate wildly. In the end, treating graphic works as real literature is to understand that all forms of literary works have varying relationships with different philosophies and movements, including feminism – real or fake.

THE ENGLISH ROSE THAT WASN'T

Hassan Mahamdallie

It is a portrait of an English Rose. The pretty blonde girl in the photograph is looking slightly upwards and beyond the camera lens. Maybe an adult standing in front of her has just said something funny or silly to get a reaction, because her eyes are twinkling and she is smiling, her lips parted revealing a slight gap between her two front teeth.

Her hair is long and curls down onto her shoulders. She is wearing a plain checked buttoned-up shirt; it looks new, perhaps purchased for the occasion. The girl is maybe ten or eleven years old, which means it is 1944 or 1945 and the German bombers that demolished houses and killed her neighbours on the road where she lives in Morden, south London, no longer strike fear. The World War is coming to a close or is just over, and maybe it is the new air of optimism amongst the adults in her family that is putting the smile on her face. Her name is Maureen Yvonne Barnett.

There was good reason to believe that things were going to improve. Although the years after 1945 saw a continuation of war-time measures such as rationing, Maureen's teenage years were materially better than the first decade of her life, that had spanned global recession and unimaginable slaughter. The post-conflict economy picked up, the Attlee Labour government introducing major reforms in state education, welfare and health. Leaders of powerful industrial trade unions were regularly treated to beer and sandwiches at Number 10 Downing Street. There were jobs to be had and the prospect for some workers of a mortgage and owning your own house.

There was a liberalisation of social norms, giving young people, particularly women, more freedom. Personal emancipation was facilitated by a bit more disposable income. As Maureen would later recall of her and her friends: 'We were young girls. We chatted to anybody and everybody. We were never ever home. We used to cycle everywhere. Cinemas, entertainment, that sort of thing.' But every evening, after a night out at the pictures, coffee house or ballroom, Maureen would return home to her 'respectable' working class home in Morden.

A heavily idealised, black and white film version of Maureen's post-war decade, that began with the defeat of Hitler and ended with the Suez crisis (that underlined Britain's inexorable decline on the world stage) runs on a continuous loop in the mythic propaganda of the Little Englander nationalists who put themselves at the head of the Brexit campaign. Political scientist Matthew Goodwin describes it as

> a particular blend of Englishness which, at times, has ventured into the darker underbelly of nationalism. It is Wat Tyler and the Peasants' Revolt, the Blitz Spirit, Private Walker, Del Boy and Fat Les all rolled into one; rebellious, angry and disillusioned but also defiant, redemptive, sarcastic, dogged, and, occasionally, triumphant.

One of the main ideological components of this Englishness is that the 'old' or 'traditional' working class of which the pleasing photo of the young Maureen might be said to symbolise, had a racial and ethnic purity — it was white. This whiteness also describes a certain shared societal outlook – respectable, proud, aspirant working class, 'bolshy' in defending its rights as 'free-born Englishmen' but also socially conservative, deferential and knowing of its place in the gradients of the British class system. The docking of the *Empire Windrush* in June 1948, carrying British passport-holding migrants from Jamaica, at Tilbury docks is seen as the dark negative – the harbinger of the coming assault upon the ethnic and cultural homogeneity of Englishness. The present-day stripping of British citizenship from the 'Windrush generation' of West Indian immigrants by the UK Tory government, should not, therefore, be seen as a series of unfortunate mistakes or the result of bureaucratic overzealousness by Home Office civil servants, rather it is an expression of a racist impulse by powerful forces to turn back the clock by physically expelling the founding generation of the modern British multicultural society.

Racist demagogues from the patrician Enoch Powell of the 1960s and '70s, to today's tin-pot version Nigel Farage, have argued that successive governments, by opening the floodgates of immigration, have displaced the 'white' working class as beneficiaries of the post-war years into an increasingly marginal and disadvantaged ghetto, encircled by dark-skinned competitors. The Little Englander project, therefore, is to somehow return to that simpler, purer, more prosperous time. Whether or not those times ever existed, let alone exactly how they would go about reverse-engineering British society back to that place, is hardly ever explicitly stated. It is more about feeding off some kind of generalised yearning. As activist and campaigner for social justice, Ann Dummett, wrote in her 1973 book *A Portrait of English Racism*:

> Enoch Powell…by referring to England's green and pleasant land as under threat, can rouse feelings instantly. For the home of the new Jerusalem to be under threat from without strikes the fear of the devil into the least Christian of men. Powell did not mean to describe present-day England as a green and pleasant land in any literal sense, nor was he taken to mean that.

Maureen, our poster girl for Englishness, returns to her suburban home after an evening at the Gaumont Cinema in nearby Wimbledon. Her family are all at home – her bookish older sister Valerie, her father Albert, 'Bert', and her mother Doris. The house is spick and span – Doris is rather obsessive about cleanliness. The front room, with its curtained bay window facing the street, is out-of-bounds except for visitors. On the back of the sofas are antimacassars – laced cloth to stop Bert's hair-oil staining the material. The family usually gather in the downstairs backroom, where easy-going Bert does his books (he earns his money collecting weekly life insurance payments from his client list in the local area), smokes his Players cigarettes, listens to the radio and plays cards with his two girls. The kitchen is Doris's domain, where a pot of tea is always on the go, in case her sister Hilda, who lives in the next road with her family, drops by for a chat.

Bert is a veteran of the Great War of 1914–18 and an unsung hero. He was born into a well-to-do family in Somers Town, behind London's King's Cross Station, and was a month shy of fourteen years old when the war broke out. Bert went to the local recruiting office, gave his age as eighteen, and signed up to the British Army. According to his sister Joan 'he was amongst the first 200 sharpshooters who went to France at the outbreak of the war. My mother sent seven birth certificates to the War Office but they never sent him home. All his life he never mentioned the war or the part he played in it'. After the war Bert joined the Merchant Navy, where he no doubt picked up the life-long habit of chain-smoking strong Navy Cut brand cigarettes. For Joan, her brave but modest brother embodied all that was the best of British: 'A wonderful man. Scrupulously clean and upright'.

For some reason, during or just after the war, Bert changed his surname from that which he was born with and adopted a new one. When he married Doris in London in 1927, the name he gave on the marriage certificate was Albert Barnett, yet his father (whom he was named after) is recorded as one Albert Brown.

This is not particularly unusual in times of chaos and rapid change. People have always seized the opportunities that wars and mass upheavals generate to reinvent themselves, including altering their official identities. Generations of men and women drawn from the countryside into work in the cities, or who migrate from one country to another, have used the cover of anonymity that urban life provides to abandon the ties of their previous existence and give themselves a chance to start a new life over again.

We do not know why Albert Brown decided to become Albert Barnett and thus pass on that invented surname to his spouse Doris and their offspring. Just as he never talked about the war, he rarely talked to his two daughters about his own family history and roots. Sometimes they would overhear adult family members talking and glean a little tit-bit of information, but they had no way of knowing whether they had heard right, or how all the fragments might possibly fit together. Maureen always held to the belief that somehow she might have a connection through her father to the Jewish people and faith, but she never managed to find out for sure. The Roman Catholic nuns who ran the Ursuline High School in Wimbledon that Maureen attended from the age of eleven, were certainly never told her father was part-Jewish, and that her grandmother was directly descended from Jews of Eastern European origin.

Those who wish to advance the notion of a distinct indigenous white working-class community that has become economically disadvantaged and politically marginalised by post-war immigration, most often point to the east end of London. In 2008, the BBC ran a provocative season of documentaries under the banner 'The White Season'. The BBC press office put out a release describing the season as:

> ...a series of films that shine the spotlight on the white working-class in Britain today. It examines why some feel increasingly marginalised... The films explore the complex mix of feelings that lead some people to feel under siege and that their very sense of self is being brought into question. And, as newly arrived immigrant populations move in, the season examines the conflict between the communities and explores the economic and psychological tensions.

A *Daily Express* newspaper journalist, commenting on one of the documentaries, *All White in Barking*, took the opportunity to argue that, 'In the Sixties and Seventies most council housing in the East End was given to large families just arrived from Bangladesh... Families who had manned the docks, lived through the Blitz and helped fend off Nazi Germany were flabbergasted to find Britain's rulers showing more consideration to strangers from the Third World'. The journalist concluded that the English East Enders had been made 'refugees in their own country. They saw one beloved neighbourhood with a legendary community spirit destroyed in the name of multiculturalism'.

Completely absent in all this is any grasp that the history of the east end of London is a history of movement and migration, and that its economic dynamism and ability to adapt, change and grow has been fuelled by immigration. The monumental economic contribution that working class

Bangladeshis have made to the east end of London, mirrors the achievement of the poor Jews fleeing anti-semitism who arrived before them, and the Huguenots fleeing religious persecution who arrived before them.

And who exactly are these 'English' East End cockneys and when exactly did they become white? If we assume that most of them have local family roots going back to the nineteenth century, what we do know is that they were regarded by Victorian society as anything but white. As academic Anoop Nayak has pointed out:

> Historically there is ample evidence to show that the bodies of the British urban poor were regularly compared with African natives of Empire in terms of physique, stature, posture, facial mannerisms, intelligence, habits, attitudes and disposition. Moreover, this 'casual residuum', as they were frequently termed, were rarely seen as 'white', but rather were imagined as part of a toiling, sweating, blackened and putrefying mass of flesh, unapologetically designated 'the Great Unwashed'.

Anoop quotes historian Anthony Wohl, who in his introduction to John Hollinghead's *Ragged London in 1861*, observes that 'concerning the pigmentation of the industrial Impoverished' it is alleged that 'the inhabitants of the slums are "swarthy", or "sallow", or have "yellow faces", or are blackened with soot, or possess "dark sinister faces" – any colour, it would seem, but white'. Anoop remarks, 'Today this may seem strange, as the working-classes now tend to be seen as the authentic carriers of whiteness, as synonyms such as being "salt of the earth" or "backbone of the nation" testify'. He concludes that 'The designation of the British working classes as white is then a modern phenomenon'.

One of those dark sinister-faced slum dwellers was Maureen's great-great grandfather, a man named David Alexander. We know a little about him. He was born in Spitalfields, east London, in 1821. Today it is a gentrified area favoured by well-heeled hipsters, but in David Alexander's time Spitalfields, and the neighbouring areas of Whitechapel and Bethnal Green, were notorious slums, known as a haunt of the destitute and criminals and ridden with diseases such as cholera. When David was aged eleven Spitalfields was described thus: 'The low houses are all huddled together in close and dark lanes and alleys, presenting at first sight an appearance of non-habitation, so dilapidated are the doors and windows

– in every room of the houses, whole families, parents, children and aged grandfathers swarm together'.

The surname Alexander indicates that he was a Jew of Ashkenazi (Eastern European) origins. Alexander was a fairly common Jewish surname, harking back to the time when Alexander the Great was a popular figure throughout the Middle East. David married his wife Mary when she and he were in their early twenties. From records we know that David was a hawker – a travelling salesman, going from town to town, door-to-door selling domestic goods to housewives. They had four children born in different towns across England – Kendal, Manchester, Northampton, and Liverpool. But by the time he was thirty, David and his family were all living back in east London; in Whitechapel, then Spitalfields, then nearby Mile End Road. He was still selling door to door, while his wife was doing piece-work sewing beads onto fabric. We lose sight of David in his 50s.

However, one of his children, Joseph, born 'on the road' in Manchester, appears in the historical records towards the end of the nineteenth century, living in Caernarfon, north Wales. What took Joseph to the entirely Welsh-speaking, Presbyterian non-conformist church-going town is not known. But we do know what he did when he got there – he married a local girl Jane Jones, the daughter of a river pilot who had drowned in a tragedy at sea when she was a child.

The young Jewish man entered the household dominated by his mother-in-law, who according to family accounts was tyrannical and god-fearing, insisting on 'putting stockings on her table legs, whitewashing the kitchen after every weekly wash' and who commanded in her will that Jane should scrub her late father's tombstone every week – 'and this was duly carried out!' Joseph and Jane started up a dyers and cleaners business in the town and raised three children. However when Joseph died young, the family was tragically broken up. His father, who had apparently never agreed with Joseph's marriage, insisted the body was transported from Caernarfon all the way back to London to be buried in a Jewish cemetery. Joseph and Jane's children were sent to an orphanage – one grew up and married a rich shipowner, one emigrated to Canada, and the remaining daughter Esther 'Hettie' Alexander moved to London and married James Brown. Hettie is Maureen's grandmother. Maureen remembered Hettie's visits during her childhood years but had only a vague idea of her gran's diverse roots and ancestry.

The fictional English hero 'Bulldog' Drummond was the invention of the successful Edwardian pulp fiction novelist Herman Cyril McNeile, known by his pen-name Sapper. Drummond's various adventures typically pit him and his gentleman friends (known collectively as 'The Breed') against a succession of (often Jewish) Bolshevik conspiracies hatched by dastardly foreigners intent on destroying his beloved England. As Ann Dummett observes, Drummond is sometimes simply described as 'a white man', but one whose Englishness sets him apart from all others: Dummett writes that

> Greeks and Spaniards were Dagoes to Sapper – greasy and 'olive-skinned' as well as untrustworthy, shifty, cowardly characters. The famous saying 'Niggers begin at Calais', was not uttered in ignorance of the fact that Continental Europeans are the same colour as Englishmen; it was uttered to convey the meaning that all who are not English are shifty, greasy, untrustworthy characters.

All this is rather unfortunate for our vision of the English Rose – given that Maureen, on her mother's side, was one of Sapper's greasy Dagoes. Doris's full maiden name was Doris Helene Draco (Greek for dragon), and she was descended from a long line of Dracos, stretching back to the original patriarch of the family, Emanuel Pantoleon Draco.

Emanuel P Draco is recorded as being born on the island of Chios (Khios) in 1838, situated in the Aegean Sea just off the coast of mainland Turkey. Historically a majority Greek island, it was famed for producing mastic gum (a tree resin much valued as a spice and herbal remedy) and for its dominance in the region's merchant shipping and trading industry. The Ottomans seized Chios from the Byzantine Empire in the sixteenth century and nurtured it as a lucrative source of wealth and taxation. However in 1821 Chios found itself at the centre of the Greek War of Independence, launched with the aim of liberating historically Greek territory from the Turks. In March 1822, hundreds of armed Greek revolutionaries landed on the island, and encouraged the islanders to join the rebellion. This in turn provoked an invasion by the Ottoman army, who put down the uprising, and set about slaughtering, expelling and enslaving the Greek population. Outrage in Europe against the atrocity became a cause célèbre across Europe, symbolised by the famous 1824 painting by French artist Eugène Delacroix, T*he Massacre at Chios*, that depicted helpless islanders being put to the sword by vengeful Ottoman soldiers.

Emanuel P Draco is recorded to have been born on the island just over a decade after these bloody events, but he did not stay there. Sometime in his twenties he left the island forever and fetched up in Liverpool, working first as a clerk, boarding in lodgings, and then getting married, raising a family, all the while gradually building a prosperous cotton brokerage company. He married a woman from Liverpool's Greek community and had five children: Panteleon, George, Basilio, Michael and Hypatia. Later in life Hypatia gained press attention when she was listed as a survivor of the 1912 sinking of the Titanic, on which she was serving as a stewardess. Her brother George Emanuel Draco, also gained a public profile (and some notoriety) as an Edwardian music hall promotor and manager. George E Draco married a Liverpudlian named Esther Pickup and moved down to Kennington in south London to become part of the capital's bohemian theatrical community. They had two daughters, one of whom was Doris Helene Draco (born in 1906) – Maureen's mother.

However, the marriage quickly went seriously wrong. George abandoned his wife and infant daughters, had a scandalous affair with a theatrical dresser, with whom he then started a new family. His wife Esther refused to grant him a divorce despite his feckless behaviour and lack of support for Doris and her sister Hilda. Doris certainly never forgave him, considering him a stain on her lifelong efforts to be seen as utterly respectable, decent and without moral reproach. However, Maureen never got to meet her Greek grandfather, and his name was rarely spoken in the family home.

Returning to the portrait of our idealised young working-class girl, we can now see that we have imposed a wholly imagined community of identity upon an individual whose scattered roots defy such simplistic categorisation. Are we really going to agree to sacrifice Maureen's rich ancestry in pursuit of artificially constructed notions of Englishness and whiteness? In reality, Maureen exists not in some narrow trickle of nativist exclusivity, but as a unique combine in a churning current of working class identities, forever mixing, merging and transforming, often below the surface, mostly unremarked upon and unrecognised, but no less real for all that.

A Coda, January 2020

A long lifetime has just come to its end. We are in Epsom General Hospital, just a few miles south of Morden. It is midday and an old woman has just drawn her final breath. All morning she had been losing the battle against respiratory failure brought on by pneumonia. Her mouth is open in death, revealing a full set of teeth with a small gap on the top row.

A few months earlier, ever since she had sensed that something was seriously wrong with her, she had begun starving herself, and her weight had rapidly dropped to that of a child. It is difficult to now imagine that tiny frame had given birth to twelve children, most of whom are presently squeezed round her hospital bed in the side room off the main hospital ward where she had been put as her condition worsened. The hospital staff had been watching all morning with growing amazement and curiosity as the woman's brown skinned sons and daughters kept arriving one after the other after the other. It is explained that they are the offspring of Maureen and her Indo-Caribbean husband whom she married in the 1950s.

The word spreads amongst the staff that the nice old English lady with her old-fashioned London way of speaking and polite manner, has passed away. Nurses and doctors pop their heads round the door to say a few kind words into the room.

Above the dead woman's bed is a hand-written name tag: Maureen Yvonne Mahamdallie.

PROMISES, PROMISES

James Brooks

In the second half of 2016, if you found yourself in the right European conference centre at the right time you might have caught a glimpse of that rarest of phenomena: a president, provost or vice-chancellor of an elite academic institution in a moment of self-doubt, contrition even. Over the past thirty years the university top brass had undergone a major makeover. A great wave of marketisation swept over the continent's academic institutions and when the fusty and/or eccentric and/or seignorial old boys fell from their perches they were replaced by smoother operators; men – of course they were still mostly men – resembling business executives. Men who were in fact business executives. Men who projected self-assurance at all times.

Their sense of self-importance was not unjustified. Universities had become central to the ever-advancing liberal-progressive-techno-capitalist project – 'centrism' to its proponents, 'neoliberalism' to its critics – which was the only political game in town in the decades before the 2008 financial crash. Centrism's central promise was that it would harness capitalism's innovative power, born of intense competition, to produce improvements in living standards for all – a rising tide that would lift all boats.

In this narrative universities and scientific institutions would collectively become something like the moon, pulling that tide up. They would no longer offer shelter from the cut-and-thrust of commercial society, as places of learning and study for the fortunate few. They would be transformed into the engine rooms of the new economy, producing both life-enhancing technologies ripe for commercial exploitation and the highly-skilled workforce needed to exploit them. This, everyone agreed, was progress and the academic and scientific Brahmins – the 'experts' – were at the helm.

Heady stuff. But what, in mid-2016, had got them so rattled? In a word, Brexit. The financial crash and the political elite's response to it – bailing out the banks and inflicting a programme of punitive austerity upon the poor – led people all over the West to question whether centrism/ neoliberalism really should be the only game in town. They returned to the abandoned positions of the left (socialism, pluralism) and the right (nationalism, authoritarianism) in a migration disparagingly labelled as 'populism' by the centrist Anglophone media.

In the early 2010s, both wings of populism started to make their presence felt at the polls, bringing the leftist Syriza to power in Greece and emboldening and strengthening the hard-right Fidesz in Hungary. The academic elite watched this commotion play out from remote boardrooms, glasses of mineral water to hand, safe in the assumption that populism was a little bump on the smooth road of progress. They went on thinking that until 23 June 2016, when the UK voted to leave the European Union. The unthinkable had occurred – the country that set the whole centrist/ neoliberal program running was disconnecting from the motherboard.

Many university leaders and senior academics lent their voices to the campaign to remain in the EU. Their institutions would suffer greatly if Brexit happened, they said. Funding for academic research would take a £750-million-a-year hit, international collaborations would be harder to come by and the UK would lose its place at the forefront of scientific innovation. This all swayed popular opinion about as strongly as a warning of disruption to imports of caviar.

On the other side of the argument, a campaign remark made by the Conservative MP Michael Gove, a leading Brexiteer, still stung. Gove answered the charge that expert economic opinion was set against Brexit with the deathless phrase 'I think people in this country have had enough of experts.' And, yeah, a lot of them clearly had.

Yet populism – centrism's imagined irrational singular nemesis – had not yet claimed its biggest prize. On 8 November the academic elite looked across the Atlantic and were dumbfounded as the bellicose braggart Donald J Trump belched his way to the US presidency. As with the financial crash, Trump's election hardly came from nowhere, but the men at the very top of the world's apex intellectual institutions had somehow not seen it coming. They had been blindsided by their faith in the steady, happy advance of liberal democracy and free-market capitalism over the Earth. Now they didn't know what to do.

All of which explains the bunkerish mood when the European Strategy and Policy Analysis System – a suitably abstruse high-level European Union organisation – met for its annual conference on 16 November 2016. Intellectuals and technocrats took turns at the lectern spelling out Where It Had All Gone Wrong and How It Could All Be Put Right. But it was left to a man for whom the term 'liberal elite' could have been invented to deliver the most succinct analysis.

Michael Ignatieff is an academic, broadcaster, author and the former leader of the Canadian Liberal Party now led by Justin Trudeau. He is rector and president of the Central European University, a private institution set up with the help of $880 million from hedge-fund billionaire George Soros. He pronounced this *mea culpa* on behalf of the academic top brass: 'We overpromised on our capacity to protect our populations with science and… walked into a public legitimacy crisis.'

The second clause is inarguable. The first may well be mystifying to anyone who isn't – as I am – a science journalist; just when did university leaders go on TV and pledge to protect the population with science, exactly? It's true – they didn't. At least not directly. But they did oversee and encourage the growth of a practice within their institutions dedicated to surreptitiously pushing that idea into the minds of the general public. I am talking about the dark art of public relations, or PR…

> The conscious and intelligent manipulation of the organised habits and opinions of the masses is an important element in democratic society. Those who manipulate this unseen mechanism of society constitute an invisible government which is the true ruling power of our country.

So wrote Edward Bernays, the founding father of modern PR, at the start of his 1928 opus *Propaganda* – a term he preferred to 'public relations' and which he tried and failed to rescue from dishonour. His words were something of a boast when he penned them – *Propaganda* was a business pitch as much as a treatise on the topic – but wouldn't be so now. We lucky inhabitants of the Western world spend an inordinate proportion of our lives passively absorbing messages of a ubiquitous media. That media and those messages are awash with PR.

How news 'content', to use the currently favoured term, appears to grow in volume while news organisations are constantly cutting staff – or in the case of local newspapers, shutting down entirely – can be partially understood with a glance at national employment surveys. In the US Bureau of Labor Statistics Occupational Employment Survey of 2017, for example, PR professionals outnumbered journalists by nearly six to one. Today every university in the UK, all of the major research funders and scientific institutions have PR teams. I would imagine the number of science PR people outstrips that of science journalists by a far greater ratio than six to one (and this is to say nothing of the pay differential, harrumph).

PR, the term, has followed in the footsteps of 'propaganda' and become a byword for manipulative insincerity and 'spin'. It's almost as if that's what the job is all about. So you'll likely draw a blank if you ring up a university and ask for the PR department. PR operatives are much more likely to work in a communications or 'comms' team, or – and this phrase has a certain wistful nostalgia to it now – the press office.

Whatever. The PR person's job is still the same: to improve the image the public has of their employer and the industry they work in, mainly by influencing media coverage. Back in Bernays' day, when PR was just a game that governments and the richest companies could afford to play, this was a creative enterprise. It involved deployment of daring psychological insights; Bernays was Sigmund Freud's nephew. Nowadays PR people – and this goes for university and science PR people – are the standard office drones of late capitalism, slouched at their computer terminals, performing repeated formulaic tasks for monthly pay cheques.

One of these tasks is writing press releases, the press release being the standard method of delivery of a piece of information into the news media and public consciousness. Every now and then what is deemed a science story will break out onto the front pages – the story of allegedly genetically engineered Chinese twins from November 2018 is an example – calling for in-depth coverage and original reporting, but much more often science stories are half-pagers that sit on the inside pages of newspapers or are linked low down on website sidebars.

For such stories, press releases aren't there to provide a spur for coverage, they *are* the coverage. Should a science press release attract the attention of a generalist website or newspaper, and even many specialist ones, it will be copied and pasted straight into the journalist's copy, perhaps with minor modifications, cut to length and slapped on the page.

This uncritical regurgitation of university messaging is precisely what university PR merchants want. Press releases are therefore written as near-perfect imitations of news stories for maximum ease when copy-pasting. *Near*-perfect imitations, mind you; they lack a sense of scepticism or journalistic balance that might risk undercutting their central claims. Still, those of a postmodern bent will appreciate the transformation of simulacra (press releases) into the things they simulate (news stories) via a process of simulation (copy-pasting).

Controlling the media message is thus rarely a problem for academic PR merchants; their problem is getting the message picked up by the media in the first place. Most big universities will produce at least two or three press releases every week, with the most popular items being in ascending order: academic awards, research funding wins and the publication of scientific studies in august specialist journals.

Did that list set your pulse racing? I thought not. Science press release material is mostly run-of-the-mill stuff, science going about its business, and of interest to few who are not scientists in the same field. When it comes to the studies, they are usually esoteric and hard to fathom. A neuroscience paper might run something like this. A group of scientists do some tests on the protein alpha-synuclein, which performs a vital function in the brain but can also form the amyloid plaques thought to be involved in the development of Parkinson's disease (it is not clear how). In these tests they identify a previously ignored region of alpha-synuclein which seems to be important in controlling formation of the plaques but also in controlling its usual work in the brain. Then...nothing. That's it. They've learnt that there are two areas of the alpha-synuclein protein that help it do its jobs (both good and bad).

How could such a humdrum study be given the jolt of excitement it needs to be transformed into news? For starters, we will need to sprinkle hyperbole liberally over the copy. The two sections of the protein the scientists studied could be grouped together and called the 'master control area', for example, which sounds much more impressive. Then it will be important to stress that the study is new at every opportunity, even beyond the point of tautology. Accordingly, the first line might read: 'A master control region of a protein linked to Parkinson's disease has been identified for the first time.'

Nice, but this is still standard PR gush, similar to that used by press officers in every field. Science PR people have an extra manoeuvre that they deploy whenever possible and not usually available to their rivals for press attention from other sectors. Rather than placing their wannabe news item in the context of the past – that is, in the context of things that have actually happened – they place it in the context of an imagined and highly improbable best-case-scenario future. Most science news is science fiction.

Such is the power of the human imagination that press-release authors only need gesture toward that future for maximum effect – the reader's mind will do the rest. Returning to the alpha-synuclein study, they only need say that the protein regions could become a target for new drugs to treat Parkinson's disease for those drugs to become a reality in the reader's mind.

Even ignoring the fact that the protein regions don't look like a very good drug target at all, seeing as they control both the pathological and vital roles of the protein, this would be a ridiculously unlikely outcome. There are myriad steps between target identification and drug approval in pharmaceutical development and every one is a major trip hazard. Under the best conditions it takes thousands of attempts and decades of expensive research to clear them all. A complex neurodegenerative disease like Parkinson's is not at all conducive to the best conditions.

Obviously, the press release – and any news stories it inspires – will not mention any of that. There's certainly no room for such rationalism in the headline, which will read 'Scientists identify new target for Parkinson's therapies'.

The utopian drug-development fantasy will be conjured elsewhere in the press release, but never clearly delineated. Mostly it will be expressed in terms of 'hope'. The world may have lost its way, but hope abounds in science press releases. It is frequently deployed in the quotes attributed to the scientists involved. That way, the hope, however ridiculous, is legitimised by expression from an expert.

Yes, that's right, the quotes you read in science news stories are rarely obtained by a journalist who's rung the scientist up, asked them some pointed questions and noted down their replies. They're lifted straight off the press release. How 'real' these quotes are seems to vary. Some bear all the hallmarks of having been written by the press-release author, some clearly result from email exchanges between the author and the scientist and some have the ring of genuine transcriptions.

Perhaps our quote will belong to the second category, the happy medium, and run like this: 'Our hope is that future research might target this master controller, to allow the development of a therapy which could tweak the conformation or stickiness of alpha-synuclein in the brain with only minimal changes to its function.'

It's a bit wordy, but it'll do. Congratulations all round, then. We've now written a perfectly serviceable press release off the back of a quite uninspiring study. Still I'm left with the question: do the scientists really hope this? It's such an outlandish scenario that I can't believe they do. Is our scientist lying, then? Did they have any qualms about that when the press officer got in touch to drum up the quote?

These are all questions which could be answered because, as you've probably realised by now, it's a real press release, produced by the University of Leeds in the UK. I picked it out at random from the homepage of the online science copy agglomerator EurekAlert! last night. It's a decent example of the kind of press release churned out by universities all over the world every day, written formulaically enough to have a fighting chance of gaining a brief flicker of public exposure via the news media.

I hope you enjoyed the walk-through. Now we're ready to examine a bigger-budget science PR production, to see how the imagined future it dreamt up actually panned out and how its implicit promises to the public were unfulfilled. For that, we'll have to be a little more selective in our choice of case study. We'll have to journey back to the halcyon days of London in 2012, when the Olympics were in town.

Heads up again, postmodernists! On 1 August, a week into the Olympic jamboree, the BBC News website published a story written largely in the future tense, reporting on an event scheduled the following day, quoting a speech yet to be delivered – quite the Baudrillardian precession of simulacra. The man delivering the speech was none other than David Cameron, then UK prime minister and former PR head – sorry, 'communications director' – of regional TV production company Carlton. 'He will address 500 leading figures from the global health industry,' the article foretold. Cameron was to announce the conversion of a urine-testing unit in the suburban London satellite town of Harlow into a world-beating bleeding-edge science hub. 'It will produce new forms of drugs and it will lead the world in the development of precision medicine,' Cameron was reportedly destined to say.

What was this hothouse of medical revolution? The National Phenome Centre, which, Cameron announced, would take over the lab space used by the Olympic drug-testing team when the Games were over. The Phenome Centre would be sustained for five years by two £5 million grants from two UK research funders, the Medical Research Council (MRC) and the National Institute of Health Research. How this centre would succeed where the pharmaceutical industry, fuelled by sums far, far in excess of those grants, had failed, was never enumerated. In fact, we can excuse Cameron's ridiculous promise of 'new forms of drugs' (the mind boggles) as a speechwriter's slip. Reading the rest of the BBC News report, it becomes clear that the National Phenome Centre was never intended to be a drug discovery lab. It was to become a research centre focusing on tracking 'biomarkers' in urine and blood samples that might furnish some insight into disease progression and susceptibility.

Even so, the promises in the media of the centre's transformative potential were grandiose. These promises appeared both in Cameron's speech and the MRC press release that was also copy-pasted into the many national media reports that followed. The 'quote' – I have to put it in quote marks, because she clearly never actually said this – from Sally Davies, then England's chief medical officer, gives a flavour. As a good science journalist, I'll copy-paste it for you: 'This research centre will transform our understanding of people's physical characteristics and disease, and enable us to pull through these discoveries into real benefits for patients. The advances that will be made by the researchers will help develop new treatments, including treatments specially tailored for the individual.'

Did any of this happen? Science PR often relies upon its promissory claims being unverifiable, either because no deadline is given for the promises to be fulfilled or because, as in the alpha-synuclein study, the promises are only vaguely alluded to. Here, neither is the case – the grants were for five years and David Cameron, Sally Davies, and all the other panjandrums who vaunted the thrilling potential of the National Phenome

Centre did so in definite terms. They didn't hope, they told us it 'will' transform our understanding, produce new forms of drugs and so on.

The Phenome Centre has done none of these things. A search on EurekAlert! for it – I'm assuming the centre would be keen to publicise the transformation of medical science it was created to bring forth – yields two results. One, from 2015, is headed 'urine profiles provide clues to how obesity causes disease', the other, from 2017, 'new urine test can quickly detect whether a person has a healthy diet'. Paradigms have remained resolutely unshifted, I would say.

In 2017, the magazine I work for, *Research Fortnight*, checked up on the centre. With its initial funding apparently winding down, we wondered what would become of it. The centre turned out to be in the midst of a transformation from a publicly supported research lab to a commercial blood and urine testing unit, offering its services to academic researchers and the pharmaceutical industry. Judging from its website, that transformation is now complete. There's no shortage of hype on its homepage, but it's not directed at the public, it's to hook potential clients keen to 'harness the vast data generated by our cutting edge multi-technology platform to inform patient diagnosis and therapy, bringing data from the bench to the bedside, leveraging research and maximising its potential impact, producing new forms of drugs'. Oh alright, I added in the last one.

It's worth highlighting the contrast between the National Phenome Centre as it existed, however briefly, in the popular imagination and the one that really existed and continues to exist now. On the one hand you have a trailblazing research institute, basking in the reflected glory of the UK's Olympic triumphs, valiantly forging ahead and inspiring 'real benefits for patients'. On the other you have an anonymous sample-testing lab in Harlow, Essex, whose absence would cause only a minor disturbance to medical science if it disappeared overnight, whereupon the lab's competitors would take over its contracts and return the bioscience industry to equilibrium.

This schema is repeated ad infinitum in modern society, largely thanks to the media's uncritical regurgitation of science PR. This is especially true in the digital realm where the promise of technology that will ease our lives and lift our spirits is made ever more fervently even as our experience of that technology grows fraught to the point of neurosis. And it still holds in healthcare. In the UK, the gradual disintegration of the National Health Service has been a sorry spectacle to witness, both directly – everybody has their horror stories – and via the media, where reports of hospitals and doctors' surgeries 'stretched to breaking point', to borrow an oft-used phrase, have become commonplace.

Yet the NHS's descent into perpetual crisis has happened simultaneously with the triumphant rise of another NHS, an NHS, which for most people, exists only in the media, mostly on TV. This is the stomping ground of David Shukman and Pallab Ghosh, the BBC's science correspondents, who deliver their pieces-to-camera from some clinical research centre trialling a new screening process to pick up cancer, heart disease, dementia, whatever it is, faster and more efficiently. 'All this may be coming to a hospital near you – and soon,' I can hear Shukman telling me in his chipper Old Etonian tones, for the thousandth time.

This artificial NHS is, understandably, where our health secretary, Matt Hancock, likes to spend most of his time. There he is, on 4 November 2019, launching a gene-testing trial and vaunting his ambition that 'every child will be able to receive whole genome sequencing'. This other NHS is 'on the cusp of a healthcare revolution,' as he told delegates at a conference, maybe also attended by 500 leading figures from the global health industry, who knows? 'Predictive, preventative, personalised healthcare. That is the future for the NHS.'

Do I need to spell out why 'predictive, preventative, personalised healthcare,' is yet another PR-fuelled future-fantasy, completely at odds with the harsh realities of medical and social care for a population burdened by the complex troubles of ageing and mental ill-health? We don't have to wait ten years to see whether Hancock's 'healthcare revolution' will arrive. It's clearly nonsense. Can't we just tag this as fake news?

Certainly, there are parallels. I think it was the technology writer Evgeny Morozov who quipped 'fake news is the poor man's PR' – an attempt to manipulate the organised habits and opinions of the masses by those who can't call upon media consultants or comms agencies or press offices to do their bidding for them. In which case maybe we can frame PR as the rich man's fake news. Maybe we can extend those programmes in which tutors go into schools to train children in how to spot fake news stories to cover PR-driven coverage too. If we want to protect them from misinformation, why don't we show them how the science establishment justifies its generous public funding by pumping out tonnes and tonnes of hot air, which is then directed into people's homes by a compliant media? Really, why not?

One reason, at least as far as science is concerned, might be that young people will rarely come into contact with a science story unless they've hunted it out. Until about fifteen years ago most people would absorb science news as they leafed through the newspaper or watched the evening news. That is no longer the case, especially for a generation used to content flooding uncontrollably into their social media feeds.

Newspaper sales are in freefall, which means that the university press-release system is feeding content to a declining number of outlets that hardly anyone reads. I do wonder why press offices are so well staffed and why they still churn so much out. I doubt they'll be closing any time soon – universities remain keen to be seen in the traditional media, no matter how small the audience – but if they do, they had a good run. Institutional press releases were setting the agenda and tenor of science coverage at least as far back as the 1980s, as the pioneering American sociologist Dorothy Nelkin noted at the time.

For decades, then, we citizens of the West had the good news of scientific progress and its promise of a brighter future as the subliminal mood music of our lives. For a while, that was fine, the promise seemed to be gradually fulfilled and intellectuals like Francis Fukuyama could theorise about 'the end of history', about how the liberal-progressive-techno-capitalist project would spread over the globe and establish itself as humanity's happy end-state. But that didn't happen. Our relationship with technology grew more complex as it started to permeate every aspect of our existence; advances in medical science seemed to grind to a halt or become inaccessible in health systems overburdened by demand. More recently life expectancy has stalled and is even receding for many in the West. Yet still the scientific establishment presses ahead with its PR campaigns, endlessly repeating a narrative of salvation by technology, conjuring visions of humanity's shining future that look ever-more ridiculous and remote to non-believers, like the desperate proselytising of a dwindling religious sect.

Yes, there are parallels, but no, science PR is not fake news. The two phenomena have converse relationships to the truth. Fake news starts with a lie and strives to make it credible; science PR takes a genuine event and extrapolates it to fantastical end-points. Both in its apparent concern for truth and its function of proselytising for a beleaguered faith, science PR has much more in common with propaganda in its earliest incarnation, when the word began its journey toward its modern meaning.

Those science press releases, all gesturing hopefully toward a future leavened of mortal burdens, are best understood as the catechisms of a modern, secular version of the *Sacra Congregatio de Propaganda Fide,* the body established in 1622 as part of the Catholic Church's drive to resist the advance of the Protestantism (the counter-reformation). When proposing the *Propaganda Fide*, as it became known, Pope Gregory XV wrote of its mission to rescue 'the sheep now wretchedly straying,' who would be placed 'in the pasture of the true faith, that they may be gathered together in saving doctrine, and be led to the springs of the waters of life.' A similar, if less explicit, rationale underlies the scientific establishment's adoption of PR. I've heard a fair few rationalisations of PR hype from those working in the academic-scientific-industrial complex. They mostly take the form of a grudging acceptance of the wild exaggerations, extrapolations and false promises of PR on the grounds that such fictions and fabrications serve a higher truth.

The higher truth is science, which is understood as a public good, a civilisational force delivering us from ignorance, the means of human advancement and so on. Science, in this context, is interchangeable with Progress – capital 'P' – which sees mankind starting down a path in the Enlightenment that leads inexorably towards a healthier, happier, more rational future – toward the springs of the waters of life, if you like.

This is such a short-sighted, delusional, Eurocentric view of history that I hardly know where to begin, but it has proved a spiritually compelling narrative for millions. Indeed, Progress – the story of mankind's salvation by knowledge, science and technology – has become one of Western secular society's sustaining myths, replacing Judeo-Christian religion and nationalism for the middle classes and supplementing those older myths for others. It is ceaselessly reinforced in the popular psyche by messages in the mass media, fed, as we have seen, by science PR.

Once the similarity of their respective missions is understood, it becomes tempting to compare the modern science PR machine with the *Propaganda Fide* and find the former wanting. The *Propaganda Fide* was, after all, a bulwark of the counter-reformation and is still going strong under a different name ('propaganda' was presumably dropped for public relations reasons). In comparison, the science establishment's decades-long pummelling of our collective psyche yielded disappointing results. The repeated prophecies of humanity's shining future were met by a collective shrug. Michael Gove called it right – by 2016 a lot of people in the UK, and not just in the UK, had had enough of experts. The academic and scientific top brass, those besuited Cardinals of the modern *Propaganda Fide*, kept promising the Kingdom of Heaven and it never transpired. Now only their bourgeois retinue keeps the faith with them.

Superficially, that's correct – does anyone not dependent on the academic-scientific-industrial complex for their salary really believe in a better, happier world delivered by science anymore? No. But in answering the question of why that is, we also discover that, in fact, almost all of us in the West retain a deep faith in the Progress myth – a faith which will be our downfall if we do not rid ourselves of it immediately.

Eurakalert! has become a considerably less hopeful place of late. Nestled alongside all those tales of targeted treatments and future therapies are intimations of apocalypse. Studies of polar ice melt, sea-level rise, wildfires, desertification, insect and animal mass extinctions are gradually gaining space on the homepage.

The terrible, inconvenient truth behind the centrist project has become inescapable – any 'progress' made by the West since the Enlightenment was built on the systematic despoliation of the natural world (not to mention relentless human exploitation in the Global South). The climate and ecological crises were not only foretold by science, but created by it.

Yet our deep faith that ever-advancing science and technology will be our salvation, not our ruin, persists. We cling to PR-driven promises of green growth and convince ourselves that we can continue to live in complete disregard of ecological boundaries, but just switch our power source. We ignore reports of the vertical leap of levels of sulphur hexafluoride, the most powerful greenhouse gas known to man, largely brought about by the expansion of electrical grids to include solar, wind and sea power plants. We ignore studies like the one published in June 2019 demonstrating that switching the UK's vehicles to battery power in line with 2050 climate targets would require twice the world's current annual supply of cobalt, and similarly deplete other precious minerals. Of course we ignore the ecological devastation wrought wherever such materials are mined.

Most disastrously of all, a deep belief in the flimsy future fantasies of science PR and a refusal to face reality possesses even the Intergovernmental Panel on Climate Change (IPCC), the United Nations body best known for its terrifying 2018 report on mankind's likely journey toward climate collapse. The IPCC allows governments to meet their carbon emissions reduction targets by deploying technologies that pull vast quantities of carbon dioxide from the atmosphere. Governments around the world have made use of this leeway and almost all now include 'negative emissions technologies' in their climate plans. There is just one small problem with this: negative emissions technologies don't exist, or at least not at anything like the scale or power needed to redress decades spent pumping carbon dioxide in the other direction. They are another of science's remote promises. The green-tech revolution factored into our plans to avert civilisational collapse is about as likely as Matt Hancock's healthcare revolution.

Are you feeling reassured? Probably not. To refer back to an earlier repository of myth (the Bible, King James version) 'there is nothing concealed that will not be revealed, or hidden that will not be known'. Our day of reckoning is near at hand.

I like to think about what life will be like then. I like to imagine that when environmental meltdown is fully upon us there will still be apostles of Progress, bedraggled little men – of course they will still be mostly men – preaching the Good Word of rationality and science and technology. I like to see them clutching dodgy EurekAlert! press releases to their chests like treasured catechisms, still blind to the realisation that somewhere along the line they started believing their own lies and mistook the artificial for the real, the map for the territory and in the process led us all to catastrophe.

I like to imagine them happy, comforted by their memories of the future.

THROUGH THE SEA GLASS

Liam Mayo

Have you ever walked along a beach collecting shells? In my home, this is one of our favourite activities. My sons, little buckets in hand, run down to where the water meets the sand, then, with the beautiful precision-in-chaos so endearing to children, carefully scour the sand for the shells that capture their attention. There are rules to this enterprise. We know the shells that are important to the local ecology need be left alone to replenish. However, those shells that are in abundance (in our place the pipi shell) are fair game. Oh yes, and any rubbish found must always go in the bin. Every now and then one of my sons will come across a colourful piece of glass, brilliantly distinguished, nestled against the white sand. 'Look Dad! Look!' How long the glass has been in the ocean, exposed to the gritty saltwater and the coarse sands of the seabed, will determine the shape it takes at the shoreline. Glass that has only recently found its way to the sea is still translucent, fine and sharp at the edges. Glass that has been in the sea longer is smooth to the touch, rounded and opaque; almost like a stone, but not quite a stone. Time, quite literally, shapes the glass. 'That's a funny looking shell.' The first time a piece of glass was uncovered we talked about it: 'It's not a shell, it's a piece of glass.' Glass that has been manufactured in a factory somewhere, by someone, used, then thrown away. 'So, is it rubbish?' Well, it is rubbish. 'Then it should be put in the bin.' Well, it may have already been thrown in the bin by someone, somewhere, but it still ended up back here on our beach. 'It is beautiful.' The colour and the way the sun light reflects against the irregular contours of the surface. 'What is glass made of?' Glass is made from sand, sand that is heated at incredibly high temperatures and then as it cools it is shaped into objects that we can use, like bottles, windows or mobile phones. 'So, we should leave the glass here on the beach then?' Well, I guess that depends on how you look at it.

To be artificial is to be not of nature, to be made by humans. More specifically, artificiality is to be manufactured by humanity as a means to replicate that which occurs in nature. Here, I seek to explore the epistemological and ontological artificialities that currently govern the human condition; the pieces of glass that have washed up onto the beach of our consciousness. In particular, I look at Modernity's constructions of subjectivity and objectivity and how ubiquitous technologies are not only inadvertently undermining the long-held mythologies of Modernity but exposing the fragility of a society devoid of sanctity at the hands of secularism; what are we to make of all these objects that surround us? My endeavour is not to add to the profound bodies of work that already exist in arenas of epistemology and ontology. Rather, my interest is change, and contemporary innovations in Western thought that make problematic the providences that govern our contemporary condition. My agenda is to pull on the threads of these interventions as a means to explore potentialities for a universalistic approach to studying the future. Indeed, this endeavour is couched in the very notion that humanity is undergoing significant transformative change – the very nature of change is changing. However, it is my hope that by corralling some of the epistemological and ontological assumptions that predicate our view of change, we may be better equipped to navigate this time of flux. I concede, and will leave you with, the ethical and moral implications of such a project; a simple question, with an understanding of the artificiality of our world, from where do we source the fundamental foundations to compel humanity through change?

Because the way in which time is experienced is a sensory matter, it is epistemologically conditioned. Time is relational and transcendent; we ebb and flow with the tides of change, we sense it, anticipate it and respond to it. These changes are rhythmic and have discernible patterns that hold powerful mythic narratives. With these patterns we may trace the manner with which reality is constructed from one epoch to the next. Modern time is framed by technology.

Technology, for the modernist, has enabled our evolution out of superstition and irrationality to dominance and universal conquest: the hunter gatherer became the agrarian, who became the industrialist, who became the capitalist. Modernist time is linear; as neat as an ice cube. Its foundations are set in the Enlightenment values of reason, rationality, anthropocentrism and secularism. Modernist time, technological time, does not seek to transcend the patterns of change, it seeks to overcome them. With technology, time can be captured, owned, and controlled. This is the myth of modernist progress.

Within this account, technology is value neutral, apolitical and functional; advanced technologies mean advancements in progress. Deconstructionists, with their variety of means for scuttling the epistemological ship, make these assumptions problematic, pointing out the potentiality for technologies to influence and subordinate portions of the community. Amongst them, Marxists, critical theorists, post-colonialist and feminist scholars, place power and the political firmly on the agenda of technology, articulating how technological determinism favours a particular worldview – usually that of Western men who preference empirical ways of knowing the world. Indeed, critiques of this nature gain currency in an epoch where the ubiquity of technologies means that existence can, for the first time, imagine itself immaterially socialised in an adjacent reality. This manifestation, whilst remaining true to our mythology of progress, implicates notions of selfhood, knowledge, truth and reality, that are intertwined in the Modernity myth – with technology those things we once held true grow more complex. This increasing complexity is powerfully linked to the manner with which we sense time; suddenly it feels as though time moves faster, decisions are more urgent, consequences more dire. For the media theorist and writer Douglas Rushkoff, we are experiencing a narrative collapse brought on by the media and culture all around us. Specifically, Rushkoff takes issue with the instantaneous and omnipresent forces of social media that are enabled through ever expanding digital technologies. American academic Tom Nichols agrees, claiming that what we are witnessing is the death of the expert: 'a Google-fuelled, Wikipedia-based, blog-sodden collapse of any division between professionals and laypeople, teachers and students, knowers and wonderers – in other words, between those with achievement in their area and those with none.'

The psychologist John Vervaeke locates Rushkoff's narrative collapse and Nichols' death of the expert, firmly within Western culture, rooted in the erosion of a unified identity once held together by 'god'. The divine, in Modernity's worldview, has become something non-rational and arbitrary, almost absurd; the minds most secure and meaningful connection is no longer with the world but with itself. He calls this, the *meaning crisis*, the collective conditioned response of anxiety, alienation, disconnection and disenfranchisement in the face of the emergent challenges owed to significant societal change. This is a loss of normative agency and emblematic of the estrangement of individuals from one another and the infertility of their ecology with the world. In these times of significant change, according to Vervaeke, we are surrounded by strangers, alone in our intent, acting with determined purpose in a world that fundamentally lacks it. We have thrown the glass out, but it has washed back up on our shore and we don't know what to do with it.

Futurist and cultural critic Ziauddin Sardar's postnormal times has provided me a point of departure in this space. By situating ours as a transitional age, Sardar has told a story of the failings of the myth of Modernity and, in doing so, speaks to the visceral uncertainty that captures the collective sense of – 'what is going on?' His litany is that of collapsing worldviews, poised eloquently between the simple symmetry of 'post' and 'normal', he articulates precisely that; that which we are experiencing is not normal, or, at least what we expect as normal – but it is not exactly abnormal either. With postnormal times, Sardar contends, we are suspended in an uncomfortable space between the no longer and the not yet. This experience, framed by poetic alliteration (chaos, complexity and contradiction) is conceptually pleasing; it provides a frame within which to shade context. And it is these shadings that help us make sense of change – globalisation enhances complexity, stock markets are chaotic and policy making is contradictory in the face of emergent challenges.

There is familiarity here; by emphasising the change of the present – ipso facto – potentialities of the future are opened. But there is risk too. If the future is both the principle for action and the active space for the realisation of potentialities, obligation is suspended. There is an unexplained cognitive dissonance between changing reality as experienced and change as imagined; the future always seems like something that is going to happen rather than something that is emergent. In this context, the future presents an epistemological obstacle to eliciting action in the present; it is a thing that is rationalised into existence, the secular bastion of hope that remains afar, an indictor by which we will progress, rather than a call to action in the present. This is using a modernist lens to fix the failings of Modernity; if I throw the glass out, it ceases to exist, a problem for someone else, somewhere else, to worry about, tomorrow. But, with this glass on our beach, in our hands, the question becomes – as my son prodded with curiosity – what do we do with it? Indeed, how are we to comprehend these postnormal times?

The critical theorist Michel Foucault affords perspective here. He reads human history through the different ways cultures have developed knowledge about themselves; through economics, biology, psychiatry, medicine and penology. This work is built upon the historian of science Gaston Bachelard's proposition of the epistemological break and epistemological obstacle – *obstacle epistemologique* and *rupture epistemologique* – in *The Formation of the Scientific Mind (1938)*. Gaston connotes the rupture of epistemology as a sporadic moment where accepted norms are distinctively broken away from. The academic A.T Kingsmith elaborates: 'the rupture is evasive, fleeting and interruptive, and makes problematic the epistemological systems of truth, reason, justice, and morality, a re-inscription of knowledge that branches off into different ways of being and thinking, theorising and living'. More than a rejection of the old, a rupture is a break away and a move beyond. Thus, the future does not arrive in a temporal sense, rather it arrives chiefly through social fragmentation. Certainly, this approach exposes the very nature of power and the role of traditional historians, as purveyors of their field, in suppressing social mutations, displacements and transformations, in favour of the continuity of long-range historical connections. The prototypical example of the construction of continuity is the manner Western knowledge is constructed – giving us the neat dotted line from Plato to Descartes to Modernity. Conversely, Galileo, Newton, Lavoisier, Einstein and Mendeleev, exemplify the discontinuity between epistemic configuration from one epoch and the next.

This illustrates the nuance between the historian of science Thomas Kuhn's paradigmatic shift and the rupture. Kuhn locates the rupture at the edge of the next scientific paradigm, quarantined from irregularities, whereas the epistemological rupture wallows in, what Kingsmith calls, the 'sea of anomalies'. As such, with each rupture a new epistemological structure emerges, and a re-reading of reality is required. This is a shift in understanding from that which has been considered normal, to the discovery and familiarisation of a new normal. This re-reading of reality is a perpetual affair; it requires prudent, conscious and recurring attention. As Paul Eisenstein and Todd McGowan argue in their book *Rupture: On the*

Emergence of The Political, epistemologies can never be natural or complete, there is no equilibrium waiting to be discovered, no totality that negates the processes of change. Rather, what we have is Kingsmith's sea of anomalies; the tide that rises and falls, the river ebbs and flows; 'From situationism's imagining of a world of random movements and structures, to deconstructionism's realising of the perpetual motion of bodies and ideas, to empiricism's envisaging of the invention of beliefs and habits – rupture's shared point of departure is a process of creativity and imagination that breaks from what is assumed to be true.'

The primary contention of the notion of rupture is that of process. This process involves memory – the non-lineal ecosystems that drive our, personal and collective, conditioned responses that are evoked by our senses. As the historian and futurist Marcus Bussey states, by giving voice to the sense of memory we begin the emancipatory process of uncovering the manner in which culture and context has altered, manipulated or crafted our personal and collective sense of present, and as such 'gain a modicum of control [and] become a little less governed by our environments'. In this way, we frame postnormal times as rupture, rather than rapture, opening a space for transformation and optimism; this is the peeling back and opening of opportunities, to new ways of knowing, and indeed new ways of being. The challenge here is to find ways to inhabit the rupture without falling back into a secure sense of identity, or nostalgia. This means we have to get comfortable with being uncomfortable; sensing the rupture is the art of acculturating to flux, dancing with the dynamics of change. Certainly, even my four-year-old son has learned that glass should be recycled.

The rupture has ontological implications. Whilst it is the construction of knowledge in the virtual realm that stimulate the meaning crisis, our imminent rupture, it is digital technologies, the vast complexity of objects designed, built and maintained that enable the transmission of virtuality, which alters the manner by which we perceive reality. Satellites, submarine cables, antennas, poles, cables, nodes, routers, desktop computer, laptops, tablets, mobile phones and modems have become the access points by which we enter and explore an ever-expanding realm, stepping from a physical world, steeped in well-defined and predictable boundaries, into a new realm of pure communication, devoid of clear boundaries, where rules are continuing to evolve. These objects, the tools of our abstraction, imply new and frequently abnormal definitions of space, volume, surface, and distance, where connection now defies the traditional meaning of community. The media theorist Allucquére Rosanne Stone calls these our 'prosthetics', objects of industrial manifestation whose intimacy with our bodies alter our perception of reality.

A great deal of research and development, design and marketing go into ensuring users seamlessly transition into new objects - adopt their new prosthetics. Design choices are aimed to de-emphasise function and emphasise the aesthetic beauty of new technologies; all the while reaffirming essentiality for modern life. Capitalist mythology buoys us here, as digital technologies become objects of our desire, hard, firm, slim, mysterious, curvaceous, spectacles of allure that yearn to be touched. The aesthetic experience merges with the act of interfacing. This puts an uncanny spin on the aesthetic experience and new forms of subjectivity emerge. As the film and media scholar, Kriss Ravetto-Biagioli points out, what characterises the new personal and person mediating screens is uncertainty about what constitutes the screen: it is both a surface and a material infrastructure; a window and a shade; an interface marked by the presence of an image and an invisible set of processes that use this same image or interface to disguise its own presence.

This places us in what Foucault called a 'fictitious position', where the viewer transforms the screen into an object, but the *mise-en-scene* installs the spectator in the non-place of pure representation of that essential absence, that never ceases to be inhabited. Thus, the aesthetic experience is altered with digital technologies; the body is now stripped of its modernist presuppositions as a locus of sensation, perception and recollection. Digital technologies, objects, are tools of abstraction; communities are mediated by technological prosthetics of presence, and the quality of our relationship with these objects remains quantifiable through the lens of modernist mythology. How are we to rationalise our relationship with objects that seemingly fragment our bedrock of our understandings of reality?

In his 1919 essay, *The Uncanny*, Sigmund Freud seeks to conceptualise the uncanny as feelings of unpleasantness and repulsion, distinct from the traditional notion of the sublime as an ennobling experience. For Freud, his undertaking was to untangle the mind's relationship with the familiar and the manner with which rationalist claims to reality are undermined through the uncanny. Throughout, the distinction between the *real* and *fantastic* aspects of the uncanny becomes increasingly blurred. In the closing, Freud denotes the uncanny as an explicitly real emotion that is nevertheless a response to the objective world, thus making it ungraspable through the clinical terms imbued through the empirical case studies of his broader canon of work; an acknowledgement that there are other forms of knowing and being outside empirical constructs.

Back on the beach we examine the piece of glass; is it glass or a colourful shell? Was it part of a glass bottle or a window pane? Or something else altogether? Where was it made and where did it come from? What was its purpose? How did it end up in the sea? How did it end up on our beach? Where did the sand that constitute its make-up come from? Where was it supposed to go? Why is it this colour as opposed to another colour? Did someone love it before it was discarded? Or did someone discard it because it was unloved?

Freud's uncanny is an embrace of the mysticism of the object, or the radical otherness of reality, bringing into focus the unknown to the knowable, the unreal to the real. The uncanny, like the epistemological rupture, provides an opening here, a crack in our conditioning, to pry open and explore deeper. It indicates an ever-growing awareness of the indistinguishability between fantastic and real stimulation and provides a conceptual vehicle to investigate our relationship with the world. The philosopher Timothy Morton argues strongly for the importance of uncanniness, for allowing space for strangeness in intimacy, in which other beings can be their strange selves, 'strange strangers'. For Morton these beings are everywhere and everything; people, animals, trees, chairs, desks, sports cars, skyscrapers, microbes and laptops. His goal is to, philosophically, make the inanimate, animate.

Bussey argues, in parallel, for an anticipatory aesthetic, that generates the space that is open and co-evolving toward conditions of reciprocal materialisations. What he is describing here is not the process of Being but the process of Becoming. We should distinguish between the two. The Enlightenment enterprise was to universalise a hierarchy of Being: God/ Man/Nature and human/animal/mineral. With this, the advancement of the sciences and the humanities, which, couched deeply in Kant's notion of correlationism, built ways of Being on the assumption that things cannot be realised until they are correlated by the correlator. This conceptually universalised human perception, from which sets of principles and values were developed and disseminated that not only affirmed human perception but reaffirmed the primacy of reality through human knowing alone. This advancement is perpetuated through the process of which Descartes terms 'the severing.'; whereby reality (the human-correlated world) and the real (ecological symbiosis of human and nonhuman parts of the biosphere) are dislocated and held at odds by an impermeable membrane quarantining the correlator and the corralatee. Being human, in this sense, is to sever ties between humans and non-humans through sophisticated instruments and scientific research of Modernity. This act of severing has moved us from Palaeolithic cultures through to Modernity, supporting our subordination of First Nations peoples and non-humans and providing us the landscape for the colonisation of cultures, the ecology and the future. Thus, this way of Being has been domesticated through Modernity's civilising process.

Quite conversely, the process of Becoming is more closely aligned to what social theorist Dianne Coole calls new materialist ontology 'a process of materialisation in which matter literally matters itself ... this is not, then, the dead, inert, passive matter of the mechanist, which relied on an external agent – human or divine – to set it in motion. Rather, it is a materialisation that contains its own energies and forces of transformation. It is self-organising, sui generis. Matter is lively, vibrant, dynamic.'

Further, and complimentary to my position on the epistemological rupture, Coole's materiality is not causally determined; forms are not as guaranteed, unassailable or as stable as they might appear. Indeed, like the recurring nature of the rupture, they need always to be reappraised within any particular context, along with their underlying ontological assumptions, lest they become reified or taken for granted. The epistemological manoeuvre of new materialism is that object relations are thinkable because they are real, even if withdrawn and unknowable. Here, we are far from the Enlightenment ontologisation of the relationship between subject and object. The new materialist ontology seeks to animate the human relationship with matter, to expand our sense of agency so to involve the interplay of human-non-human in co-creative works of materialisation. If new materialism is moving to a process of becoming, then our notion of subjectivity too becomes a process; fluid, pores, open and coexistent.

Social theorist, Ananta Kumar Giri, calls this weak ontology 'which urges us to realise that ontological cultivation is not only a cultivation of mastery of the self, but also cultivation of its humility, fragilities, weakness, and servanthood facilitating blossoming of non-sovereignty and shared sovereignties... Weak ontology helps us realise that both identities and differences have inbuilt limitations and they ought to realise their own weakness as a starting point for communication and sharing through cultivation of weak identities and weak differences'. This weakness suggests new possibilities for subject formation. Morton's notion of the 'mesh' is relevant here, as it describes the interdependence and interconnectedness of all living and non-living things in a way which gives equal value to the holes in and the threading between actors within a network. In doing so, Morton keeps open a space for the uncanniness of our intimacy with the world and with other beings.

Morton's position is one of objective universality; 'the hard matter of home is also the surface of some star – at once right there and somewhere, anywhere else.' He posits that the mesh is 'vast yet intimate', it simultaneously extends outward and inward, with no centre, edges, order or hierarchy. Morton points to the world of biology, applying this system of view to lifeforms; lifeforms are made up of other lifeforms, the theory of symbiosis and lifeforms derive from other life forms, the theory of evolution. With the mesh, Morton claims, any notions of 'inside' and 'outside', 'close' and 'far', 'large' and 'small' lose their meaning as relative terms ; 'the world looks as it does because it has been shaped by life forms every bit as much as life forms have been shaped by their environmental conditions'. Thus, according to Morton, we need to find new ways of being together in the world – subject and object – that go beyond modernist constructs of the self and self-interest.

In the present context, we reflect on our relationship with digital technologies. I shift my thinking from seeing my mobile phone as a tool, as a device, as a piece of technology, rather as an object that shares the 'mesh' with me. It, along with my computer, my modem, indeed, every other part of technology that I come in contact with, all hold space and are part of my universe. They are designed in offices, crafted in studios and constructed in factories; they have their own distinct subjectivity, and they have their own place in the coexistence of my reality; they exist as much as I exist. When I think of my mobile phone in such a way, its birth in the factory, its delivery to me in the shop, I am forced to conceive of its death; what happens to it in death. I may throw it in the bin, it may go into a land fill, indeed it may be recycled, but it continues to exist elsewhere, out of my purview. Its matter, its energy, its essence, although in a different embodiment, goes on in our shared universe. In reflecting upon this, I give voice to the object; the mobile phone exists both in present time, but also in past and in future time (the mercury in its battery will last up to 250,000 years).

Yet, object universality, within the confines of Modernity, poses problematic moral consequences. The synthesis of subject and object, human and object, whilst claiming equal ontological standing, may be misconstrued as the malevolent process of reification; the reduction of one entity to another's fantasy about it for example. Critics of new materialism and object orientated ontology point out that, in this proposed framework, when executed through a quasi-religious and premodern discourse, human agency is reduced to thing agency. Personal and political responsibility is difficult to sustain with a flat ontology, they maintain, as agency cannot be located outside the human sphere, in the material, non-human world. The philosopher Slavoj Žižek, in his book *Absoute Recoil*, calls this 'a kind of spiritualism without gods'.

However, this very critique fails to acknowledge the confines within which it operates; it is a criticism that continues to reinforce the frameworks that have been in place from the Enlightenment, and the frameworks that are now failing to respond to transformative change. Object universality is a quest to experience reality unmediated by signifiers, to do away with the confinements of Modernity (and postmodernity) – kick off our shoes and run our toes through the sands of the real world. Where Modernity has created distance between us and the things of the world, new ontological approaches offer us the opportunity to regain intimacy with our world. Agency here becomes about how we qualify (and quantify) the value of our relationship with objects; the lens through which we examine ethics and morality shifts from the agent to the relationship's agents maintain within one another. To achieve this however, I argue, requires a new mythological underpinning to guide our process of Becoming. We need to undo the rationalism that has sanitised our view of the world. That is, we should seek to re-mystify the world.

Vervaeke remarks that while it is necessary to feel that the world is consistently intelligible, it is also necessary to have our sense of the world pulled periodically from underneath us: 'Insights emerge from the wreckage of this experience. It allows our perspective to reframe itself around a fuller appreciation of reality, like stepping from behind a camera, or losing your footing only to regain it with more traction'. Without a doubt, the world view of Modernity is collapsing and leaving in its place a void yet to be filled. This is not to say that Modernity itself is collapsing. Of course, it may reimagine itself and grow through this period of change. But our current Modernist lens is becoming increasingly opaque; washed by the salt and sands of the sea. My endeavour here has been to highlight the artificialities of Modernity's constructions of subjectivity and objectivity and the variety of ways that contemporary innovations have sought to reconstitute our ways of knowing and being in the world. Specifically, the manner in which ubiquitous technologies have exposed the fragilities of modern society underpinned by secularism.

The way we know and be in the world is artificial; it is made by humans. The ubiquitous technologies that support this way of being and knowing are also artificial. We share our world with objects, yet, whilst we approach them as tools, they will remain outside of us, othered in a manner that subjugates their existence. What is required is a shift from Being to Becoming. Understanding this, we may see the current epoch of transformational change as a crack – an opportunity – to pry open and explore deeper the epistemological and ontological artificialities that have long governed us. Moreover, it is my hope, that through this understanding, we may be better equipped to navigate these postnormal times, toward a universal approach to futures thinking. The question remains, however, understanding the artificiality of our world, from where do we source the fundamental foundations to compel humanity through change?

Back on the beach, crouched down in front of my four-year-old son, toes curled in the soft sand, he looks at the piece of glass laying in the palm of my hand, 'So, we should leave the glass here on the beach then?' I give it back to him, 'I don't know', I say, 'What do you want to do with it?'.

ARTS AND LETTERS

SHORT STORY: THE MARCH *by Naomi Foyle*
SHORT STORY: HUNGRY SEASON *by Shah Tazrian Ashrafi*
FOUR POEMS *by Mozibur Rahman Ullah*

THE MARCH

Naomi Foyle

This is a story about a boy called Hamid. One might argue that it starts fifty-six years before he was born, during the Nakba of 1948 – in Arabic 'the catastrophe', the founding of Israel during which over five hundred Palestinian towns and villages were wiped off the map, seven hundred thousand Palestinians were driven from their homes, and over twenty thousand Arabs were killed, including in what historian Nur Masalha describes as 'scores of massacres'. But it's also true to say that, like a shooting star briefly glimpsed, the span of a short story can be a streak of light within a much longer narrative arc. So, let's say this story begins on the last Friday in April 2018, when Hamid is 14, a boy living in a house in Shejaeeya, a working-class district in the East of Gaza City, with his parents, his two little brothers and younger sister, and his grandfather. His father is a mechanic, though there isn't much work at the garage anymore, so the family sometimes has to get help from charities or the Ministry of Social Affairs to pay the bills. His mother looks after the house and the children. They aren't an especially political family, but no Palestinian can avoid politics. Since the end of March, after prayers on a Friday, the whole family, along with Hamid's uncles, aunts and cousins, has gathered up cushions and a picnic and gone out to the tent camp at the border to join the Great March of Return.

As of the time of writing, early 2020, the March has been suspended and, due to the coronavirus pandemic, may not be resumed for some time. But when this story starts, there were five tent camps in all, stretched along the border from North Gaza to the closed Sufa crossing near the old airport. Hamid's family, arriving in two old cars, one driven by Hamid's father, the other by his uncle, always go to the one closest to their house, south of Gaza City near the Karni crossing, also closed for years. On that April day, as they have done every Friday since the March began, they park up then join the people walking down the dusty road to the site, a river of people bearing a flotilla of flags: the red, green, white and black sails of Palestine rippling and shining in the breeze.

It's a slow procession, and Hamid begins to feel frustrated by the pace. As the tops of the tents come into view above the heads of the marchers, he dances ahead, cutting through a group of youths and nimbly swerving round a fat lady in a niqab and her pram.

'Hamid!' his mother barks, loud enough for the Israelis to hear. He bows his head and slows to an exaggerated trudge. Marching in place, like a robot, he lets the family catch up. His mother grabs his elbow.

'You could get lost in a minute, Hamid.'

'Help your mother carry the picnic,' his father orders.

He's already carrying a backpack full of water bottles. How can she not understand he's excited? The camp is enormous, like a festival: thousands of people congregate here every Friday, some of them staying all week. Each of the tents is named after a village in '48, and the old people who were expelled from that village gather in and around it with their families, whole clans pitching up, some sleeping there, some couples even getting married there. Outside the tents there are stages where Hamas officials and the protest organisers give booming speeches in front of big pictures of Dr Martin Luther King, Jr. and Mahatma Gandhi. Hamid's grandfather has explained who they were: great leaders who had freed their people by leading famous protest marches: King from a town called Selma – it sounds like Hamid's sister's name, Salma – to Montgomery in America, to demand voting rights for African-American people, and Gandhi to the sea in India, to defy British tax laws and gather salt, free from the shore, as God intended. In Gaza, as his grandfather said, fishermen can no longer fish, teachers can no longer teach their students, doctors and nurses can no longer save lives. There is only electricity for a few hours a day, three- or four-hour periods of power interspersed with blackouts lasting at least twelve hours, and up to eighteen hours in the winter. Whole streets are flooded with sewage. The shops are empty. Nothing is how God had intended it anymore, except for the will of the people. God, his grandfather says, intends them to resist the Israelis and demand their Right of Return. And that, God willing, is what each Palestinian will do, down to the last breaths in their bodies.

At last they reach the Al-Lidd tent. It is already packed with people, and the shady spots beneath the olive trees are all taken. There's a little bit of shelter in the shadow cast by the *portaloos*, but no-one wants to sit there. They find a clear stretch of ground and Hamid's mother and aunties lay out a picnic cloth and cushions. The sky above is a brilliant blue, and though the sun beats down on their heads, a light breeze refreshes their faces.

'I can smell the thyme in my mother's garden,' Hamid's grandfather says as he sits down on the green plastic chair Hamid's cousin had carried to the site. The old man always says this when the wind is blowing from the North. Hamid can smell it too, a fine savoury thread weaving through the gusts of fried falafel and roasted corn, tear gas and burning tyre rubber. The breeze also carries the shouts of the protestors, throngs of them running at the Israeli fence, and above his mother's head he can see clouds of black smoke rising from the no-go zone. But what is his mother doing? Unpacking a picnic basket.

'You marched from Al-Lidd,' his mother says as she sets the olive oil and za'atar on the cloth beside the eggs and lentil salad. 'And now we're marching back.'

No, they aren't! They're sitting down! The protest is called the Great March of Return, but his family has spent every Friday sitting around the tents, eating, gossiping and listening to the speeches. How was that anything like his grandfather's experience of being driven out of Al-Lidd. Hamid's heard the story countless times; he knows it by heart. It was July 1948, during the Nakba. The temperatures were up to 35 degrees, and the people were fasting for Ramadan, but the Israelis forced them out of the town and onto the road. Hamid's grandfather was seven, and had seen his great-great-grandmother die on the march, sitting down at the side of the road, pressing her fist to her heart, gasping, and then collapsing slowly to the ground as her family burst into tears and lamentations. Hundreds of people had died on that march, their bodies buried in the corn, or just left to rot by the road. Babies had suckled the last drops of milk from the breasts of their dead mothers. At last the Arab Legions picked up the survivors and took them in buses to Ramallah, from where Hamid's grandfather had eventually wound up in Gaza.

The old man is smiling at some neighbours. He'll be joining them soon, exchanging stories of the old days. Hamid's heard all those tales a million times too. He itches to be moving: running up to the fence with his friends from school and their older brothers, armed with slingshots, ducking through the smoke from the tyre fires, aiming rocks at the snipers high in their towers, and at the hills beyond them. His friend Mahmoud has bragged all month about his aim, gloating over the joy of planting a stone in his own land.

'Maama,' he begs, as his grandfather reached for a pitta bread. 'Can I go watch the March, please?'

'No, Hamid.' His mother slaps his little brother's hand to stop him squabbling with Salma over the picnic cutlery. 'You're too young.'

'I'm not too young,' he sputters. 'I'm fourteen! Mahmoud and his brothers are there. Girls are going up to the fence! It's a protest. We all have to do it, or it won't work! You must be the only mother in all of Gaza City who won't let her son even watch.'

'Hamid,' his father warns. 'We talked about this, remember?'

His face burning, he stares down at the olive dish. His father had taken him aside when the protests began, and explained that, while the family would be going every week, they would stay seated at the tents. The Israelis had already taken Hamid's uncle from them, his mother's brother Muhammad, killed in the Israeli bombardment at the end of 2008, and her best friend Farah, who was killed with her parents in the bombs that rained down on Shejaeeya in the summer of 2014: his mother didn't want to risk losing a child also. When he was older, he could make his own decisions about how to resist. But for now, he had to obey his parents. Hamid only really knows Muhammad, a thin young man with a pencil moustache, from his photograph in the living room, but he remembers his mother's tears at the funeral, which had made her hands all wet when he'd come running to comfort her. He hasn't seen her cry since though, even after the massacre.

Because that's what it was. The bombs that fell on 20 July 2014 didn't just kill Farah and her family: over ninety people died in Gaza that day and night, sixty of them in Shejaeeya. Hamid doesn't like to remember it: the terror of being trapped at home, the whole house shaking, car alarms going off in the street, Salma and the other little ones crying and clutching at him on the sofa as he tried to be strong and protect them, his baby brother

screaming in his mother's arms, his grandfather praying as photographs fell
from the walls, the glass shattering on the floor, his father going to check
outside as the bombs moved further east, his mother pale-faced with the
unspoken fear he wouldn't come back. Finally, his father returned, saying
it was safe to leave, and they fled with some food and nappies, blankets and
pillows, through clouds of dust and mountains of rubble to the Shifa
hospital, where they were sent to sleep with other survivors in a primary
school. They returned home a few days later, thanking God that their house
was still there. Farah's house was demolished though and, four years later,
Salma has only just stopped wetting the bed and his eight-year old brother
still wakes up screaming from nightmares. Hamid feels different too. He's
jittery. He used to like going to school, but now it's hard to concentrate in
class, and when he's walking home, if an ambulance siren or other loud
noise goes off suddenly, his heart races and his body runs hot and cold. To
let off steam he sometimes goes out in the street with Mahmoud and
throws rocks at walls. His mother, meanwhile, is always ordering him
about. His father says she gets angry quickly because she's afraid, but
everyone in Gaza is afraid. Why, when people were finally *doing something*
to show they weren't just mice in a cage, was she being so over-protective?
Did she want to live like this forever? Didn't she want Palestine to be free?

'We are doing it, Hamid.' His mother wipes Salma's face with a damp
cloth she'd brought in a plastic bag. 'We're here, aren't we? Every week.
You're fifteen next month. I've said you can go to the edge of the high-risk
zone then, with your father. But you are not *ever* to go into the no-go zone.
Not while you're living under my roof!'

'Hamid's growing up, Maryam.' His grandfather brushes a pitta crumb
from his beard. 'Let him go, daughter. To watch only. I'll go with him.'
Grasping his cane, his grandfather begins raising himself up out of his chair.

'Ya Abbi!' Hamid's mother's eyes flash fire at her father, but her husband
gently holds her wrist.

'Let them go, habibti. His friends are all there. And he needs to see it.'

Her mouth tightens. But she pulls Salma into her lap, kisses her small
head, and says no more.

His body fizzing with excitement, Hamid leaps up and helps his
grandfather to his feet. Together, his grandfather's hand resting lightly on
his shoulder, they pick their way through the seated protesters, and join

the edge of the crowd of onlookers, journalists, paramedics and protestors spilling in and out of the high-risk zone. They are half a kilometre from the border. Ahead of them, visible between the billowing black smoke of the tyre fires, a towering wire fence stretches in either direction like a giant roll of steel wool: their cage, keeping them trapped in Gaza, an open air prison where everyone is serving a life sentence for the crime of being Palestinian. Behind the grey mesh barrier, with its movement sensors and facial recognition trackers, are the Israeli snipers, invisible in their laddered white turrets, and beyond them the hills and fields the Israelis have stolen; in front is the no-go zone, a flat barren stretch of land, three hundred meters wide, where no Gazan is permitted to tread or to till his own soil. Today that land is alive with fire and movement: youths dashing out to throw more tyres on the fires, paramedics in white jackets disappearing into the smoke, girls in hijabs and keffiyehs walking straight out to place flowers on the fence. His grandfather shakes his shoulder, points, and laughs: a few metres away a young boy is stuffing a tall green onion down the front of his white face mask, a novel method of protection against the tear gas billowing ahead.

'Palestinian genius!' His grandfather chuckles leaning on his cane.

That boy's only eight or nine, and his parents let him protest. Hamid scans the area for Mahmoud – is that him? He wants to run and find out, so badly his chest hurts. But his grandfather leads him on toward an ambulance and together they watch two paramedics dash out into the no-go zone with a green stretcher. The noise of the crowd pulses through Hamid like a heartbeat: everywhere people are yelling and screaming and chanting 'Return'.

'Look, Jiddi!' Hamid tugs his grandfather's sleeve. 'He's nearly there!'

A youth with a slingshot is zig-zagging through the tyre fires, his red shirt consumed by the smoke, and then reappearing, smaller and smaller as he heads for the fence. Then people are pushing Hamid and his grandfather out of the way – the paramedics, their faces streaming with sweat, are returning, carrying a man who's been shot for daring to venture out on his own land. Hamid catches a glimpse of his bloodied shirt, before the roaring, heaving crowd knocks him sideways and jostles him over the stony ground. He searches for his grandfather, finds him and grabs his hand, raising it high.

'Return!' he shouts until his throat is hoarse.

Then, out of nowhere, white lightning blasts through his right thigh and a high thin scream, his own scream, fills his ears until they pop and everything goes black.

That's the start of Hamid's story, then. It's based on UN, television, alternative media and human rights agency reports of the Great March of Return, and on published interviews with wounded Gazans. Statistics differ, but at least 256 protesters, including at least 42 children, were killed on the March and, according to Medicin Sans Frontiers, over 35,000 people were injured, many seriously. Israel has attempted to justify this violence by claiming that the protestors were all 'terrorists', but reading accounts of the March and comparing the casualties on both sides it's obvious that Israeli lives were never in sufficient danger to justify these mass shootings: over that same period eleven Israelis were injured and one Israeli soldier was killed – shot by a Palestinian sniper outside the protest sites in what independent investigators have deemed a separate incident. One could certainly argue the protests were not entirely peaceful: some youths and Hamas members approached the fence with slingshots and Molotov cocktails and fire-kites and fire-balloons intended to torch Israeli crops. Some protestors also achieved their aim of breaching the fence. But the vast majority were empty-handed and none carried guns. According to the Belgian-based NGO International Crisis Group, the two Hamas gunmen killed on the first day of the March were operating separately from the protesters while a United Nations Human Rights Council (UNHRC) report produced in February 2019 concluded that of the 183 fatalities in 2018, only two could be justified under international law. In December 2019 the International Criminal Court also cited the violence at the fence when announcing their decision to pursue an investigation into Israeli and Palestinian war crimes. Despite this international opprobrium, though, Israel pursued its open fire policy, week in, week out, with impunity. As the UNHRC report makes clear, no-one on the March was safe. Paramedics, including twenty-one-year-old Rouzan Al-Najjar in her Red Crescent white coat, and journalists, including Yaser Mourtaja in his Press flak jacket were killed. People were lethally shot while standing around having a smoke, running back to the tents, or lying wounded, face-down on the ground. People in wheelchairs and on crutches were killed, as was a child who was standing alone performing a traditional dance with his hands in the air. A schoolboy distributing sandwiches three hundred metres from the fence was shot in the face, sustaining permanent hearing loss. Snipers shot another boy who was delivering onions against the tear gas at the same distance from the fence, making him one of the many March lower-limb amputees. In one instance, a man was shot a kilometre away from the fence, just as he arrived at the site. On the deadliest day of the March, 14 May 2018, as – in contempt of international law – Donald Trump and Binyamin Netanyahu presided over the opening of the new American Embassy in Jerusalem, Israeli snipers, in what can only be described as a shooting frenzy, killed at least sixty protesters and injured nearly 3,000 others. Many of the injuries sustained over the course of the March were life-changing. By December 2019, one hundred and fifty-five people had lost limbs, over twenty were paralysed, and over twenty more had lost an eye, or both eyes, to rubber bullets.

Yet people kept coming, every week. They knew the risks they were taking, but after enduring a decade under siege, including two major bombardments and many random air strikes, they were fed up with living in fear. It's a vital fact about humanity, seen time and again in history: when everyday life is miserable but just about bearable, most people trudge along just trying to survive; but when existence becomes terrifying and hopeless, large numbers of people shed their fear and rise up. Take WWII for example. As the war went on, the Allies' so-called 'strategic bombing' campaign, culminating in Dresden, where 25,000 people died in a firestorm, increasingly targeted civilian areas, with the explicit intention to crush morale by destroying people's homes and making them fear for their lives. The result though was the opposite: the ruthless bombardment only strengthened civilian resolve.

In Palestine, decades of Israeli atrocities, from the Deir Yassin massacre in 1948 to Shejaeeya in 2014, to the continuing shooting of children, have not succeeded in crushing the Palestinian spirit. In Gaza, in response to eleven years of economic blockade and on-going military assaults on homes, hospitals, electricity plants and agricultural industry, the people rose up in their own Arab Spring. Inspired by two journalists, Ahmed Abu Rteima, who conceived the idea for the March in 2011, and Muthana al-Najjar, who pitched a tent near the border in early 2018 and lived in it for a month, ordinary Gazans spontaneously began to gather near the fence to plant olive tree seedlings, a symbol of Palestinian existence, which the Israelis can never uproot, no matter how many bulldozers they drive over the land. The protests grew quickly, though with that success lost its grassroots leadership: Hamas took control of the organisation of the March when it became clear how popular it was. Still, the Great March of Return remains a watershed in Gazan resistance, for eighteen months attracting tens of thousands of unarmed civilians prepared to risk their lives to demand their human rights. Unsurprisingly, given the 'war of narratives' at the heart of the Israeli-Palestinian conflict, their courage and determination are largely misreported in Western mainstream media. A BBC documentary on the events of 14 May presented the day's carnage in misleading context, focusing on Israeli fears and isolated, often ambiguous, examples of Palestinian violence, and avoiding discussion of the blockade and the legitimacy of the protesters' demands. By the end of 2019, online reports in English had dried to a trickle, the fates of tens of thousands of protesters left wounded and bereaved barely registering on the world's conscience.

Six weeks later, Hamid, now fifteen, is still stranded at the start of the story. It's a day he keeps replaying in his mind like a video game, stuck on Level One, as he lies on his bed and stares up at the ceiling, prickly sweat gathering underneath his pyjamas and pain devouring what's left of his right leg.

Mahmoud has visited, once, before Hamid said he didn't want to see him again, and he said that standing by the ambulance was actually the most dangerous place to be: the white coats of the paramedics made them easy targets. But Hamid knows that the Israelis could have shot him anywhere: by the youths stuffing their pockets with rocks near the water station, in the shade beneath the gnarled old olive tree near the stage. No, he thinks over and over, if he could go back and live that day again, he would not have gone to the high-risk zone at all. He would have said, 'Thank you Grandfather, but it's too crowded, and too hot, you'll get tired. I'll stay here with you. Here, have some more hummus. Tell me again about the death march from Al-Lidd.' Because worse than the throbbing pain of his stump, worse than the fire eating what's left of his thigh bone, worse than all that is the pain that overcomes him whenever he looks at his grandfather's chair in the living room. It hurts so much to look at that chair, its squashed cushions and faded headrest, sitting empty now beneath the framed photograph of Al-Lidd on the wall – a black-and-white shot of a palm tree, small stone houses and streets his grandfather remembered playing on – that he doesn't go into the living room anymore. He just stays in bed.

His father has told him his grandfather wouldn't have suffered. That as the paramedics were rushing to Hamid, the old man collapsed, falling to his knees and keeling over just like his own grandmother had done east of Al-Lidd, dying of shock, right there in the dust. His father looks one hundred years old now, his face seems to have caved in, and he always seems to be blinking back tears. Though his mouth sometimes twists into a smile it's a false smile, forced onto his face in order to make Hamid pretend that everything's going to be okay. He comes and sits with Hamid in the evenings, holds his hand, tries to get him to practice getting into the wheelchair, going outside. But Hamid doesn't want to go outside. The roads and pavements are potholed and rough, so he can only get as far as the corner store, and besides, he doesn't want everyone in the neighbourhood to look at him and pity him, or whisper to their children, 'Remember the story of the rabbit who didn't listen to his mother and got into trouble?' His father says it was the Israelis who killed his grandfather, not Hamid, but that's just part of the whole 'let's pretend' game he's playing. His father also says things will be better when he gets his prosthetic leg, but that's not true. He's looked it up on his phone: his stump will hurt even more, with sores from rubbing against the prosthetic. Even if it doesn't hurt, he won't be able to play football, not properly, or ride his bike, and little children will still be frightened of him. It took Salma and the others nearly two weeks to come near him again when he arrived home from Al-Shifa hospital; and though Salma likes to show him her colouring books, at night she's started wetting the bed again.

Anyway, he hasn't even been fitted for the leg yet. Meantime, his grandfather is dead, his father is a grey ghost, and his mother is a silent pillar of nerves. When she brings him his food, she's so tense that the soup spills over the tray. She stands and waits until he mutters "Shukran", then sits in the chair in the corner, playing with her rings and watching him eat. Afterwards she makes him change his compression garments, the two sleeves the hospital gave him to keep his stump from swelling up too much, and when, wincing and groaning, he's unrolled the dirty one, she scoops it up under her arm to be washed – along with Salma's bedsheets, she reminds him. Otherwise, it's as though she's ignoring him. He can't ignore her, though. He hears her talking sharply to the children, and, sometimes at night, shouting at his father. She doesn't have to shout at Hamid, though. He knows it's all his fault. For being impatient. For not waiting until he was fifteen to go to the high-risk zone. Just like it's all Hamid's fault that now he won't ever be able to work in his father's garage, where you need to be strong and fit to change tyres and lug engine parts about; won't ever have a family of his own – who would marry a man with one leg? He'll always be a burden on his parents. As well as the wheelchair, he has a pair of crutches, and he can get about if he has to, to the shop or to school, if its open, but mostly he doesn't want to. Mostly he lies in bed playing stupid mind-numbing games on his phone. Or he just watches the ceiling fan, tears trickling down his temples into the pillow as he remembers the frail grip of his grandfather's hand, their joint fist raised up high to tell the Israeli snipers: we're here.

'You have to do it for him,' his father says in the car two weeks later, the first day they drive to the rehabilitation centre. 'Your grandfather wanted you to see the March. He wanted you to have courage. He died resisting the Occupation, a shahid in our family, alhamduhlilah, like you are, and he would want you to keep on resisting. So, you have to do all the exercises the doctors teach you. Do you understand, Hamid?'

Hamid stares out the window at the grey rubble of Al-Nazzaz Street. Farah and her family had lived in a house on the corner. Opposite, the body of a pregnant woman was pulled from beneath the remains of her home. Families are living in the bombed-out ruins, carpets hanging on laundry lines for walls, children running around barefoot, each still with two legs. Should he praise God for that?

At the rehab centre, he sits in the waiting room playing Tetris on his phone. A young woman in a white coat calls them in to her office. 'Hi Hamid. I'm Sara,' she says. He grunts. He wants to keep playing his game as she checks his notes on her computer, but his father makes him put his phone in his pocket. She takes his leg measurements, then tells him about desensitising his skin in preparation for the prosthesis. He takes the cloth she gives him and dabs his stump, biting his lip as a bolt of pain rockets up the bone.

'Do you have any questions,' she asks.

He looks down at the tired linoleum. 'When will it stop hurting?' His voice cracks. He sounds like his little brother. Like a baby. He hates that. A tear runs down his nose and he sniffs and wipes it away with his sleeve.

Sara is silent. His father puts his arm around his shoulder.

'Everyone's different, Hamid,' she says at last. 'I can't say how it's going to be with you. I just know it's very hard right now, but, Inshallah, things are going to get better. We're going to make you the best leg we can. In two months, if you do all the exercises we teach you, you can start wearing it. You can join our soccer team, too, and our night classes. We have a course in electronics that's very popular. You could learn how to fix mobile phones. How does that sound?'

His mouth twists. He's always going to be in pain. It's his punishment for killing his grandfather. Why is he even here? He ought to have died on the March, shot in the heart, not in the leg, and his grandfather should have lived, saved by the paramedics who would not have been desperately trying to stem Hamid's bleeding. His mother would have preferred that, he knows. Snot and tears are drooling down his face now, and his father pulls him into his chest.

'He's still finding it hard to adjust. And he misses his grandfather.'

'I see, I see,' Sara says. 'Well, just start with little steps, Hamid. Keep washing your leg.'

He doesn't want to look at his stump anymore, let alone wash it, but his father makes him, every morning and evening, as part of their prayer ablutions. His father also drives him to the rehab centre for the next two months. His mother is talking more to him now, nagging him to follow all of Sara's instructions. On the day his leg is scheduled to arrive, she scolds him, warning that he'll never get anywhere in life if he doesn't go back to school as soon as possible. His father, though, acts very cheery. And, in her office, Sara is positively beaming.

'Hamid,' she says as she presents him with an ugly plastic and metal leg, 'this is a special leg, one of a kind. Made in Gaza. We want to test drive it with you and if you like it, we'll put it into mass production.'

It looks like a normal false leg, clunky and awkward like the ones he's seen people using in the neighbourhood and at the beach. There's a large black plastic socket at the top, lined with felt, and below it a metal knee and a metal post that ends in a black plastic foot. But Sarah is smiling like she's invented a fence cutter that will tear through the Israeli barrier in thirty seconds flat.

'It's a SmartLeg, Hamid!' She claps her hands. 'It's connected to a special app we've developed to help you keep track of your walking.'

'I already have a step monitor on my phone,' he mutters.

'This is different. Our app reminds you to wash your leg and do your exercises. You can monitor your pain levels too, so you know in advance when to stop walking for the day and prevent getting sores. Plus, you get rewards when you meet your targets. See?'

She shows him on her own phone. It's a pretty basic game. If you follow all the rehab instructions and walk the prescribed number of steps, you get gold coins you can spend in a shop on comedy and music videos, or what Sara calls 'fun English lessons'.

'And ...' she taps fast on the screen, 'watch this!' She gestures at the leg, and the black thigh socket suddenly lights up: a zig-zag pattern of small blinking red, green and white lights.

'Whoah! It's a Palestinian SmartLeg!' His father applauds. He and Sara are laughing. Hamid sinks a little lower in his chair.

'You can programme the lights to come on when you hit your daily target, or whenever you like.' Sara tells him. 'We just want to see if the app helps motivate you. You can give us feedback, to improve the rewards or the features. Okay?'

He looks at the leg. 'Can I make it so the lights don't come on?'

Sara exchanges a glance with his father. Her eyes are still bright but her smile is fake now, he can tell, fixed on her face with a bit of sticky tape. 'Yes. Of course. If you want.'

He prefers it that way: he doesn't want everyone staring at him anymore than they already will be.

'Okay. I'll use the app.' He digs in his pocket for his phone.

'Good boy, Hamid.' His father hugs him and rubs his hair with his knuckles, as though he's won a race. 'But first let's try that leg on for size!'

That part of the story is clearly made up. Not quite science fiction – it's too low-tech for that. But the sophisticated 'SmartLegs' being developed elsewhere to aid better functionality would be too expensive to produce in Gaza, where the Artificial Limbs and Polio Centre makes prostheses with German materials imported through the Erez port. Treating over 3,000 amputees a year, the Centre manufactures and installs new limbs, and provides physiotherapy and training in how to use them. Coping with the influx of injured people from the March has been a big job for a team of five technicians, and their work will soon be supplemented by that of a new medical centre, the Hamad Hospital for Rehabilitation and Artificial Limbs, which, in response to the growing need in Gaza, will soon be providing free care for amputees.

Physical wounds, though, are only half the story. Although rehab clinics in the Strip also provide mental health support for wounded people and their families, interviews with young Gazan amputees suggest that some sink into a deep and lasting depression. The problem is endemic, and spreads far beyond the frame of Western psychotherapy. In Gaza, as Canadian psychologist Dr John Soos has observed, 'post-traumatic stress disorder' is a meaningless term. For one thing, there is no individual 'disorder' to treat: the source of the suffering is political, the collective punishment Israel inflicts on a captive civilian population. And neither is there anything 'post-' about their pain. 'Homelessness,' Soos points out, 'multiple deaths within families, severe injuries, and the ever-present threat of renewed Israeli bombardment create a psychological climate of ongoing continuous, collective trauma'. For mental health workers, this trauma is compounded by their need to remain open to the suffering experienced by their clients. Data is difficult to gather because of a taboo on discussing mental illness, but all the available evidence indicates that record numbers of people in the territory are suffering from anxiety and depression, leading to mounting numbers of suicides, especially amongst the young. And, as if being subjected to devastating military assaults and a near-complete economic embargo wasn't enough to cope with, right now, in mid-March 2020, the Strip faces the very real possibility of a public health Nakba. The West's bad case of 'coronavirus anxiety' pales in comparison to what Gazans now fear: at the start of the COVID-19 pandemic, into the most densely populated place on Earth, already suffering severe electricity and medical shortages, the Israelis allowed just two hundred testing kits for 1.8 million people. Inevitably, the disease has come to Gaza, prompting renewed international calls for the blockade to be lifted: as long as it lasts, containment and treatment will be virtually impossible.

At time of writing, that's a nightmare yet to fully break open. Here in this story, Hamid and his father have arrived home from the rehab centre, Hamid using the new leg and his crutches for now. It's dark in the living room, because the electricity is off, which is normal, but it's also very quiet. His mother isn't there to greet them and his siblings must be playing in their rooms. Something else is different too. It takes him a moment, but then he realises: his grandfather's chair is gone from its shadowy corner. And on the wall, where the photograph of Al-Lidd once hung, there's just a cream-coloured rectangle, framed with nicotine stains.

'Maama,' he exclaims. 'Where's Jiddo's chair? And his photograph?'

'Maryam!' his father calls. His mother comes in from the kitchen.

'Don't shout,' she says. 'I'm right here.'

'What's going on?' His father sounds stunned. 'Where's your father's chair?'

She purses her lips. When she speaks, it is calmly, as though she's teaching them a lesson. 'The Imam said we need to move on. No one was sitting in it, so I sold it. We can use the money. And we need the space for Hamid to practice walking.'

He can't believe it. 'I can practice walking outside!' he explodes. 'And what have you done with his photograph?'

'I said don't shout,' she warns, her eyes dark. He glowers at her.

'Where is it, Maryam?' his father insists.

She lifts her chin. 'I threw it away.'

'What?' his father sputters in disbelief. 'That's Al-Lidd, Maryam. That's your home!'

Her jaw is set so hard she doesn't even look like his mother anymore. It's as if some stranger has crept into their lives and stolen her place. 'No, it isn't,' that woman insists. 'Gaza City is my home. Al-Lidd was just an old man's memory. We're never going back there. Don't you understand?' She shakes her finger at them. 'The Jews won! They took our land, and we're never getting it back!'

'No, Maryam.' His father's voice is low, but his anger is rising with every word. 'We will return. If not us, then Hamid, or his children. It's our right, and if we fight for it long enough, we will win it. You can't kill that hope for your children.'

'It's fake hope,' she snaps, flinging her arms in the air. 'It kills us. More and more of us, every Friday. It took your leg, Hamid, and it killed your grandfather. The Jews won't stop until we're a nation of cripples. We have to give up hope.'

'What are you saying, Maryam?' His father raises his hand as if to block her advance. 'We can't let the Israelis win. They might crush our bodies, but we will never let them crush our spirits!'

'Don't blame the Israelis, Ahmad.' His mother's eyes narrow and her voice is quiet but honed to a steely point, a dagger aimed at his father's heart. 'You let them go. "He has to see it," you said.'

'Stop it!' his father commands, his face flushed. 'Stop it. You have to let go of this blame. All that happens is Allah's will! That's what the Imam said!'

'Yes, so we have to accept that Allah wants us to suffer!' She exclaims as if in triumph, throwing up her arms again. Her eyes are wild. It's frightening. Hamid has never seen her like this before. 'He has sent the Jews to punish us!'

'Are you crazy, Maryam.' His father grabs her wrists and pulls her arms down. 'For what are we being punished? For being Palestinian? The UN sent the Israelis. Allah wants us to resist!'

Hamid looks desperately round the room. The photos of his uncle and grandfather are still on the bookshelf. But the wastepaper basket is empty and the picture of Al-Lidd is nowhere to be seen. 'Where is it?' he shouts, banging one of his crutches on the floor. 'Where's the photo?'

His mother wrenches out of his father's grip and spins to face him. 'It's gone, Hamid. It's gone.' Tears are streaming down her face, like a flood down a cliff. She reaches up and clasps his face in her hands, gripping his cheeks and gasping through her sobs. 'You can't live in the past. You have to fix your mind on finishing school and taking that training course and making a life here!'

'Why have you done this, Maryam?' His father yells. 'And why today? The boy's just got his new leg! We should be celebrating!'

'I am celebrating!' She pushes Hamid away, waves her hands and screams at his father through her tears. 'It's a fresh start.'

Hamid is already walking, awkwardly, to his bedroom. He shuts the door and sits down on the bed. His whole body is on fire. His parents' screams penetrate the walls and upstairs the children are starting to cry. He unstraps the new leg and rolls up in a ball on the bed, a pillow over his head.

He lies there for five minutes, his stomach churning and his stump throbbing. Then the radio comes on: the electricity is back and the keening beats of Mohammad Assaf's Arab Idol hit, 'Raise the Keffiyeh', reach his muffled ears. From under his pillow, Hamid reaches out and turns up the volume, loud enough to drown out his family. Then he sits up, blinks in the light and takes out his phone.

He pulls up Google Images and taps in 'Al-Lidd'. There are hundreds of images: maps and old photographs, colour ones of the old Arab ruins, a soap factory, an old woman with a key, and black-and-white ones of the town in the twenties and thirties, and of the Death March, families walking hand-in-hand down the road with their belongings piled high on their heads. He scrolls through for a while, then gets up and puts the leg back on. Ignoring the pain in his stump, and leaving the radio on, he opens the door and moves as quietly as he can down the hallway to his father's office.

He's allowed to use the computer for schoolwork, so he knows the password. He's not allowed to use the printer without asking, but his parents are still fighting, his father shouting 'You need to see a doctor, Maryam!', his mother crying and shrieking 'What doctor? I'm dead, Ashraf, dead! No doctor can bring me back to life!' They won't hear Hamid print out his grandfather's memories, and his birth right, as many photos of Al-Lidd as he can until the ink cartridge runs out.

The ending of the story is approaching now. Often in the writing of stories, the ending arrives first, or very early on anyway. Then it's just a question of getting there. For Hamid, though, stuck in Gaza, stuck in his bedroom while his mother paces round the house, clattering as she cleans, ordering the children around, refusing to say sorry for getting rid of his grandfather's things, 'getting somewhere' doesn't feel like an option. The evening of the big fight, Hamid sticks all the photos of Al-Lidd up on his bedroom wall, then sits and waits for his crime to be discovered. He doesn't get punished though. Where, previously, his father always let his mother make the decisions about disciplining the children, now he tells her that Hamid has his retroactive permission to use the printer. The next day he even goes out and buys a photo frame for Hamid. But otherwise, his father isn't around so much anymore.

In the weeks after the fight, Hamid's father comes and prays with him in the morning, but rarely in the evenings. In the evenings he goes out to visit relatives or to the mosque. He wants Hamid to come to the mosque too, but Hamid doesn't like praying in front of other people anymore. When his mother is out, he prays in the living room, where the chair used to be. It doesn't feel like God is listening though: his leg still hurts, his mother is still angry with him, Salma still wets the bed, his little brother still has nightmares. Soon Hamid can't stand being in the house, even alone in his room. He can't go to school while he's recuperating, but he goes outside more now, to practice walking. On Fridays his father goes with him, takes him for falafel and gives him pocket money; other days he goes alone. He can wear a pair of jeans, to cover the prosthetic leg, and though he wobbles a bit sometimes, people don't stare at him too much. He uses the app to log his steps and when he gets home, if the internet connection is strong enough, he spends the gold coins on music videos. His mother nags him to learn English, but what's the point of that? He's never going to get to travel.

Though his leg remains painful, over the next couple of months his strength improves. At the start of October, Sara says he can start to plan longer walks. At home, he looks up Al-Lidd on his phone again. On the map it's called 'Lod' and the Israelis seem to have built their separation barrier into the app, because it refuses to calculate the distance or directions from 'Lod' to Gaza City. But, using a ruler on one of the maps he's printed out for his wall, Hamid calculates that it's sixty kilometres from his house to what will always, no matter what the Israelis call it, be his grandfather's hometown of Al-Lidd. Based on his pain threshold, and the rate at which his stump develops sores, Sara said he should walk no more than two kilometres a day with his SmartLeg. So, he programmes the app to reward him when he hits that target. By early November, he'll be in Al-Lidd.

He starts out in the neighbourhood, walking down the uneven pavements, past the corner shops and farmers carts, the mobile phone shacks and groups of youths laughing and smoking in doorways, stopping to rest on the low wall around the junior school, then walking home. That route gets boring quick, so he starts taking the bus, first out to the beach, where he walks along the crowded promenade and back, children dashing past him with their buckets and spades, seagulls screeching overhead as the fishermen come back with their meagre catches. When he was a child, he wanted to be a fisherman, but what's the point when the Israelis won't let you take your boat out more than a few metres into your own waters? When he was a kid, he also loved the beach. Now, though it's the same as it always was, full of people, sunning and swimming and eating roasted corn and ice-cream, he's different. He can't wear shorts or run in the sand. There is a boardwalk for wheelchair users that stretches out over the sand to the edge of the sea, but he doesn't use that. He can see the sea fine, and anyway, Al-Lidd is inland.

Then one day he bumps into Mahmoud and his brother, who ask him if he's down here for the amputee games?

'What? No,' he says, and they point to the sea, where some young men on crutches are splashing and dancing in the waves, their stumps sticking out of their shorts.

'They're on the football team. Heroes FC,' Mahmoud says. 'Are you going to join?'

'No.' He curls his lip. 'That's for people with crutches. I'm using my new leg.'

'That's cool, Hamid.' Mahmoud glances down at Hamid's jeans, then up again. 'Do you want to come for an ice-cream?'

Some people stare. Some people look shifty, as if they've got somewhere they urgently need to go. Mahmoud's brother is one of those. 'No, thanks,' Hamid says. 'I have to keep walking.'

'Okay. Call me, okay?'

'Yeah, sure.'

After that, he decides to go further afield. One day he ventures North, spending some of his pocket money on a taxi all the way up Salah El-Din street, getting out at the turn off into Beit Hanoun. He walks along streets lined by the jagged empty shells of houses and apartment blocks, past bomb sites still heaped full of concrete rubble, bent iron girders and splintered bits of furniture. It's like being in Shejaeeya, except he doesn't know anyone who died here. The Israelis have made him feel like a war tourist in his own country. At the edge of the town he looks out over the fields toward the

fence in the distance and hurls stones at the lights of the Erez Crossing.
When he gets home that night, his mother asks where he's been.

'Out.'

'Out. Out. Just like your father.' She folds a napkin and puts it in a
drawer. 'Did you eat?'

'No,' he mumbles.

'Well, you missed dinner.' She goes to the door to the living room.
'There's food in the fridge,' she says over her shoulder.

There isn't much there – what's the point of a fridge without electricity?
– but he isn't very hungry. He takes some leftover maftoul to his room. He
listens out for his father, but falls asleep before he comes in.

The next day, with the rest of the money his father has been giving him,
he takes a taxi all the way to Khan Yunis in the south. It's like a smaller
version of Gaza City: masses of tower blocks built back from the coast. It's
the first time he's been there, and he just walks around the beach for a
while. On Friday, his father seems pleased that he's been 'out exploring' and
gives him more money for taxis. So, he returns to Khan Younis: it's a relief
to know he won't run into anyone he knows. Next, he goes to Rafah, right
on the border with Egypt, and looks at the gate. It's open more often these
days, but you need a visa to go through it, and a lot of money to bribe the
officials to bump you up the queue, and not many people have either of
those. He's just got enough money for a couple of taxis a week and the
occasional falafel. If he needs to buy anything else, he takes a pitta and
hummus from home. After seeing the gate, he starts taking cabs for shorter
distances, getting out at a village or rural junction and walking alongside the
fields and olive orchards. Once he walks down a gravel road to the border,
not too close, but close enough to see the fence. He walks too far that day,
more than two kilometres, and his leg hurts so much the next day tears keep
springing to his eyes. But it doesn't matter. He doesn't care. He takes more
painkillers, that's all. He's getting closer to Al-Lidd. That's what counts.

Then it's November. He's been from North to South, from the beach to
the fence, he's seen all of Gaza there is to see. And his app tells him he is
only three and a half kilometres from Al-Lidd.

That day, he waits until after dinner to go out. In his room, he puts on a
pair of shorts under his jeans. Then he makes a final adjustment to the app,
puts the phone in his shirt pocket, and wraps his keffiyeh around his neck.

He opens the door, then stops and turns back to the bedside table. He takes the photo out of the frame his father gave him. It's of the Al-Lidd Death March, a boy holding his little sister's hand on the road. He finds a pen and writes 'For Salma, with love always, Hamid' on the back, and leaves it on his bed. Then he takes a photo of an Al-Lidd street scene from the wall, similar to his grandfather's picture, with a palm tree and houses, folds it in four and puts it in his shirt pocket, next to his heart.

'Where are you going?' In the living room, his mother pulls on her cigarette. She's started smoking indoors. She's also painted over the space where her father's photo used to hang. It's as if her interior decorating plan is to allow nicotine to spread evenly over the wall.

'Out.'

She stares at him through the smoke.

'To meet Mahmoud,' he says.

She stubs out the butt. 'You're friends with Mahmoud again?'

'Yes,' he mutters 'I saw him down at the beach.'

She sighs. 'Okay, Hamid. But you're not to go far. No driving in Mahmoud's brother's car. And be back by nine, or I'm taking that phone off you, I promise.'

Outside, he takes a deep breath. It's a cool evening, the twilight is falling, and the streetlights are casting a hazy orange glow over the people taking their evening strolls. He joins them, his heart, for the first time since he was shot, floating softly like a cloud in his chest. It's exactly three thousand, four hundred and seventy-eight meters from his house to the tent camp: he has done parts of the route lots of times plus measured it all out on Google maps. That's more than he's supposed to walk, but he's been pushing himself as he gets toward the end, and he's impatient now: he can't wait until tomorrow.

His stump chafes in the socket of the leg, but he savours every step. It's like walking through a dream. Cars are honking, people chattering, motorcycles revving their engines, the smells of roasting doner kebab, tobacco, apple shisha, and petrol drift on the air, but all that is happening as if at a great distance. He's walking down his own road, a dusty country road with corn fields on either side, leading him toward a palm tree on the horizon, its dark silhouette curving over the roofs of white stone houses, shining ahead in the moonlight. Alsoup ahead, his worn grey jacket and keffiyeh always just visible in the shadows, is a slight old man, walking with a cane, tapping out the route.

When he gets to the tent camp, he veers right. There are still people living there, waiting for Friday. He wanders along the edge of the high-risk zone, searching for the spot. Is this it? It's hard to tell. It's not like his blood is still staining the ground. But it's close enough. He takes out his phone, checks the screen. His heart sings. He's got twelve metres left to walk, and then he'll be stepping inside Al-Lidd, walking down its narrow winding streets, searching for a house with an open door, an old man sitting in a blue armchair inside.

It's getting dark now, a hazy darkness speared by the cold white lights falling along the length of the fence in the distance. Hamid sits down on a nearby log and reaches into the back pocket of his jeans. He takes out the pair of wire cutters he bought in Khan Younis and puts them down beside him. Then he tugs off his jeans. As the cool air nibbles his bare skin, he folds up the trousers, places them neatly at the base of the log, and feels around on the ground for some rocks. He stashes the stones and the wire cutters the pockets of his shorts. Then he feels in his shirt for the photo of Al-Lidd. It's too dark to see it properly, but the shapes of the white houses are dimly visible. He holds it up at arm's length and gazes at it for a minute, framed by the dusk and the fence and the hills; then he puts it back in his shirt pocket with his phone and stands up. He looks down past his red and white keffiyeh at his legs. One flesh and bone, one mostly plastic and metal. He can't run on it, for fear of falling over, but he can walk well on it now, wherever he wants to go. He stretches, takes a deep breath and inhales the scent of thyme from the North.

This is the end of the story. I expect you know now, maybe have done for a while, what Hamid does next. And yes, he does. Facing north, he walks into the no-go zone. At the thirteenth step he takes, his phone buzzes in his shirt pocket and the little bulbs inset in the socket of his prosthetic leg blink on: a band of red, green and white lights, floating in the darkness, steadily moving north, toward Al-Lidd. That's the image I must leave you with, though: I can't tell you what happens after that. This story, which treads and transgresses many borders, is a fiction written by a British-Canadian woman living in Brighton, based on her imperfect and third-hand knowledge of Gaza, and her reasonably informed understanding of the Israeli-Palestinian conflict. Though international observers, as witnesses and solidarity activists, do have a role to play in the long arc of that violent narrative, what happens next is, ultimately, for the people of Palestine and Israel to decide.

HUNGRY SEASON

Shah Tazrian Ashrafi

In the initial years of catching the addiction, it took Nahin around ten minutes to yank the life out of an otter. Slimy. Glossy. Squeaky. Puppy-faced. Puppy-eyed. Chirping. Purring.

Curiosity-spun whiskers. Moon eyes.

Ten minutes. An otter-shaped leaf. Cascading from the universe's branches.

Now, it took the fifteen-year-old boy only five, at most. Years of practice seeped perfection into his bones. Sheer repetition governed the movements of his life-taking limbs. A redundancy lodged inside his nerves had spun a well-deserved skill—claiming firm grip on a shimmering, slippery, smooth-furred, brown otter with one hand and showering on it blows with a sickle, or at times, an axe or machete, with the other. All along the alkaline of its blood salivating in his mouth.

Squirming nuisance. Thin stream, thick stream, fast stream. Red, limy menace. Clumps of black in the red, red world. Spritz of life on his dark skin. Last cries of a life. Flight to another world.

His father, Abdul, always wondered where his otters had disappeared, that too, ritually. Finding no other plausible answer every time one went missing (even though they remained chained in a hutch in their little otter republic with virtually no autonomy). He soaked up the treacherously credible words of Nahin with utmost belief. Nahin would tell his father that sometimes it had been the work of the elusive grey wolf that ventured into their compound in the dead of night and sometimes the ubiquitous monitor lizard; he would tell him that he had witnessed the horror of the fictitious abduction over and over. A memorised script.

Grey wolf.
Monitor Lizard.
Plucking otters.
Out of their immobile republic.
Mobile republics attacking an immobile one.

Abdul did not have the slightest inkling of the fact that his favourite otters—aqua puppies that helped him catch fish from the wildly snaking, precarious, mangrove-poked rivers of the Sundarbans—always ended up in his son's digestive system. They disappeared, true, but they did so in perfect deception, in close proximity to Abdul, roiling among the fleshy insides of his son, sliding away into complete non-existence. His otters, their smoky souls to be specific, caressed Abdul without his knowledge. They said countless Fuck you's to his son in their shrill otter language, before taking flight to another world. Raindrops in reverse. An orchestra of flying otters.

Abdul used to take Nahin on his fishing expeditions into the heart of the Sundarbans (the mangrove forest that fringed their village) on days he did not have school. Screeches of monkeys, birds, boars, and deer seamlessly blended into one music, and reverberated throughout the long, undulating, curvy, splintered limbs of the forest. At times, the intermittent roars of tigers also punctuated the note. Nahin would carefully observe how the otters quickly flitted across the small boat as soon as they were liberated from the hutch, and leapt into the saline, emerald waters, creating wild splashes, shattering still images of trees, in desperate search for fish. He revelled in the observation—the otters, with their quick, little claws and mouths, claiming firm grip on silver, scaly, thin fish, catching the sun on their wet backs, their piercing cries suffused with excitement. The splashing sounds dominating the ambience muffling the throaty songs of storks and herons.

Immobile republics being temporarily mobile.
Laying siege to an aquatic republic.

After the otters procured fish, a certain amount of the haul would go into their systems as reward. Abdul sometimes provided them extra fish out of sheer affection. He felt indebted to them, as they helped his livelihood stay afloat by deftly snatching fish from the hands of the tributaries and rivers. He did not like to keep them under his leash; he believed they deserved freedom and to live with the larger part of their otter universe. But, then their freedom also meant Abdul's misery. Heavy losses in the market would drive him into the belly of poverty. Now, because of the encroaching salinity of the waterbodies and diminishing survival rates of fish, he was only midway to reaching its belly, but inside its mouth, nonetheless.

Stench-filled, suffocating, hot air, lightless world.

Nahin killed only one otter a week because the population of fish in the zigzagging rivers was dwindling and Abdul was not a rich fellow. Abdul had to depend on his otters to catch those tricky, scaly beings hiding in the skin of the Sundarbans—that much Nahin understood. Although his conscience was claimed by an unsettling fixation for an even more unsettling act, it knew its limits. It knew that daily disappearance would mean the birth of unflinching suspicion in the heart of his father. Even one disappearance per week was somewhat enough to get Abdul riled up, since he had to empty his pockets at the end of every month to buy a new otter. Nearly hunted to extinction, otters were not readily available, which is why he had to depend on smugglers who brought them from West Bengal, and not for a modest price.

Before every killing, the thought of how the otters helped Abdul earn a livelihood for them, the puppy-eyed innocence of the creatures flashed itself in Nahin's mind.

A quick, summery, slim, glaring blade.

A flitting skin of the sun.

But the curiosity-streaked eyes, the dark muzzle, the rapidly-moving limbs, the wise whiskers, the carpet-smooth skin, the irresistible ensemble of the creatures brushed the thought aside and held him captive.

That glaring blade, lost.

The fire of hunger, found.

The frustrated, bony Abdul, denuded of strength and energy, powerlessly accepted the ritual of weekly disappearance. After all, he did not have a companion — only a young son —, came home late and went out to work very early in the morning. He needed enough rest. Lack of sufficient sleep always messed with his head and digestion; he knew it very well. He could not let them risk his already-at-risk job and starve his little family of two. Even though enough measures were taken to safeguard the otters' hutch, one went missing every damn week. Abdul had no idea, but Nahin owned his own pair of keys to the hutch.

Owing to the disappearances coupled with the diminishing population of fish, Abdul always remained drowned in the stinging waters of a morose state, his worn-out mind pregnant with exasperation and despondency. Why couldn't his otters stop vanishing? Why did he have to keep buying a new one every month? Couldn't the grey wolves and the monitor lizards have mercy upon him? Didn't God understand that without the otters his livelihood would crumble to dust?

Nahin could sense that; the hands of misery choking his father. But he could also sense the need to satiate his addiction; this tentacled addiction of hunger that governed his psyche, laved his conscience with its slender, hunger-soaked limbs. Once, Abdul came up with a pilot plan of keeping the hutch under the bed that he shared with his son for a few days. The plan failed; the stench of excrement and the creatures' body odour, alongside their constant murmur and buzz annihilated the possibility of a healthy sleep. Nahin was in a fix while the plan breathed, which was approximately for five days. He was worried he would not get an otter that week because the possibility of getting caught red-handed while taking out an otter from the cage loomed large then. But after the plan's bones withered away, compromising the safety of the immobile republic, he found solace in the bubbling prospect of an afternoon feast.

His desire reared its heads.

Looked forward.

Their veins throbbed.

Steadfast, unflinching gaze.

***

On a hot July morning, when the tide was low and the air was imbued with birdsongs and a mob of smells emanating from various leaves that the Sundarbans had to offer, Abdul, alongside Jashim—his neighbour, a fellow fisherman —, ventured into an inlet with high hopes of catching scores of Tilapia and Maagur fish.

"Why do you buy a new otter every month?" asked Jashim as he and Abdul released their otters into the olive waters and they started working their ways through the grey, soggy banks detecting the presence of a miniature civilisation of fish.

Abdul turned to him, squinting at his dark figure against the fiery sun, and replied, "What can I say? One disappears every week, *bhaijaan*. Every week!"

Jashim grew suspicious hearing his reply, as anyone would. How could an otter go missing every week from a locked cage?

"How so! It sounds impossible. I mean, look, it doesn't happen to the rest of us. Even if it does, it is usually once every three months or so," Jashim said, a frown plastering his sweaty face, the din of the otters at work growing loud in the background.

"I don't know. My son says he has seen monitor lizards and grey wolves taking them"

"Did you ever see it?"

"No, I cannot manage to stay awake at night. I have to rely on my son's information."

"Keep the cage inside your house then, instead of that hut!"

"I can't. They smell like shit."

Their conversation was leading nowhere; it was a fruitless interaction. A barren dialogue off set and forgettable before the ripe bearing of the otters' work. As they hopped on the boat, their mouths full of clay-tinged fish, light reflecting off their scaly bodies as though they were heavenly blessings, both Abdul and Jashim shoved the dilemma at hand into a corner alive with the residue of such fruitless conversations.

Today, they would glean a pleasant earning from the market.

***

An afternoon exhausted with laziness. Devoid of activities. Gravid with snores and recesses. Haze of slumber cupping the atmosphere in its palms.

In the forest.

A tiger letting out grumbles. Lying on elementary mangroves. Breaking them under its feral weight. Its cubs sleeping on its belly. Inside, a deer, a monkey, a half-eaten boar. A cement-hued crocodile. Drunken with the afternoon haze. Bathing in the afternoon sun. A river pirate's leg inside its being.

In the skirting village.

Smell of lunch—meat, vegetables, fish—climbing the air. Haunting the nostrils. Sickle, rusty bicycles lying about. Under the clutches of inactivity. Chickens and their hens stationing themselves inside coops. Empty streets. Shining under the blaze.

Rivulets of sweat gathered on Nahin's skin as he pinned a wood-brown otter to the ground. Witnessing the unfolding horror, the rest roared forth a crescendo of shriek from within the cage. Otter-canons. Letting out invisible surges. Sound, their ammunition. Nahin pressed its belly with his knee, exerting significant force so it would stop clawing at his skin. Blobs of sweat slowly dripped off his forehead and crashed into the otter's gaping eyes steeped in pain. It flinched. He reached for the rusty sickle with his right hand, and then, after momentarily wielding it in the air for reasons unknown, ran it through the otter's throat. Splotches of dark blood splattered his face and white shirt. His hands were catching the wild frenzy of a deluge flowing out of its throat. Then he amputated its limbs and skinned it for his weekly, raw feasting. A few minutes rolled by, and, as if propelled by divine intervention, Abdul stormed in, a long, thick stick in his hand, with a motley crew of armed neighbours, shattering the lazy haze of the afternoon.

He, like the others, stood shocked witnessing the scene: his fifteen-year-old boy eating the meat off an otter's bones, his face smeared with its blood, its furry skin lying on a bloodied patch beside him, its eyes and claws here, its muzzle there.

"Hay Allah, what is this? How is this possible?" some screamed. Some threw up. Some simply ran away.

But Abdul stood motionless, glassy eyed, his mouth gaping.

He had decided to come home early that day, since he felt feverish whiling away his time in the fiery hotness of the bazar. As he approached home, he heard the cries of his otters inside the hut — where the otters stayed. Fearing that it might be a dangerous animal that had intimidated the otters inside, he ran to his neighbours' houses desperately and formed an armed mass before storming in. He could never fathom that the animal he had been fearing would be none other than his own son.

***

A few months later, Nahin passed away as a result of a long, vicious illness. Of course, it had a lot to do with the fact that his diet included otters. He died a painful death. Rapid convulsions followed by vomiting throughout days and nights. It was not known why his body decided to act up suddenly, though. He had been a popular consumer for a long time, why had there been no illnesses or anything before? No one knew, no one cared to know. What only mattered was that he was gone. Fifteen years of existence. Smoked out of this world.

Perhaps, when he was foaming at the mouth in the hospital bed as Abdul screamed his heart out, the phantoms of all those otters that he had feasted on mocked him and worked their ways inside his body as they would have dove into the river, pursuing fish, instead to jerk the shadowy hint of life out of him. Perhaps, they cried a little for Abdul, whose grief would aggravate leading a solitary life without a family. But the joy of witnessing their killer's death overpowered their glum sentiments for Abdul, the one who had trained, fed and adored them for their brief stint in this realm of the mortals. Turbulent. Loud.

The day Nahin was surrendered to the belly of the copper earth, to another world which shared no bridge of coexistence with this one, Abdul, pulverised by grief, killed his otters. The remaining seven of them.

Abdul and his beloved creatures were threaded together by the fellowship of grief. He, by his son's death, and they, by their impending deaths playing out in front of them. The thatched roof of the hut witnessed how Abdul cried when he hacked at their slender, little bodies with his machete and how they cried receiving the blows too hard for their soft bodies. The raucous coalition of grief lodged itself in the hut's essence.

He ate one each day. For a week. Living the secret life his son had led and finding solace in the shadowy presence of Nahin that came with the act. The act that repeated and repeated.

Departure. Seven otter-shaped leaves. Falling off the branches of the universe. Immobile republic in flight. To another world.

Aerial republic.

Only its vestiges—republic of skins and bones—remained in this world.

FOUR POEMS

Mozibur Rahman Ullah

Crystal Library

A library of crystal
Where the sun shines calm & still
For laughter like an apple
And for her fair head resting
   Against my shoulder

She turns to me, and says
You must learn to relax.

And then — What is love
But small-talk.

And I say,
But small talk makes me feel small.

So she says,
Then write!
   And write in CAPITALS!

Will that make me feel tall?
She laughs, and says no.
That's a joke.

So I laugh.

Don't you know how to be human?

I did once – that was a long time ago when I climbed walls and flew paper planes and watched the red glow of my blood in the night and then flung the torch light to the bright moon and the bright moon shone back.

And then I caged my heart,
And opened my mouth.

She looks at me.

Or my heart was caged.

When you fall, she says.
I will catch.

Then she adds,
Write from where you are,
From your heart,
For your heart has always been warm.

Your heart won't enslave you
But your mind and your eyes might.

And then – turning serious
She asked – am I thy love?
And I said yes, our hearts are tied.

In your tender dew I came alive.

Lies Inc.

Towards the flame you fly
Drawn by the story, the hype
Virtue, they say, is its own reward
Then when the going gets tough
They stab you in the back

Time after time
Suicide, cancer
And the rotting of the mind

They smile at their guile
And laugh at your lack of spies
Then you are exhibit A

Pinned down
Like a fly
In the centre of a web

Nothing is true
For everything now is a lie

Telemachus

Orphan boy
You watch the great waters
For a sign

Sailor he says,
   Is there any news of my father?
My mother pines
And our home is without a guardian
And forty men sup and dine
   They eat up all our substance
   They are the wolfish kind
   Nothing they do comes to any good
   Our house comes to ruin

Athena, for it was she
Hidden in sailors garb
Looked at him with her calm grey eyes

I came from a land distant and far
They say that he fought armies single-handed to a standstill
And bewitched by sirens
   He slept under a moon-lit dream
   But his heart aches for Ithaca
   Land of his fathers
   There he was born
Now he sails to you
On the foam flecked seas

Sailor, says Telemachus again
Will you stay, will you rest?

You have your father's manners
But I cannot rest
My ship sails tomorrow

But bring me a laurel wreath
To lay at the goddess's feet
And we will chant a hymn

Rouzans Song

Introduction

This is a poem about a young Palestinian nurse who was killed during the Great March of Return in Gaza.

As Salaam al-Alaikum

My name is Rouzan al-Najjar
   From Khuzaa in Gaza
I am a daughter of men
   And a daughter of Palestine

My father is Ashraf al-Najjar
And my mother Sabreen al-Najjar
I am the eldest of six
And I am a medic

When I was young
We slept as one family
   In one bed
Tallest to shortest
Eldest to youngest

All of us here are Najjars
We fled Salamah by Jaffa
The day of our Nakba
And the day of our tears.

And though we dried them,
We remembered.

This is a burning land
An enclosed land
A land under siege
   Our land is a blister
But the sea breeze still swings
   Through my hair

And the oranges from Jaffa
  Are sweet to my tongue
As his looks are

Our Nakba has not ended
  It blasts us here still
Khuzaa is now buried
It's buildings bull-dozed
There was a battle here
  And I saw my friend torn apart
  Her blood wetting the dust
  Amongst the dead and dying
    In the streets.

I dried my tears
And I commended her to Allah.

My father sheltered me
  And I grew up as slender as a rose
  My laughter was as the bubbling brook
When my mother's face would darken
  I would move worlds

It was not in their shadows
  That I lived
  But in their light

I do not whisper
And nor do I shout
With my friends
  There is laughter
  There is talk
  And there are jealousies
I was as a lily amongst the thorns

I said to my friends, smiling
  Perhaps I will become a shaheed
And then they frowned and said
  Do not seek martyrdom

For Allah does not love those
   Who martyr themselves.
And I replied,
  I do not seek martyrdom
  I seek to add my voice
    To a just cause
  And my hands
  And my song.

For all women are my sisters
As all men are my brothers
Our neighbour is not a stranger
And to the stranger we offer
   Our olives and our bread

We are beset by perils
And all paths are perilous.

This is a land beloved
   By two people
For the land loved them both
And pledged its troth
But we are walled off
   From each other

Who is the groom?
And who is the bride?
And where is the wedding?

I hear only voices crying
   In the wilderness

And they said,
  We commend you to Allah.

He said, she did not know us
   But she treated us like we were
   Her own brothers
   She was as a dove to our sorrows

I am a difference
And aim to make a difference
My blood be upon it

I said to my father,
　Give me away
And he said,
　I will not give you away
　You are my only daughter

And I said to my father again,
　Give me away
And he said,
　I will not give you away
　You are my light
　　In this darkness
　Because of you
　　There is warmth

Then I said to my father,
　I have listened to thy words
　And it is to thy words I hearken
　Call me not a rebellious daughter
　　Who makes an ornament
　　Of herself
　But obedient

And I said to my father a third time,
　Give me away
And he said, I give you to life
　Allah will shelter you
　As He has sheltered me
　And you will be
　　The daughter of men

I taught myself as Allah had taught me

I taught myself by the light of a kerosene lamp

I bandaged the wounds of my friends - and of my foes
I was as swift as a gazelle
Amongst the rocks

I was as a lily amongst the thorns

And they called me a lioness
   Amongst the lions.
And they said, I was reckless
Then they cautioned,
   Your first priority is your own self, and the safety of your own self. This
path is perilous. It is beset by perils. If you live, others will live. But if you
die, who will you save then?

They said, bend a little
As the bullet is on its way to you.

I said, the bullet chose me
Because I do not know how to bend
Why should I change? It is not I that should change, but the world.

And they said,
     Allah Malik al-Mulk

He said, I hope we do not get shot.
And I said, If I die, then so be it
   We die as friends.

But I am no martyr
For I love life
It is as honey to my lips

My lover is my friend
And I am a friend to all lovers
Those who love the wheat of life
I am an army to myself

And the sword to my army
I am my own sword
 And offer myself to my own people
When my life ends
Make my life a perfume
For those who know me
   And for those who do not.

Wreathe my name in roses
And anoint it with myrrh
Then cast it upon the sea
And commend me to our Lord.

   Say, that I was faithful
   And say, that I was true.

No, said the wall
   Which walls off time
And No said the barbed wire
The watch towers shook their heads, and glared.

She is not the measure of mercy
Nor an angel of mercy though she has the face of an angel.

She was a shield terrorists held in front of them.

She was a bandage that terrorists revived themselves with.

She nurses vipers at her breasts
This is a land of dragons' teeth.

She did not lead but she was led
   To walled up horizons
   To a moon locked up in rocks
   To a nest of thorns

She is a dead end
That ye should not follow
Bury her name

Forget her face
Remember her shame

Ye are a pathology
We aim to cure
Aye, the medicine is bitter
But ye shall swallow it
Time is on our side

And then all the clocks
In Gaza whirr and clang
And their bells begin to toll

Tomorrow is full of fragments
And doors open and close in the sky
    Where our hands cannot reach
    Even when we jump

The sky, that is as hard as a wall
There, in the glare of the Israeli sun
Our history is erased
    Brick by brick

We bang on the walls because we are suffocating.

We throw stones at the walls because they make us eat bricks.

We set fire to our hearts because once this was a land full of olives.

    And the sun shone on all.

O my Friends,
O my Countrymen,
O thou World
    Hearken to my plea
    And be thou my witness:

Brothers and sisters of my heart, children of the sun, listen not ye to the
whisperer, he that knots hearts and minds, he that grows within walls and

silences, and that makes victims of us all. We are victims of silence and walls but we will not go in silence and we will break down walls, for though we are weary, we are taller than our shadows.

Dedication
Dedicated to the memory of my mother, who could not read English, but would have understood.

REVIEWS

GHETTO STORIES *by Marie Michalke*
A CIRCUS OF BOYS *by Arsalan Isa*
COVID-19 ENTERTAINMENT *by Khuda Bushq*

GHETTO STORIES

Marie Michalke

In the autumn of 2018, I headed to SOAS's brand new Brunei Gallery lecture theatre for a reading of Elias Khoury's new book *My Name is Adam*. The English translation had just been released and the author was touring the UK to promote his book. As expected when a living legend of Arabic literature appears, the room was packed with students, lecturers, activists and readers. Khoury spoke with great caution, every word seemed deliberate; yet, every now and then he made a joke with the interviewer or with himself. The questions led Khoury into his past. He talked about the work at the PLO (Palestine Liberation Organisation) newspaper *Palestinian Affairs* with his friend, the famous poet Mahmoud Darwish. When he spoke of the novel's main protagonist Adam Dannoun, it was in the same manner as he spoke of Darwish. I tried to untangle which protagonists were real, but I instead started getting disoriented in the process.

During the Q&A, a man raised his hand and asked about a character in the book he knew from New York, blind Mahmoud. For some moments, Elias Khoury on stage and the man in the audience had their own private conversation about an old friend. Meanwhile, I lost track of who was a real person and who was a character. Perhaps it was true and Adam Dannoun was the actual author of the book which is what Khoury claimed. Retrospectively, I am sure: for Khoury, the protagonists of the book might as well have been real. Just as the novel is actually not his creation, but the collective story of the people of Lydda. The book hooked me with its philosophical argument that 'fiction is truth's first cousin' and imagination and reality are actually twins. I bought a copy and Khoury signed it for me, I think he was slightly amused by my disorientation.

After that, when I read *My Name is Adam,* I felt I was reading someone's secrets. The book is the first part of a trilogy called *Children of the Ghetto.* It consists of a preface, a manuscript of a novel about the seventh century poet Waddah al-Yaman, and Adam's memoirs. In the preface, Khoury claims that fictional author-protagonist Adam wrote the manuscript and the memoirs. Themes of narrative unreliability, alienation, and the fragmentation of memory are clear early on and travel through the story.

Elias Khoury, *My Name is Adam: Children of the Ghetto*, MacLehose, London, 2018.

On the first pages, Khoury describes how he met Adam Dannoun, the author-protagonist of his book. He admits his confusion: was Adam an Israeli Jew, who had acquired a perfect Palestinian dialect, or a Palestinian who had mastered flawless Hebrew? He could not place Adam and thus distrusted him, after all, there was a slight chance Adam could be a spy. A few pages later, Adam reveals how he plays with other people's perception of his identity.

'When I was asked who I was, I'd run my fingers through my curly hair and say one word (Ghetto), and the listener would understand that I was assigning myself to his memory, not my mother's. It was of course a silent lie, but only if we believe that the clouds are lying if they don't bring rain.'

Adam actually grew up as a child of Lydda. To him and all its inhabitants, Lydda was a city under siege, a result of the Nakba, and a ghetto. But when asked where he was from, he would wrap the name and characteristics of the ghetto he was from in silence. This leaves Adam's listeners to interpret the word 'ghetto' through their own understanding: the traumatic Jewish history in central Europe with the Holocaust at its dark centre. Adam turned himself into a child of Jewish immigrants from the Ghetto of Warsaw. This habit of concealing his identity helped him escape the discrimination Palestinians in Israel face on a daily basis.

His silence concealed the differences between the Lydda and Warsaw ghettos, and this concealment demonstrates how subjective identity is. In the scene above, Adam tricks both his Israeli colleague and Elias Khoury, because they understand the Israeli and Palestinian identity as mutually exclusive. Instead, Adam's identity is fluid and can change with time and circumstances. He focuses on the emotional experience of the victim and draws parallels between human suffering; this is how Adam turns himself from a Palestinian from Lydda to a Jewish descendant from Warsaw into an Israeli/Palestinian exiled in New York. This switching of identity is more than just convenient for Adam. It is a coping mechanism: if he convinces himself he can be someone else, he does not need to confront his painful memories.

My Name is Adam is a continuous exploration of the internal reactions to trauma, how people deal with horrific experiences and unthinkable violence and continue with their lives. The novel shows how identity is constructed, it is imagined; but it becomes real through the consequences of that imagination. Sometimes, the horrible experiences a person has to live through because of their ascribed identity is how imagination turns into reality. Adam's silence translates these traumatic, unspeakable experiences that often lie at the core of collective identities. For example, 'Ghetto' is everything his Israeli listeners need to hear, to understand his family's past in Warsaw. The word is loaded with emotions and memories unnecessary and often painful to say out loud. This silent understanding between people of the same community based on their traumatic past or present is audible through Adam's writing. Adam is a Palestinian in Israel, his suffering during the Nakba, an event denied by many parts of the Israeli society, remains unacknowledged. Adam says 'My tragedy isn't in need of recognition, and whether they acknowledge it or not, it is engraved on our souls and places'. The novel scrutinises what we mean by identity and leaves the reader and Adam feeling like it is arbitrary and unreal.

When I started reading Adam's memoir, I struggled at first. Initially, I disliked Adam's narration, he was bitter. He was lying to himself and to me, the reader. The lie was not present in what he wrote, but in what he left unsaid. He pretended to be self-reflective. But his memories and reflections seemed tainted and retrospectively corrected by his own world view. As he went deeper into the project of collecting the story of his life, he was forced to reassess his understanding of the past. During his memoir, he interrogates all aspects of his self-perception, even his fake Jewish one. This process demands a lot of energy and strength from Adam, it is self-therapy. He strives to overcome his coping mechanisms of changing his identity and altering his memory.

To understand his past, Adam recollects the stories and memories of the inhabitants of Lydda about the Nakba. After the founding of Israel, the city's small Palestinian population remained under military rule from 1948 to 1952. This military rule enforced the conditions of a ghetto for the inhabitants: they were not allowed to move outside of its fences without permission from the military, they did not receive supplies from outside, and were left to fend for themselves with limited resources. The result is isolation, a form of exile. In a podcast interview from 2018 with Nora Parr, Khoury explains why Lydda was no exception; ghettoisation was the experience of nearly everyone remaining after the Nakba. He explains that not many people, not even within the Palestinian community themselves, know about the lives and conditions of Palestinians living in these ghettos after 1948. *My Name is Adam* wants to give a voice to the stories that have been overlooked.

Through this theme, the novel inverts the Palestinian story of exile and refugeehood; instead, it tells infinite stories of the struggles of the remaining Palestinians. It aims to look at exile not through displacement and departure, but from a place of encroachment and confinement: an unexpected, neverending exile because it is done at home. Even after the restriction of movement was lifted, the Palestinians found themselves alienated in an unknown land between new people, longing for the homeland, which now only exists in memory.

The novel approaches the Nakba and political violence through emotions and experiences and not through precise dates and facts. Facts are interpreted in myriad ways, especially when they concern the history of Israel and Palestine. Many memories and struggles of the remaining Palestinian population of this time are orally transmitted and not documented in an official document. The dominant narrative of the founding of Israel did not leave space for the suffering that came with it. This can be read as an imposed silence, or muteness, on Palestinians within Israel based on their identity; their experiences remained unheard. This book is an alternative understanding of dominant history told through the memory of Adam, the first child of the ghetto of Lydda. It is a translation of this muted experience into words, a rendering of emotions and trauma written between the lines of official documents.

Telling the story of Palestinian collective memory is only half of what the book seeks. For me, different ideas of translation inform the core of the book as well. Translating always means there is the doubling of voice. Not only the voice of the author who co-wrote the text, but also the voice of the translator. Furthermore, the translation is only one version of the source text, one of countless interpretations and perspectives.

I first read *My Name is Adam* in translation by Davies Humphrey. Khoury is not an easy-to-read writer in Arabic, but Davies is accustomed to Khoury's prose as he was his translator for *Gate of the Sun* and *Yalo*. He is perfect for the job also because he translated what is often called the first modern Arabic novel, *Leg over Leg* by Ahmad Faris al-Shidyaq. The book is known for its complicated prose, its many rhythms and rhymes, its lengthy listing of synonyms and mixing of genres. *Leg over Leg* might have been an influence on Khoury's style of writing as well: each version of a story is a synonym of the next. In an interview in 2014 with the *American University in Cairo Press*, Davies says he is guided by the rule of function in his translation: he models the English version of the text along the function of the Arabic one. He continues that a good translation for him is when a text is able to echo the style of the author. In the case of *My Name is Adam*, the style of writing is a reflection of the particular way of storytelling: the narrator's constant reflection, investigating every thought, mirrors his repetition of different versions of the same story.

These many stories are based on witness reports. Khoury explains in an interview with the *Paris Review*, that for some of his book projects he works with oral histories. He would talk to survivors of the Nakba and their descendants and weave their memories and stories together in his novels; a translation of memory into literature. The result is a multiplicity of perspectives and understandings which resemble a narration – not a narrative – of an event. A translation is a version of a source text, it does not contradict it, rather it broadens its meanings. There is no singular voice or author; instead, an infinite amount of stories told by different voices complement, build on, contradict and expand each other. The many memories of different people broaden the identity of the author so that the book is not written by one person, it is written by a myriad, including the translator.

Khoury echoes texts that process the experience of the Palestinians within and outside of the borders of Israel, before and after the 1967 war. He mentions Ghassan Kanafani's famous *Men in the Sun*, he draws a parallel between himself and Emile Habibi, author of *The Secret Life of Sa'id the Pessoptimist* and he mentions Anton Shammas's *Arabesques*. But throughout the book, he also makes connections to a Jewish heritage. After all, the trilogy is called *Children of the Ghetto*, just like Israel Zangwill's classic. The book talked about the generation caught between the ghetto with its deprived and impoverished Jewish community and the new opportunities in London. He mentions the Israeli writer S. Yizhar often. Adam also talks about Yizhar's book *Khirbet Khizeh* in which the author reflects on his experience of being a soldier during the establishment of Israel and the Nakba in Palestine. By connecting Palestinian and Israeli and British-Jewish fiction with each other, Khoury brings the emotional experience of the protagonists closer, without denying the individual horror of the events on which they are based. He breaches the distance between what it means to be Palestinian and what it means to be Israeli and breaks down barriers between these identities.

The strength of this book lies here: it forces us to reconsider what we thought being Palestinian or Israeli means. I don't believe that books can change set hearts, but literature has the power to make other perspectives understandable and tell different sides. It can make us think and reassess. *My Name is Adam* is a push to reconsider assumptions of identity, especially important within Germany, the country that inflicted the Shoah on European Jews. Germany has a complicated relationship with the Palestinian call for human rights. I remember some uncomfortable discussions with Antifa supporters, mostly with members of the 'anti-Deutsche' group. For them, Israel is the celebrated exception to their strict ideology of no borders and no nationalisms. In 2019, the German government legally outlawed the BDS (Boycott-Divestment-Sanctions) movement as inherently anti-semite. This decision equates the Palestinian civil society's movement for human rights, right to return and self-determination with anti-Semitism. But it comes as no surprise. As part of an anti-racist network, *Junge Islam Konferenz*, I started understanding racism through the experience of the Muslim community in Germany. I recognise how many groups and individuals in German society, not only the far-left ones, encounter Muslims with suspicion of being anti-semitic.

This suspicion is a consequence of a reductive – and frankly, racist - idea that all Palestinians, Arabs and Muslims, are believed to be in conflict with Israel and thus must hate all Jews. They suffer under the 'Generalverdacht' to be anti-semitic by nature. This adds considerably to the discrimination the Muslim community already faces in Germany. In German politics and public discussions, it is still debated whether Islam is compatible with 'the German identity' and Christian values, ultimately labelling the Muslim community in Germany as foreign to German society.

Reading more books like Khoury's *My Name is Adam* is important, because they radically question identity, exploring its limits and grey areas. Unravelling one's identity and scrutinising one's belief system is a painful process, but, in the end, it cannot be avoided. At the moment, Germany deals with its own identity - and in extension the Israeli and Palestinian identities – on a superficial level. There yet has to be a meaningful confrontation of the underlying reasons and ideologies of the Holocaust and its connection to current anti-Semitism and racism in German society. Instead, anti-Semitism is outsourced to the Palestinian, Arab and Muslim communities, which in the dominant view are considered inherently anti-Semitic and are conveniently outside of German self-understanding. This way, Germany avoids the problem of looking at its own white-Christian anti-Semitism and Nazi history in current attacks. I am aware that there is a real problem of anti-Semitism within Arab communities; but in Germany, white-Christian anti-Semitism and racism enabled all attacks on Jewish and Muslim lives within the last year alone and there were far too many. I am thinking of Hanau, of Halle, I am thinking of the soldier Franco A., of 'die Gruppe S', and of 'Revolution Chemnitz' amongst many more. Instead of actually reconciling Germany's own history and relationship to the Jewish people within its state borders, the unconditional support for Israel is slowly buying a clean conscience from historic guilt. Accepting that the victim can also be the oppressor is a lesson taught by the novel as well.

My Name is Adam makes clear, for example, that to show solidarity (at least to some extent) with the German–Palestinian community is more valuable than guilt-guided solidarity with a far-right, ethno-nationalist government. This would also require a re-evaluation of the founding process of the state of Israel and the exclusive ethno-nationalist values at its core.

In a *Paris Review* interview, Khoury says 'the conflict is still essentially an ethical issue. When you have a victim in front of you, you must identify yourself with the victim, not just show solidarity.' For Khoury it is all about identification; he writes in a way the reader sympathises with Adam and feels with him, and consequently with the many voices narrating their intimate anecdotes. Through insights into personal reflections, he unravels the human emotions behind the label 'Palestinian'. He achieves this by adding another layer of meaning to the silent understanding of the word ghetto. With the memory and stories from the inhabitants of Lydda and Adam himself, he expands the Jewish history by the experience of the Palestinian people who remained after the Nakba. It parallels the human encounter with suffering while still acknowledging the difference in each individual experience.

A CIRCUS OF BOYS

Arsalan Isa

Most of us are fortunate enough not to have experienced an exile. Somehow, Maazan Maarouf has snagged two. His double exile begins as a Palestinian refugee in Lebanon, where his family fled the siege of Tel al-Zaatar to Beirut, and continued as a political refugee in Iceland. In an Al-Jazeera *Poets of Protest* documentary from 2012, Maarouf is filmed walking in Reykjavík. Wrapped in winter clothes that shield from the Icelandic cold, his long, curly hair bounces distractingly in the wind. He admires the snow, eagerly imparts his observations, but seems preoccupied, a vigilant traveller shooting weary glances. He says, 'Beirut resonated between a city that was mine and a city that was rejecting me.'

Maarouf, who initially gained recognition for his criticism in Arabic magazines and newspapers, has had some strange misfortunes. In 2013, a thief in Stockholm stole his backpack which contained a notebook with 27 finished poems. He turned to prose as a kind of recovery. His luck improved, and *Jokes for the Gunmen*, his first short story collection, won the Al-Multaqa prize in 2016, and then, in 2019, Jonathan Wright's translation of the book was longlisted for the Man Booker International.

Maazan Maarouf, *Jokes for the Gunmen*, translated by Jonathan Wright, Granta Books, 2019

Maarouf describes his art as a 'mission of how to reconstruct the dirt, this is poetry, maybe to make a rose out of dust.' This idealism, seeking to transmogrify the mundane, would otherwise feel dated and naive; post-war humanism that tastes of didacticism and moral authority, yearning for an era before truth became passé. But in *Jokes for the Gunmen* this moral imperative chills when it appears in a child's voice. Suddenly the search for stability and honesty is sombre. Think of Greta Thunberg and child warriors. Conviction in unexpected bodies. It's a refreshing rejection of chic-nihilism. This collection of twelve stories isn't a study of war or a simulation in absurdity. It's an odd, boyishly wrangled fantasy that grieves lost childhood. Call it a comic plea that cautions against miscommunication and the violence men inflict on each other. Yes, war is present and pervasive, but only as a soundscape or as a circumstance. Maarouf describes war as a 'scenography' or as a 'pinned background'. And this is where the stories excel, rather than fetishising settings, Maarouf downplays them. Instead of focusing on the gratuitousness of violence, its arbitrariness and alleged absurdity, Maarouf pushes details; a father drooling at the edge of a bathtub, the turning handle of a gramophone, a secondhand matador's suit.

The author's impish voice spindles from farce to severity. His images are odd. Their bizarreness captures the most vivid feelings. In 'Matador', the narrator describes the experience of sitting in a fully air-conditioned room, 'you feel like an ant that has swallowed a pin and can no longer move.' The humour allows the development of meatier themes around humiliation and honour; men who cannot cry, a father asking his son for his limbs, an uncle beating his nephew on the face. Maarouf's images feel parachuted in from the Roald Dahl universe, and they explore masculinity in a quirky way. After a beating, the narrator in 'Matador' says of his uncle, 'I stood facing him, defiant as a young bull without horns.' The humour also works as a distancing tool – if you can't talk about it then joke about it, invert it, reconfigure it – and somewhere we're waiting for the characters to talk meaningfully with each other, but they can't. There's something very male about this – a reluctance to talk candidly, to confess, to become visibly vulnerable, and even though Maarouf is aware of these dynamics, and shows their pitfalls, the humour only perpetuates this alienation; and suspiciously, we feel it has something to do with male relationships with mothers – quite a few of the stories have a nurturing mother in the background that these men can access for emotional safety.

In the first three stories of *Jokes for the Gunmen*, violence appears at home, between fathers and sons, and through the enforcement of masculine traditions: honour, dignity, status, and purpose. These traditions, and their accompanying behaviours, cause immense, often invisible, damage by turning men against each other. It's comical, but also alarming to see tough men rendered ridiculous in their pursuits, unable to communicate with each other. Their grand ideas are parodied and their strength is reduced to a hopelessness they can't articulate. They can't seem to wake up, connect with their real selves, and overcome the nonsense. We want to kick them in their shins to stir them awake.

In 'Jokes for the Gunmen', the title story, the boy-narrator admits that, 'power was the most important subject, as far as we were concerned, during the war'. Especially as it concerns fathers, and the power they wield at home. The narrator dreams for his father to have a glass eye. He hopes the eye will make his father powerful and the gunmen in his neighbourhood will stop beating and harassing him. The story excels in its inversion of traditional masculinity. A boy witnesses his father's humiliation and wants to restore his family's dignity. He adopts the bravado and machismo of a boy who rationalises that violence commands fear and respect. He tries to safeguard his father's honour. The stories the son spins about his father violently beating him, how he was kidnapped, how he was a major player in the war, complicate the narrator because they demonstrate the depth of his compensatory delusions. To fulfil his duty to the family, the boy feels he needs to exercise violence, and endure beatings to defeat this unnamed threat. Sadly, the lingering violence and tragedy isn't the war itself, the mortar shell that kills his brother or his father's humiliation by the gunmen, it's how these characters change, how they cope with their delusions, and how they are driven to actions that will later haunt them through recurring dreams.

The power dynamics and definitions associated with masculinity, how they are practiced and fulfilled, are exceptionally well explored. We learn how the projection of masculinity isn't strength as such, but it's the failure in processing emotions, a protective shield that also functions as a coping strategy. Also, it is the repression of fear and vulnerability, the generation of toxic myths and delusions, all to compensate for a fundamental deficiency, either in control, status, body, or strength. Maarouf equates, without stating it so clearly, masculinity with weakness, not with power. This kind of masculinity functions as a proxy and construct, not as an essence that is innate to men.

What is most alarming is how a boy's sense of play and imagination is coupled with an adult's ability to execute violence, but unlike a self-reflective adult, Maarouf's boy-narrator seems blissfully aware of the consequences of his words and actions, and this is devastating. The man that the boy is becoming – strong, defiant, able to confront adversity, to administer and deliver violence, to curtail chaos, a man's man, is at the cost of his humanity and his compassion. When the son loses an eye, his father reassures him: 'You're a big boy and from now on you won't just be a boy. You'll be a man.' A man is equated with survival. The journey into manhood is marked by the presence of pain, yet the father later dreams for his son's original eye to be returned; he both admires and laments the ritual of manhood that comes with loss, with a diminished humanity, but recognises that something essential was stripped away from his son in the process.

Does this strike the right tone on the crisis of masculinity? At the end, are these boys to blame for the monsters they become? Is blame a useful, equitable word? This understated journey into the origins of toxic masculinity is refreshing, but only as a cautionary tale. What can these men do, when they aren't given an opportunity to develop, to socialise through emotions. When the father gifts the son a pepper plant, the son tries to conserve water by spitting on it and this compassionate gesture is misunderstood, only to result in the son's beating. Intergenerational violence has been thoroughly documented, and abuse has legacy, it carries, sprouts, travels, changes hands, morphs, grows, seeks out new hosts, desires belonging, and violence is never eradicated, once administered, it only reappears elsewhere. In this sense, the story isn't prescriptive but representative. It doesn't offer any solutions. The ugliness of the world that Maarouf summons is at times fatalistic, and unsurprising for someone who is suspicious of peace. Maarouf describes his first experience in Iceland in an interview with the Reykjavík Grapevine: 'The peace was confusing. In Lebanon, you walk in the streets and wonder whether the car you're passing by has a bomb inside it.'

'Matador' feels like a Sisyphean story. The narrator's uncle buys a secondhand matador suit and sets out to become a bullfighter by strangling cows in a slaughterhouse. Throughout the story he dies multiple times and is unable to achieve his goal, only to come back to life and try again. He relentlessly pursues an impossible ideal. He fails, but persists. Sisyphus is a prototype of unflinching, stoic, and relentless masculinity. A man, often illustrated as chiselled and hyper-masculine, is forced to repeatedly push a stone uphill to no palpable gain. He is condemned in a present so present that it annihilates everything else, either a perfect torture, or the pinnacle of neo-capitalist productivity. Productivity for its own personal sake; for process, for procedure, for purpose. Interestingly, this is King Corinth's punishment by Hades. So why then, has the myth of the 'single-minded and obsessively focused man' penetrated so deeply into popular culture? Where hyper-specialised labour, requiring obsessive and compulsive behaviours to master, are applauded? What's really at stake here? Is this an internalisation of a symbolic urge to narrow in, centre, focus, overcome adversity, exert dominance, and invade? And this specificity, this specialisation, can be visualised as a pin-point, as a compression, as an enclosure, as a man chasing the art of bullfighting to the point of neurosis. The uncle continues to die and come back to life, each time he returns with an inexplicable urge to be a bullfighter, to defeat 'cows' and fulfil his dream. Eventually, he stops coming back to life, but instead his nephew adopts his dream with a twist, he wants to be buried in a boxer's gloves. These characters, trapped in a Sisyphean cage, cannot see the limitations of their desires. Both of them seek fulfilment in feats of strength and violence, both are unable to acquire this state. Ironically, neither of them are able to see that there's more to their condition than fighting; their masculinity is defined by the force they can exert around them. Violence doesn't fade, it passes down from one family member to the other, creating a cyclical niche for itself. It is repetitive, undefined and seemingly pointless. Yet it is necessary, imperative to the fulfilment of something – a delusion, a myth, a thing to be held in the face of the uncertain and the absurd. A coping mechanism to deal with the onslaught of reality.

Maarouf does an excellent analysis of the relationship between a father and son in 'Jokes for the Gunmen', through an ironic and devastating inversion, but there's a palpable absence of female characters in the story. Not that every story necessitates a gender balance, but the only time a woman appears is in the form of a cliché; a traditional nurturing mother, who fades into the background, and who is rendered voiceless and formless. This is the biggest drawback to an otherwise extraordinary story, because it's not done ironically or as parody, it simply feels overlooked, and makes us question if Maarouf is only interested in these issues as they pertain to men, even when they are universal, ubiquitous, and cut across gender and identity. Unfortunately, this isn't the only story in the collection that casts women in this role. In 'Matador', the only woman in the story is the boy's mother. She nurtures her brother, encouraging his dreams by feeding him and performing the stereotypical role of what a maternal woman symbolises in these circumstances; obliging, agreeable, nurturing. In another story, 'Gramophone', a woman is only introduced through her role as a mother, as an appendage to her husband. It is still too early in Maarouf's career to ascertain how he will continue exploring gender. This might be one of the key reasons that *Jokes for the Gunman* was overlooked in favour of *Celestial Bodies*, another Arabic novel which explores gender more fully, for the Man Booker International Prize.

But there is a great deal to enjoy in *Jokes for the Gunmen*. Come for Maarouf's mischievous voice, with its absurd logic and fiendish images, and stay for tales of resistance and loss. Overall, an interesting study of sensitivity and maleness. 'Jokes for the Gunmen' is a story that will stay with me for a long time. If only the other stories were as fully fleshed.

COVID-19 ENTERTAINMENT

Khuda Bashq

One of the more interesting lessons to come out of the COVID-19 pandemic was the realisation that time was in fact not exactly what we needed. Books collect dust, endless hobbies wait in Sisyphean anticipation to be explored, and Netflix cries out for your attention, or at least your continued cash for subscription loyalty. After all, once you do find something worth bingeing on, after a few hours playing in its trap, it asks 'are you still watching?' Taunting you for the great ruse it has pulled over your eyes. More sinisterly, the devil's greatest trick pales in comparison to the one played by Capitalism. The abominable truth is that we cannot help but want what we cannot otherwise have. A need that falls short of our reach is, well, I suppose its rather boring. And at the moment I'm so bored that even the existential dread of my own, inevitable end cannot move me to take out the rubbish. For I, and by a social-distancing compliant extension, 1.7 billion other people on this planet are in quarantine, lockdown, or some other form of isolation and movement control. So at least there is a comfort in the knowledge that I, we, are not alone in our aloneness. Beyond the obvious disruption of work and life, how are we to bide the time. How can such strictly enforced monotony be confronted, engaged, or navigated? How will entertainment save us at this moment of great need? Can we even be entertained in such dark times?

The feat put before our sources of entertainment is not an easy one in any sense of the word. Our attention spans are at their most apathetic. We grieve, in our forced hermitage, the murder of our fair motivation, but in light of its now being an ex-motivation, couldn't be bothered to do anything about it. Anxiety stabs at our side because 'things should be happening' but they aren't. But if we knew how to deal with anxiety without exceptionally addictive and questionable side-effect latent drugs, the world would be a far greater place than we all know it is capable of being. A false FOMO (fear of missing out) for a world that cannot exist beside COVID-19 conjures the thirst that compels a shipwrecked survivor to drink vast quantities of sea water. Suddenly, yes while I have always wanted to sit around and binge watch that one show or finally watch all the films of my favourite franchise back to back, I can't. At least not comfortably.

Some would claim entertainment is an escape. With little desire to resurrect this debate here, let's give it the benefit of the doubt. Yet a problem still remains. How do you escape when you are imprisoned within the very escape you had so desperately desired? We can reinterpret the deeper terror within the 1959 episode of *The Twilight Zone* titled 'Time Enough at Last'. Mr Henry Bemis' final sobs of anguish are less over the loss of his visual aids or the books he's longed to escape within, but instead more that he has no one to speak with about these tales, to seek comradery, to distil then infuse meaning into the world, a practice we often take for granted. To get through the hashtag #StayHome, our entertainment may need to do more then allow us to escape our momentarily not-so-busy lives, but provide us with some meaning and perhaps direction. The metaphorical gymnastics required here will take the best of the best. The greatest performances, writing, editing all stirred into quality production. But Hollywood, like various governments and businesses held their breath, afraid that the world after COVID-19 would be drastically different and perhaps they would be unable to get on without their out-of-date ways. The entertainment that chose to fill this vacuum is a bit harder to shower in praise. Unfortunately, upon looking back on the things which have entertained us during these Covidy times, I'm afraid this doesn't give a good prognosis on the state of the art of entertainment.

'Weird Al' Yankovic's 1984 song 'Nature Trail to Hell' gives us a meta look into the blending of reality and escape found at the cinema. The song is framed as a trailer for the next great American slasher film where an escaped convict proceeds to slaughter a troop of cub scouts on summer camp in glorious, gory 3-D. The film within the song is mentioned as 'good clean family fun' tailored to entertain everyone since it is nothing more egregious than the 'if it bleeds, it leads' content seen on the six o'clock daily news. The commentary made here rings true to date, if not presently taken to a comically absurd level. The joke is seen in a variety of memes featuring a character laughing as they read a story they believe to be from a parody news source, such as *The Onion*, only to find out it is an actual story brandishing the covers of the likes of *The New York Times* or *The Guardian*. As COVID-19 spread like flatulence in a room with poor air flow, the news as such had nothing to report on barring how much we didn't know about the virus and how embarrassingly incompetent our politicians were at responding to it. That isn't news, that's *schadenfreude*. And even for those of us who delight to dabble, excessive amounts leave a bad taste in the mouth. As the news plays out in a fantastically cliché, yet dreadfully dull re-enactment of the media as in every end of the world film, why watch the boring version run a mobius script on 24/7 news television? Perhaps there are lessons, yet more importantly, meaning to be found in how we all imagined this end to go down.

The first few days into our eventual end of times a la COVID-19, the memes joked that we imagined our apocalypse attire to involve tight leather and recycled armour, all completed by a mutant deformity. Instead we find ourselves in the comfort of pyjamas. What was supposed to be steampunk and *Mad Max* (1979) was actually more *The Big Lebowski* (1998). Thankfully, science fiction filmmakers and writers have done a lot of groundwork for us. We can choose our own apocalypse. End by natural disaster as in *The Day After Tomorrow* (2004), *San Andreas* (2015), or *Geostorm* (2017). End by AI or robots, such as anything from the *Terminator* franchise, *The Matrix (1999)*, or *Transcendence (2014)*. End of the of the world by way of nuclear war or economic collapse (rather similar situations when you think about it) as depicted in the *Mad Max* films, *Elysium* (2013), or *Turbo Kid* (2015). End by nature striking back as seen in the *Planet of the Apes* films, *12 Monkeys* (1995) or *After Earth* (2013). Yet many of these films fall sort in delivering the type of entertainment we need during COVID-19 isolation. A vast majority of end of the world films age very poorly due to bad graphics and even worse dialogue. They either focus too much on what is happening, be that by trying to pseudoscience their way to a proper set up or abandoning this to focus on making it all spectacle, or are forced to focus on the characters, where you might manage to salvage a good drama out of the film.

Even end by the more topical deadly disease such as seen in *Outbreak* (1995), *Cabin Fever* (2002), or *Contagion* (2011), leaves much to be desired. First off, locating the patient zero is made far too conveniently and vaccine production appears as simplistic as operating an Easy-Bake Oven. Second, the lack of facemasks (forget about N-95 variants) and the frequent flow of hand sanitiser play second fiddle to every character's disregard for social distancing, proper sneezing technique, or really any elementary form of disease prevention knowledge. And seriously, what is it with the characters' obligatory need to make-out when an ominous, faceless disease is running about. The convenience of disease logic and the idiocy of characters make these sorts of film not only a waste of your overly abundant time, but a case of distress and frustration for COVID-19 plays by its own logic that even has those familiar with other coronaviruses of future's past (SARS and MERS) hesitating to the response of 'what exactly is going on?'

Interestingly enough, the best end-of-the-world films come in the variety of the most outrageous apocalyptic scenarios. These are your zombie or supernatural monster invasion flicks. Classics like *The Blob* (1958), *The Mist* (2007), and even *Children of Men* (2006) also fit on this list. What makes these films so wonderful is that they know they can't trick the audience into believing the scenarios as real possibilities. Instead of trying to give you an explanation, they leave it vague or straight-up don't tell you how it all happened. They leave it to you, the audience, to fill in the blank or imagine your own logic which is going to be far more powerful than anything they try to sell you. When successful, these films focus on characters. The problem that arises from these end-of-the-world films is two-fold. First, the central thesis of most of these films is that the real monsters are the humans which, after enough horror marathons and binge watching of the AMC series *The Walking Dead*, is not good for the spirit stuck in the situation brought on by COVID-19. The second piece of the downside to these films is that they are virtually inescapable and while this unsatisfying ending can be fun every once in a while, this is not particularly brilliant in light of the state of the contemporary world. *The Return of the Living Dead* (1985) and *The Crazies* (2010) leave us with hopeless endings. Perhaps it is because the scenarios devised for these films are so fantastical, how can you ever go back? Therefore, dropping a bomb, or we didn't actually kill the menace, or no characters surviving the film leaves the audience momentarily shocked.

This is fine, if they can then leave the theatre and go back to their real world. Yet here we are locked in our rooms, afraid of everyone watching films that essentially posit that every human is horrible and that our situations are pretty dire and inescapable.

Just as COVID-19 itself arose from China, another great crisis also arose when they started closing cinemas. Closing the cinema houses in China at the beginning of the outbreak, alone, cost the film industry over $5 billion. Where politicians lacked the ability to act as the world fell apart and closed up, film studio moved quick to pull their line-ups. Some film releases all the way into the summer of 2021 have been delayed. Numerous film festivals have been cancelled including the internationally famous SXSW and Cannes. It is not unrealistic that 2020 may be the year without films, heaven forbid the Oscars be cancelled, and miraculously not due to their ratings from 2019's contest. Even studios with the contingency of a streaming platform, like Disney, are pulling film releases, not wanting to take the hit in sales from releasing them online only. Yet, while the studios hold out for a return to normalcy, streaming services such as Netflix, Amazon, Hulu, and many more are taking full advantage of their situation. At the moment this looks even more calamitous as the quality films made by artists, supposedly are sticking to the studios as they wait out the storm. The problem is that the young and the hungry will take what they can get and Netflix and Amazon are happy to saturate the seas with chum.

What is nice about the Netflix, binge model, is people don't like commercials, and like things broken up into episodes. Now sitcoms don't work with today's audiences so we need long continuous stories. This is great for novel adaptation and gives me hope for the Netflix version of *The Lord of the Rings*. A great example of this is *The Haunting of Hill House*. Though as it stands Netflix's good to bad is about a 20/80 percent split. And the small slice of good stuff is based on prior source material or the occasional good writer/filmmaker/acting that managed to join the Netflix Empire. The bad part, I believe, is the result of the unholy marriage of postmodernism, short attention spans, and the digitisation of our lives.

To illustrate this unholy marriage, we can focus on Netflix which is setting the standard for streaming services (Hulu is almost a carbon copy, but with higher standards, thus less content. Amazon and other, not-just-streaming companies, tend to put more effort into the quality of their content, perhaps they are interested in awards, perhaps they don't want to play the mudslinging game Netflix has set up). Netflix began just as video rental began to fall obsolete and Netflix is guilty of at least having a backstabbing hand in the death of those businesses. It was a cleaver, prototypical Silicon Valley-esque story. Why leave your home to go to the video store, when you could just get DVDs in the mail. And forget late fees, just return it when you want another and we will send you the next one on your list. And if you keep the movie, no big deal, you just pay the monthly subscription price and no harm, no foul. Then came streaming and Netflix was king by default. But they, as during the mail in rental days, didn't have original content, so they had to buy old series lost to syndication. For many years (and it still shows today) Netflix was synonymous with the nostalgia network. *Friends, Seinfeld, The Office, 30 Rock,* and all the live studio audience and quirky fourth wall breaking your heart could desire. Netflix has survived by making good deals with good content producers. This is how, once they started making their own stuff, they made a pivotal jump. Suddenly the nostalgia network was making its own shows and a few, very indy, very cliché films. Luckily, they had deals with Marvel and managed to buy up several properties that had lapsed after the great film studio franchise race that rang in the twenty-first century. This was largely motivated by superheroes and classic film-worthy literature needing a new interpretation. This also gave a boost to foreign content, which for Americans is British television, and for the rest of the world are dramas in non-English languages, getting good mileage out of the historical drama genre. But the original content coming out of Netflix is another problem entirely.

The dark times began rather recently. Short attention spans meant people want episodic film content. And it is also a natural reaction to every blockbuster being three or more hours long. The art of editing is wasted on the youth. The digitisation of our lives has made it so that content needs to be continuous, like our 'stories' on social media, and focus on real people. And postmodernism did two things. It destroys morality, after all, isn't good/bad, right/wrong in the eye of the beholder? Postmodernism also made it so that there are no good guys and no bad guys. This brings us to the next chapter in the Netflix hijacking of our entertainment. During our COVID-19 hiatus, perhaps you came across the increasingly popular original series *You* (although it is based on a book). In the three seasons and counting of this series, we follow our 'protagonist' as he stalks a girl, making quippy references to the canon of Western literature, and killing people who mildly present a bad influence to the object of his obsession. We relate to our protagonist because he is attracted to pretty people. He is also very smart, like we all wish we were, introspective, but not without flaws and ironic weaknesses. After all, if we are to have blemishes, can't they at least be well accounted for in the writing. He uses psychopathic manipulation and technological knowhow to make the pretty girl fall in love with him. This is a very brief gist of a series that thinks it is more clever than it actually is (and I've suffered through the whole bloody lot). What is troubling is, why is this show making me want to feel for someone who in my heart I know to be a bad guy. Just because he is horrendously average, the narrator, and somehow all the other people, he comes in contact with are bottom-of-the-barrel of human morality, do I need to cheer for him? Think about this while I discuss the other Netflix anomaly that is getting way more attention and views than it should be.

Social media, and by extension, the world has fallen in love with *Tiger King*. *Tiger King* is the latest of Netflix's interesting experimentations with the genre of documentary. Since attention spans require episodic content (and hey, it happens to keep people watching), the Netflix 'documentaries' are like limited series events of multiple episodes. *Tiger King* follows in the vane of *Abducted in Plain Sight* and *Don't F**ck with Cats: Hunting an Internet Killer*. In these documentary series, the point appears to be, as though postmodernism was invented yesterday, to celebrate people who have committed acts that we would otherwise abhor. The audience is asked to sympathise with murders, rapists, and criminals. To embrace the tragic flaws of being human. We are forced to humanise what cannot be forgiven by typical ethical standards. Then they pin the 'wrongs' of the 'protagonists' as the result of mental illness, which is obviously poorly understood by the filmmaker, yet like a true social justice warrior, they think we should, as a society, already understand it better. These documentaries fundamentally fail because we shouldn't try to humanise inhuman crimes. They succeed, I hope, only because they manage to hold our jaws ajar long enough to hold our attention for fifty minutes.

Tiger King is the epitome of this Netflix 'documentary' phenomenon. The Tiger King, Joe Exotic is so esoteric and beyond what would be considered socially acceptable (you know by the evil Establishment, man) that you are expected to love this 'underdog'? Joe Exotic is an exotic animal breeder and salesmen. He is gay. He is a polygamist. He has a mullet. He loves guns and has many, one always kept as his side. He has an internet show. He once ran for the US presidency. And most of all he speaks his mind. He is half Donald Trump, a populist product of anti-establishment sentiment and crass rhetoric. And he is also half Donald Trump, a manipulative impulsive narcissist hiding behind America's demented notion of freedom and his own celebrity. The only thing worse than him, is the rest of the cast surrounding him. Be that the yoga guru misogynist gun freak, aka the other exotic animal guy, or the archnemesis of Joe, the hippie, potential husband murdering, animal print wearing, animal rights activist trying to shut him down. The whole documentary is focussed on terrible human beings committing heinous crimes, resulting in broken lives, empty ammunition cartridges, and the revelation of a messed-up subculture that speaks to America's contradictory love for freedom, guns, and justice. Justice being defined as killing the other guy before he kills you, I think? But no matter, because we get plenty of cute tiger cub glamour shots.

This man, the Tiger King, must gain the praise he gets in much the same way the show Jerry Springer gained popularity in American homes. So begins a long history of social popularity that results in the election of Donald J. Trump and God only knows where it goes thereafter. We can watch as our fellow man descends into madness, so that we might feel better about our own, less than ideal, lot. Joe Exotic is deified in memes which are a fitting form of entertainment for my generation who is contributing to the through the roof increase in screen-time over the isolations induced by COVID-19. Memes are the apotheosis of a generation raised on such entertainment peaks as *Family Guy* and Judd Apatow films. Comedy from reference to pop culture. Something that doesn't age well, but that's okay, because more and more content will always be being produced in this nonstop always connected world we find ourselves in.

Luckily, boredom provides lovely fodder for our screen anxiety. You know the condition that infects more and more of us each day. Driving a need to wake our phones and check our social media feeds. Laughing at memes, cooing at images of cute animals, or partaking in the latest video challenge. Among ways to find entertainment in the dullness of COVID-19 are to post images of you staying home, for you are the hero by acting responsibly as per the designates of some hashtag's decree of what is and is not justice. And now thanks to TikTok we can all partake in a global talent show. Lip sync a popular song in a funny costume or with a creative dance or make us laugh with your own comic sketch. But you don't need to be an artist per se. You could do the emoji challenge. Where a song plays and you are presented with a random assortment of emojis. In one version, with every bass beat, you are to stretch your face to meet the emoji or, in another, it is the various hand emoji symbol which you must copy with your own. While the proliferation of social media usage always coincides with increases of narcissism, there might be hope in how we use social media during virus induced isolation.

Where social media prior to the outbreak of COVID-19 was the essence of self-importance, in times of isolation, it is nice to see that people are not so much speaking of themselves, but to others. There is a notion of community that has infected social media. Posts are engaged and people communicate more it appears. Instead of the motivation of attaining the status of trending or the accumulation of likes, people seek each other out in these times. As a community, those on social media, the only place where social distancing and sterile technology can be insured as a companion to public gathering, there is hope that we might help each other out. A novel dream for the old-fashioned notion of society. And thanks to camera filters and TikTok, we are somewhat challenged to do it creatively. #StayHome may be the most powerful movement to come about in modern times. A truly global commitment to ending the spread of COVID-19. Yet we speak in memes and emojis, a language that demands interpretation and therefore does the opposite of what one might think language ought to. That being the seeking of understanding. For as we are communicating more, which is good, are we understanding less? And this is the greatest calamity we will face well beyond COVID-19 and our entertainment crisis.

We can thank higher powers for the internet and social media, for it might be the only thing keeping us going completely mad from the isolation we find ourselves in during these Covidy times. Yet in the hieroglyphs and uncertainty of the times we find ourselves in, we all too easily forget about those who are not able to engage in this super community. First, there are the essential workers, who must risk and work tirelessly for the rest of us to keep ourselves safely isolated. Then there are the poor, who cannot afford to isolate. Those unfortunate souls that no matter the crisis, the structures remain in place to keep them where they must remain. And our entertainment continues to attempt to spirit us away from the escape we are confined within. Some of this time needs to be reserved for reflection. And maybe some entertainment can be found beyond what is popular. Hopefully the ennui of these isolated times will inspire us to do better and create better entertainment that provokes us to action. Maybe the new wave of art to come after COVID-19 can seek to motivate improvement in the world, rather than attempting to escape it.

ET CETERA

LAST WORD: ON THE DISAPPEARING NORMAL *by Samia Rahman*
THE LIST: TOP TEN SPARKS FOR THOUGHT ON AI *by Wendy Schultz*
CITATIONS
CONTRIBUTORS

ON THE DISAPPEARING NORMAL

Samia Rahman

Waking up on 23 March 2020 to a surreal new reality, it felt like we were in a scene from a film: let's call it Locked Down in London. Except this was not a disturbing nightmare or one of those apocalyptic TV serials. This was really happening. 'Well, this is all a bit postnormal,' I thought. But then I didn't really understand, let alone appreciate what postnormal times was all about. Despite my best efforts to learn about complexity, contradictions and chaos, it was all too speculative for my evidently arrested development to contend with.

Of course, some of it did make sense. It's true that history is accelerating in a way that was incomprehensible half a century ago, perhaps even a couple of decades ago. Things that used to take months or years, such as receiving a message from someone on the other side of the world, are now occurring over days, maybe even seconds. But aren't 'these times' always postnormal, in the eyes of every generation? My six-year-old nephew often asks me what life was like in The Olden Days and I am in awe of my nine-year-old niece's tech savvy that far outstrips anything I am capable of even now, never mind when I was her age. Life seemed a little postnormal before it became, like, really, post-normal. For the physicist Carlos Rovelli, all of reality is a consequence of interaction, negating entirely the notion of 'here' and 'now', because there is no such thing as the directional flow of time, or even the existence of time; fundamental physics after all, does not distinguish between past and future. He argues that it is far better to understand the world as 'happenings', as we know the rate that time passes varies according to altitude and speed. By viewing time in this way, we create space for the complexity of our existences, our emotions, and our approach to what we otherwise perceive of as the 'normal' passing of time.

But, the happenings of right now are definitely not in any version of my understanding of normal when we compare it to the Before Times. Here we are, cast into an unreal existence that throws everything we took for granted into question: the norms of our societies, our values and who we are. The shock has reverberated in every possible way, from a deeply personal to a societal and global level. But perhaps we are a little hyperbolic in our distress at the loss of our natural state. Instead of viewing this as a battle between life and death, we might do better to remind ourselves that death comes to us all. This is the feature of these times, a reminder that every one of us is mortal. The shock comes with the fact that we have been yanked out of our comfortable bubbles and forced to confront our mortality.

Our new normal comprises a global effort to support our health systems, to buy more life, more time. And if there is anything good that has come out of this, it is that perhaps we will look hard at what is important to our societies and take the opportunity to manifest change and renewal. How many workers were told it was unfeasible for them to work from home? And then, in the blink of an eye we are all magically working from home. But again, the machine is relentless in its artificial drive for normality, as employers worldwide spared no thought for the anxieties, pressures and struggles of workers and expected them to carry on as normal. Are we absolutely not in the grip of a disorienting pandemic, wrenched into the most unprecedented moment of our generation, often cut off and far from those we love and fearful of this unconventional enemy that is all round us? We are rendered helpless, and yet plunged into uncharted territory, juggling home, kids, cabin fever, in our attempts to keep calm and carry on. Meetings that could easily have been emails are not cancelled, merely postponed and converted into Zoom conference calls as data security and privacy concerns fall by the wayside. Wellbeing and mental health do not feature despite an already fragile climate.

We can talk about everyone pulling together, and calling on the blitz spirit, but let's not romanticise the past, which, do I need to remind you, is ostensibly an illusion, a convenient memory function to assist humans as they grapple to comprehend their incomprehensible existence. Poverty and class divisions were as pertinent then as they are now. After all, who isn't able to show resilience in their spacious suburban semi-detached home complete with garden, compared with a family crammed into a one-bedroom flat in an urban sprawl. Just as they did then, today people are turning on each other, egged on by a hysterical media. How dare my neighbour take a stroll, pedestrians accuse runners of breaching social distancing etiquette, locals are launching vigilante campaigns against those who dare to venture into their territory for fear they are bringing the 'plague' with them. Yet, just as before, there is also the solidarity that comes with being in a worldwide existential crisis as communities pull together in wave after wave of breathtaking humanity. Every Thursday at 8pm almost every single household on my street stands at their front door clapping, cheering, and singing for those who are at the front line of this fight and no that's not a tear in my eye. This scene is replicated all around the country, all over the world. It's emotional. A moment when we can forget social distancing and self-isolation, and remember how we once enjoyed evenings with friends and family, danced and socialised, a wistful memory in these strange times. But we need more than applause, we need everyone to think about who they voted for, we need to remember which employers are treating their workers shoddily, and we must never forget who, in a time of crisis, revealed themselves to be the helpers.

This unreality is a humbling experience for humanity. Has it sunk in yet? We are not a master race. It's time we listened to nature, to remember to listen to 'experts' such as those who warned that this threat was coming and implored us to be more prepared. This mess has been exacerbated by the mistakes made by governments who under-estimated the threat that was posed. We should work together now to collaborate instead of compete. To be humble and accept our weakness – that is what I hope will come out of this.

The twenty-first century has seen two seismic events that dramatically impacted our lives. Both times we have failed collectively. For a short while after 9/11, the US held the sympathy of the entire world, but instead of reaching out, they chose to bomb and kill. Iraq became a catastrophe and we are still reeling from the consequences. In 2008 the financial crisis was an opportunity for politicians to evaluate and transform the economic system but it was business as usual. The banks were bailed out, heralding a decade of crippling austerity that caused untold misery to many and brought the NHS to its knees. By the middle of the next decade, the top 1% in the UK had made enough money to pay off the government debt. Meanwhile, the rest continued to foot the bill. Anger with the present economic system was deftly re-directed with the help of a fear-mongering right-wing press, creating fertile ground for insidious populist movements such as Brexit here and Trump across the pond.

We are now in the middle of the third seismic event of this century and judging by our reaction, we have been slow on the upkeep. In the first week of lockdown, thousands of teachers in the UK received a letter from the Education Secretary thanking them for their efforts. Really? The same politicians who decimated the health and education system? The same politicians that cut public services by up to 40% are now praising care workers, bin men and other public service workers who haven't received a pay rise for years. The lowly paid, the unskilled, the migrants, all those who are keeping essential services running as the economy grinds to a halt. The mantra of the last decade is that if you are poorly paid then that's because your job has no value, and therefore you have no value.

Suddenly, those unskilled workers are heroes for being at the frontline, lauded by the same tabloid media that demonised them, for keeping the country from falling apart. Forty years of neo-liberal orthodoxy has been washed away in favour of state intervention. We are all socialists now. Those people saying the government is doing all it can to protect livelihoods must realise this. They haven't done it for altruistic reasons. They've done it because there is no other choice as they desperately strive to keep our broken economic system from complete collapse. Imagine if wages and jobs had disappeared and you still had to pay the mortgage and rent and bills. How long do you think before disaffection became full scale revolt? Maybe it still will; we can only hope. There are plenty more people who, betrayed by their government, have nothing to lose.

Within a matter of days, the lives we know have gone, temporarily at least. You're not going out for dinner any time soon. You're not getting the builders in to create that new extension on your house. You won't be going on that family holiday to the South of France this summer. Twenty-first century materialistic capitalism has been postponed, for now anyway. The artificial world has become our reality and the virtual world our lifeline.

And what a lifeline. Social media got me through the first week as hilarious memes perfectly captured the surrealism of our collective experience.

Making Day One immeasurably lighter, Kevin Farzad, Iranian singer and songwriter, tweeted the most relatable quarantine experience on the beginning of the onset of numbness, grief and disbelief:

My Quarantine Routine.
I just wanted to share what works for me.
This is just to give me structure and a sense of stability.

9am – 2am: wake up and stare at my phone

Variations on lockdown schedules flooded social media, helping us all feel a little bit better about the extent of crazy we were faced with. As shock and disbelief subsided, social media users explained how the hours of each day would slip by in a miasma of paralysis and existential dread:

Unknown tweeter:
7am: Breakfast
7.15am: Dessert breakfast
8.30am: Panic snack w/news
9.45am: Chocolate
11.30am: Snack while standing up staring
12.30pm: Lunch w/small dessert
2.00pm: Post nap luncheon
4.30pm: Trail mix
6.00pm: Dinner w/weird vibes
10:00pm: Ice cream

Social media has stepped into the breach of the new social distancing normal. As a result, we find ourselves permanently online courtesy of a dizzying array of apps that promise entertainment as well as the chance to connect. With so many people isolating alone it has become a thing to organise a virtual coffee and catch up with a friend or a dinner date with a romantic interest. I've been assured that Tinder-ing is as buoyant as ever, with singletons navigating these new charters and bringing a whole new meaning to the notion of being locked down.

We're adapting well to our new normal. The news has become essential viewing as we follow the twists and turns of this gripping plotline. Truth is stranger than fiction they say, but that was before. Terms such as flattening the curve have become essential to our discourse as we study the graphs and calculate the death-tolls every day. Statistics hold a morbid fascination, perhaps filling the void for sports fans looking for a winner in every scenario. Is the winner the one with the best infection to death ratio or the most spectacularly flattening curve?

There are winners and losers already in the new 'entertainment'. For smug celebrities and social media influencers, so used to fans obsessed with their every artificial, contrived and airbrushed move, nightmare scenarios are coming true. They are being ignored, made irrelevant by the all-consuming spectre of COVID-19 that has sucked up every second of airtime in the jostling world of Instagram likes and internet views. Instead of adulation and fawning, no ones cares and they are getting desperate, resorting to barrel-scraping gimmicks to get attention. Millionaire actor Gal Gadot was one of the first off the starting blocks, recruiting a bunch of other tone-deaf and clueless celeb mates to put together a cringe-worthy rendition of the song 'Imagine' by John Lennon. With ill-advised lyrics yearning for a world 'without possessions' just as people were losing their jobs and facing financial despair, the artificiality of celebrity culture was made all the more stark and ugly.

We are living in a new age, in postnormal times, where old orthodoxies have been replaced by a new normal. When this is all over can we ever get back to 'business as usual'. Do we even want that? Surely not. There must be a reckoning. We must not forget what came before. And with a new public awareness of the artificial constructs of capitalism that have exacerbated our plight, there yet may be a chance. For what will public opinion be once this is over? The politicians will gaslight the public, blaming anyone but themselves and will try to go back to the way things were but public opinion can and should push back. What would you choose? Life or the economy? You can't bring back life.

We humans are arrogant. We fell for the false belief in our own superiority. And now? Consider how the world has been upended and the fault lines in our fraught societies exposed. A British friend went to Uganda for a work trip in late February, planning a March safari holiday in Kenya before returning to London. By the time he was scheduled to arrive in Nairobi, African countries were closing their borders to those from the epicentre of the virus, Europeans. How ironic. Power dynamics have become skewered and the current chaos problematises the usual prevalent populist stereotypes. It turns out that the corona originated in China but was spread around the world by middle class (predominantly) Westerners hopping on flights to various parts of the world. The fault lay with the globalised elite, not the usual scapegoats: 'unskilled' migrants and asylum seekers seeking a better life in accordance with neoliberal capitalist calls to aspire.

An organism that emerged only a few months ago begs to differ. Perhaps now we can remember to respect that organism and acquiesce to the demands of nature instead of putting our needs first. Let's not revert to the Before Times. It is, after all, the human brain that determines what we call the flowing of time and the sense of the speed at which it appears to proceed. Artificial constructs that champion productivity to the detriment of humanity and neoliberal values of 'time equals money', must surely take a step back in the new re-ordering of priorities. In these less than normal times, all delusions of what went before must pass and healing, however long it takes, must be allowed its journey.

TEN SPARKS FOR THOUGHT ON AI

Wendy L Schultz

> I like to think…
> of a cybernetic meadow
> where mammals and computers
> live together in mutually
> programming harmony…
> …a cybernetic ecology
> …all watched over
> by machines of loving grace.
> Richard Brautigan, 1967

In April 2020, one could be forgiven for wishing that artificial intelligences were running the world. Organic intelligences are only too often demonstrating organic incompetence generated by running organic decision-making through organic ignorance. Humans have dreamt of building a better decision-maker for centuries – creating their own false gods to invoke, in the Old Testament; devising humanoid robots and living marionettes in *The Book of a Thousand Nights and a Night*; describing robotic workers, helpmeets, and colleagues, and the three laws to control them, in Isaac Asimov's robot novels; and evolving the planet-governing Minds in Iain M. Banks Culture novels. We dream of creating an Other on whom we can rely, perhaps because we are so aware of our own flaws and frailties.

Bad news: we will undoubtedly incorporate those flaws in any intelligence we create. Partially good news: more interesting artificial intelligences may evolve on their own – and develop their own unique array of flaws besides which ours might merely be spitting into the wind.

We can hope that their virtues will include charity and kindness – in the months and years to come, we will need it.

In approaching the possibilities of artificial intelligence, we must first ask: how is it born, and how does it grow up? Then, what purpose(s) might it serve? Where will it fit in with human beliefs, cultures, and people? Finally, how could AI help in the COVID-19 pandemic? The following ten sparks for thought are ordered to address those core questions.

HOW

1. Top-down, centralised, programmed

Building a better brain! A great ambition. The traditional approach relies on a symbolic representation of the world – a set of rules describing how the world works, and the creation of algorithms to generate responses according to those rules. This approach attempts to model human performance. Typical examples include 'expert systems', built up from observing proven rules of effective practice followed implicitly or explicitly by experts, or by modelling finely observed and accurately described systems. The flaws in this approach are computational limits - so many rules for so many potential situations! – and the built-in biases of the human programmers. On-off/black-white/algorithmic decision-making leaves little space for nuance. When quantum computation becomes widespread and practical, offering the programming option of maybe/both combined with massive processing power, this top-down approach to AI might once again become interesting. But would a quantum-processor-based AI simply be inherently indecisive? Maybe?

2. Bottom-up, distributed, emergent

Situated intelligence provides an alternative approach that starts small and evolves in complexity. Build something that senses its environment, with a few simple guiding rules and goals – and let it learn. Machine learning is basically a bootstrapping mechanism for creating AI. Initial results applied to robotics created artificial insects, artificial puppies, and smart search algorithms – Alexa and Siri and hey, Google. Baby programmes are embedded – or situated – in a dynamic environment that they can sense, respond to, and manipulate. Each interaction teaches the software more about the environment and the possibilities for interaction and the potential range of results. To date, all examples are deliberately designed by software engineers.

But could situated intelligence evolve on its own? Peter Cochrane, former Chief Technologist at BT Labs, has pointed out that the human intelligence is distributed and networked: individual brain cells are dumb; the brain is intelligent. That intelligence is based not simply on processing power, but also on sensors – the ability to perceive and interact with reality. The internet is also composed of distributed interconnected nodes, soon to surpass in number those of the human brain. And we are giving it senses: the cameras and microphones on our smartphones, the smart wifi home sensors, environmental monitors connected to the internet – we live enmeshed in the internet's increasingly sophisticated senses. At what point will the machine learning capabilities built into the internet, coupled with incoming data, challenged by relationships with seven billion inquiring humans, just wake up and start learning with the entire planet as its sandbox?

3. How intelligent is intelligent – will AI actually be only an 'artificial stupid'?

Vonda McIntyre's 1989 novel *Starfarers*, set on an immense habitat/ spaceship, introduces 'artificial stupids' – robots of limited intelligence devised specifically to handle ongoing maintenance and chores. This provides an early signal for an ongoing debate in the AI community – should stupidity be built in, in order for artificial intelligence to more closely resemble human intelligence? Human intelligence is constrained – constrained by imperfect memory, imperfect perception, imperfect performance, and cognitive bias. Free of these flaws, AI could potentially outperform humans by many orders of magnitude. Thus the idea of introducing artificial stupidity: it might make artificial general intelligence safer by limiting it in the ways humans are limited. The downside? Hobbling AI with biases and built-in imperfections also potentially hobbles its ability to support better decision-making for humanity.

WHAT

4. Servant, companion, lover, benevolent overlord?

What might AIs be to humans – how might they fit into our relationships, our social connections, our cultures? As none yet exist, we can only fall back on fictional explorations of the possibilities. *Iron Man*'s (2008) AI character Jarvis is designed by Tony Stark ('genius, billionaire, playboy, philanthropist'), but programmed to evolve. Jarvis is a good fictional example of how massive processing power connected to multiple sensory inputs – video and microphone feeds, laboratory sensors – might nurture growth of an AI. While modelled after an old family retainer and designed to be a digital servant, Jarvis is in many ways Tony's closest, and perhaps most reliable, companion and friend. In much the same way, Samantha in the movie *Her* (2013) begins as an AI-powered virtual digital assistant – a more effective Alexa or Siri – and evolves into an independent sentience who first falls in love with her human clients, and then transcends their merely human intelligence. Samantha does so not only through massive distributed processing power and distributed sensor feeds, but also and more importantly, through simultaneous interactions with a multitude of human beings.

At the other end of the spectrum are the immense Minds of Iain M. Banks' Culture novels, the powerful artificial intelligences whose 'bodies' are kilometre-long spaceships, or entire orbital stations. The Minds are amused by human culture and tolerate humans as entertaining residents. They absolutely control the structures that are their bodies, and by doing so enable humans to luxuriate in heedlessness without reaping the consequences of their own ignorance. The technological evolution of Minds leads 'to a state in which humans don't only do less, but also think less in a world of more and more intelligent objects.' The Culture seems very much like Brautigan's 'cybernetic ecology, ... all watched over by machines of loving grace'. Sounds relaxing, doesn't it?

WHERE

5. Culture and ethics — Buddhist AI? Quaker AI? Islamic (halal?) AI?

Whether an AI is deliberately programmed, or evolves from a dynamic relationship with the wider environment and human demands, what might be its philosophy? What cultural perspectives and moral frames might it apply to its interactions with the world and us? Critiques abound regarding the in-built bias of machine learning algorithms — the techbro worldview coded into microprocessors. Perhaps with Buddhist or Quaker starting assumptions, humans would not need to worry about AI dominating humanity; it would prioritise mindfulness, meditation, the resolution of conflict. What would an Islamic AI be like? That is, what characteristics might render an AI halal — and what might make it haram? Similar questions are being asked elsewhere in our emerging digital life. The worldwide Islamic economy — worth nearly US$4 trillion and growing —provides financing based on shari'ah law; the Shariya Review Bureau has certified several cryptocurrencies as compliant and halal; Islamic digital startups like CollabDeen proudly proclaim that they are melding faith and lifestyle in their on-line collaboration platform. What might be the decision rules, perspectives, and behaviour of an AI who is among the faithful?

6. Cranky, funny, loving — what will be our individual experience of AIs?

Zooming in from wider questions of worldview, culture, and morality, to those of psychology, what will the personalities of emergent AIs be like? In the film *Interstellar*, the humans could adjust personality settings like independence, humour, sarcasm. Will AIs have personality menus? Or, more likely, if they evolve into sentience, will each have its own unique immutable personality? Douglas Adam's *Hitchhiker's Guide to the Galaxy* depicts a lugubrious AI robot, Marvin, whose permanently depressed perspective colours his every utterance. In contrast, the *Iron Man* movies suggest that Jarvis contains built-in algorithms for critical thinking and humour, which have evolved along with his other capabilities. The result is an AI executive assistant with a wry, critical, and sarcastic view of its progenitor/boss/owner. The AI Samantha in *Her* begins as upbeat, cheerful, and helpful – and grows affectionate and profoundly loving. What do we want of the AIs of the future? Do we want them to recognise and experience human emotion – to reflect our own feelings back at us and to encourage them?

AIs might well evolve their own unique emotions but would we ever be able to understand them? In William Gibson's *Count Zero*, the Tessier-Ashpool AI known as The Boxmaker lives out its days in a room in Villa Straylight on an orbital station, carefully and almost meditatively creating glass-topped boxes filled with objects of everyday life, some cast-offs, some antiques, some human and personal, some objets d'art. Is the assembly random? People read deep meaning into the boxes and their contents. But the question is, does the Boxmaker itself invest great meaning in each box and what it contains – that is, is it deliberate art? Or just a random collection of junk which humans perceive as art? This is perhaps the greatest and most subtle version of the Turing test for genuine intelligence.

7. Smarter – or just different?

Both of the previous sparks for thought frame the culture and personality of AIs as at least human-adjacent: our silicon relatives. But the story of the Boxmaker raises a different question. What if AIs are entirely alien instead, and beyond our understanding? Would we want such entities making critical decisions for humanity? The Minds of Banks' Culture books frequently remind humans how ineffably superior Mind intelligence is to human intelligence, and it is so palpably true that humans find competition moot. The books convey the sense that during any human-Mind conversation, the Mind is also engaged in millions of other activities –humans require only a small percentage of a Mind's mental activity. That a vast thick culture exists above and around merely human culture, carried out in conversations over light years among the Minds, simultaneously blazingly fast and of patient, extended duration. The tone and tenor of that magisterial conversation is hinted at by the names the Minds give themselves: Frank Exchange of Views, A Series of Unlikely Explanations, Unfortunate Conflict of Evidence, Irregular Apocalypse, and Prosthetic Conscience, are examples. Each name almost makes sense to humans, but each clearly fragments larger lattices of thought. Will we simply be the wrasse to AI whales?

8. Our silicon better half?

While we are building evolving computer networks, we are evolving ourselves as well. Scientists have experimented in brain-computer interfaces since the turn of the century: Kevin Warwick implanted microchips along the nerves in his hand; Braingate implanted a microchip array in a human brain. Developing an 'exocortex' is the logical next step – expanding the capabilities of the human brain by direct link-up to external memory and processing technologies. This could be any combination of artificial external information processing devices that augment a brain's biological cognitive processes. For example, an individual's exocortex could consist of linked external memory modules, processors, Input/Output devices and software systems that would interact with, and augment, a person's natural brain functions. It is one short step from exocortexes becoming commonplace, to humans linking intimately with emerging AIs. The relationship could be the best of both worlds: extending cognition and processing power for the human, and offering the AI a nuanced and mobile sensorium with which to experience the world. AIs might be less the civilisation-ending threat that some analysts perceive; and humans more the global problem-solvers they need to be in an era characterised by climate crises, environmental crises, and now epidemiological crises.

COVID-19

9. Problem analysis or problem solutions?

Epidemiologists were overjoyed by the possibilities inherent in big data and massive computational analysis applied to public health challenges. Rapid processing and analysis of a country's worth of personal health data, compiled from your Fitbit or AppleWatch, opens up the capacity to spot previously unrecognised patterns and relationships across environmental conditions, lifestyle, diet, stress, and genetic characteristics. Using an AI to run data pattern-identification and analysis non-stop across entire populations could create a daily 'weather report' for health – what illnesses are cropping up where, and why. This daily report could also warn of shifts in external conditions – pollen, new food fads, stress-inducing events – that could in turn create new ill-health hotspots. Should such a big data-health AI stop at simply identifying emerging health problems like pandemics? Or could we ever trust one enough to grant it the powers to offer individuals incentives for lifestyle changes, or to implement health policy initiatives for communities and countries? This could end the politicisation of health and environmental issues. Except, of course, for the politics of the AI itself – what moral and ethical frames might an AI invoke if faced with questions of medical triage?

10. The ultimate epidemiologist – or the start of the Surveillocene?

The immediate question is whether machine learning – really the practical capability that is the closest we've come to AI – can be effective at helping humans cope with the COVID-19 pandemic without laying the foundation of an overbearing surveillance society. The WHO, public health experts, and doctors all hammer home the need to test, identify, trace contacts, and quarantine in order to control COVID-19. Those needs cry out for digital solutions: there most definitely is an app for that. In fact, several exist, among them South Korea's COVID 100m app, and the Kings College's COVID Symptom Tracker at covid.joinzoe.com. Analysts have also been identifying potential hotspots by combining searcher location data and specific Google search terms, eg, 'I can't smell' plus fever. A genuine Artificial General Intelligence could sift through mountains of public health and personal health data and identify epidemiological patterns before most humans finished formulating a question. The problem, of course, is the data. Is the trade-off of public health security worth acquiescing in the loss of control over our data – particularly over data as personal as the state of our bodies? Could we trust an AI with our data? Who will in future watch the watchers – will it be machines of loving grace?

CITATIONS

Introduction: Certificate of Authenticity
by C Scott Jordan

For more on the philosophy of authenticity see Jean-Jacques Rousseau (1754) *Discourses on the Origins of Inequality,* (Hackett, London, 2011), Søren Kierkegaard (1849) *Sickness Unto Death*, (Penguin, London, 2004), Martin Heidegger (1927) *Being and Time*, (SUNY Press, Albany, 2010), and Authenticity entry of the Stanford Encyclopedia of Philosophy at https://plato.stanford.edu/entries/authenticity/; Karl Marx's quote on history's repetition comes from Karl Marx, 'The Eighteenth Brumaire of Louis Napoleon', *Die Revolution*, (New York, 1852), available at https://www.marxists.org/archive/marx/works/1852/18th-brumaire/ch01.htm

Artificial Defined by Jeremy Henzell-Thomas

In explaining the origin of English words, including their Indo-European roots, I have consulted various sources, including John Ayto, *Dictionary of Word Origins* (Bloomsbury Publishing, London, 1990); *Chambers Dictionary of Etymology*, ed. Robert K. Barnhart (Chambers, Edinburgh,1988); Joseph T. Shipley, *The Origins of English Words: A Discursive Dictionary of Indo-European Roots* (John Hopkins University Press, 1984); *The American Heritage Dictionary of Indo-European Roots*, ed. Calvert Watkins (Houghton Mifflin Company, Boston, 2000; The Online Etymology Dictionary, Merriam-Webster Dictionary and Wikipedia; Andrew Lawless, *Plato's Sun: An Introduction to Philosophy* (University of Toronto Press, Toronto, 2005); Michael Pakaluk, *Artistotle's Nicomachean Ethics: An Introduction* (Cambridge University Press, 2005), 5; Jeffrey Barnouw, *Odysseus, Hero of Practical Intelligence: Deliberation and Signs in Homer's Odyssey* (University Press of America Inc., Lanham, Maryland, 2004), 250; Allen Verhey, *The Great Reversal: Ethics and the New Testament* (William B. Eerdmans Publishing Co., Grand Rapids, Mich., 1984), 141; and Jeremy Henzell-Thomas, 'Armonia: Fitting Together in a Plural World', Inaugral issue of *Armonia* Journal

(March 2017) at https://armoniajournal.com/2017/03/10/armonia-fitting-together-in-a-plural-world/.

On Artificial Intelligence and related questions concerning human faculties, I have referred to the following sources: Zbigniew Brzezinski, *Between Two Ages: America's Role in the Technetronic Era* (Penguin, 1978); Julia Bossmann, 'Top 9 ethical issues in artificial intelligence', World Economic Forum, 21/10/2016 at https://www.weforum.org/agenda/2016/10/top-10-ethical-issues-in-artificial-intelligence/; Ana Santos Rutschman, 'Stephen Hawking warned about the perils of artificial intelligence – yet AI gave him a voice' (*The Conversation*, 15 March, 2018) at http://theconversation.com/stephen-hawking-warned-about-the-perils-of-artificial-intelligence-yet-ai-gave-him-a-voice-93416; the Stanford University '100 Year Study of Artificial Intelligence' at https://ai100.stanford.edu/history-1; Kelsey Piper, 'Why Elon Musk fears artificial intelligence', *Vox* 2/11/2018 at https://www.vox.com/future-perfect/2018/11/2/18053418/elon-musk-artificial-intelligence-google-deepmind-openai; Jean Schradie, *The Revolution That Wasn't: How Digital Activism Favors* Conservatives (Harvard University Press, Cambridge Mass., 2019); Bernard Marr, 'Is Artificial Intelligence Dangerous? 6 AI Risks Everyone Should Know About', 19/11/2018 at https://www.forbes.com/sites/bernardmarr/2018/11/19/is-artificial-intelligence-dangerous-6-ai-risks-everyone-should-know-about/#752e5bac2404; Kabir Helminski, 'The Spiritual Challenge of Artificial Intelligence, Trans-Humanism, and the Post-Human World' at www.sufism.org; Clive Thompson, 'How to Teach Artificial Intelligence Some Common Sense', *Wired* 13/11/2018 at https://www.wired.com/story/how-to-teach-artificial-intelligence-common-sense/; Richard Fletcher, 'Google Boss: Artificial Intelligence will do more for humanity than fire', *The Times*, 23/1/20; Ian Sample, 'Powerful antibiotic discovered using machine learning for first time', *The Guardian*, 20/2/2020 at https://www.theguardian.com/society/2020/feb/20/antibiotic-that-kills-drug-resistant-bacteria-discovered-through-ai; Lou Del Bello, 'Scientists Are Closer to Making Artificial Brains That Operate Like Ours Do', *Futurism*, 28/1/2018 at https://futurism.com/artificial-brains-operate-like-humans-close; Martyn Thomas, 'Human error, not artificial intelligence, poses the greatest threat', *The Guardian,* 3/4/2019 at https://www.theguardian.com/technology/2019/apr/03/human-error-not-artificial-intelligence-poses-the-greatest-threat; 'How AI will go out of control according to 52 experts', *CBInsights,* 19/2/2019 at https://www.cbinsights.com/research/ai-threatens-humanity-expert-quotes/; Laurie Nadel, 'The Artifice of Social Media and the Dehumanizing Factor', *Higher Journeys,* 24/8/2016 at http://www.higherjourneys.com/artifice-social-media-dehumanizing-factor/; Jeremy Henzell-Thomas, 'The Power of Education', *Critical Muslim 14, Power,* April 2015 (Hurst, London), 65-86, and Introduction to CM 15, *Educational Reform,* July, 2015; Iain McGilchrist, *The Master and his Emissary: The Divided Brain and the Making of the Western World* (Yale University Press, New Haven and London, 2009) and 'The Battle of the Brain', *Wall Street Journal* (2/1/2010) at https://www.wsj.com/articles/SB10001424052748704304504574609992107994238; Karim Douglas Crow, 'Between wisdom and reason: Aspects of 'aql (Mind-Cognition) in Early Islam', *Islamica* 3:1 (Summer 1999), 49-64; Guy Claxton, *Hare Brain Tortoise Mind: Why Intelligence Increases When you Think Less* (Fourth Estate, London, 1997); F. David Peat, *Blackfoot Physics: A Journey into the Native American Worldview* (Fourth Estate, London 1994).

On other manifestations and applications of the 'artificial', I have referred to Jeremy Henzell-Thomas, 'Out in the Open', Introduction to *Critical Muslim* 19, *Nature,* July-September 2016 (Hurst, London), 3-24; Elie Dolgin, 'The Myopia Boom'. *Nature,* 18/3/2015 at http://www.nature.com/news/the-myopia-boom-1.17120; Aisling Irwin, 'The dark side of light: how artificial lighting is harming the natural world', *Nature,* 16/1/2018 at https://www.nature.com/articles/d41586-018-00665-7; 'Why Artificial Light is Bad for You.' *Solarspot* Blog at https://solarspot.co.uk/general/why-artificial-light-is-bad-for-you; Holly Strawbridge, 'Artificial sweeteners: sugar-free, but at what cost?', *Harvard Health,* 8/1/2018 at https://www.health.harvard.edu/blog/artificial-sweeteners-sugar-free-but-at-what-cost-201207165030\; '4 Things to Know About Artificial and Natural Flavors', *Ameritas,* 25/5/2017 at https://www.ameritasinsight.com/wellness/artificial-natural-flavors; Liji Thomas, 'Are Artificial Food Flavors and Colorings Harmful?' *News*

Medical, 14/11/2018 at https://www.news-medical.net/health/Are-Artificial-Food-Flavors-and-Colorings-Harmful.aspx; on the artificial heart, https://en.wikipedia.org/wiki/Artificial_heart, and on the 'artificial smile', http://bodylanguageproject.com/nonverbal-dictionary/body-language-of-the-artificial-smile-or-fake-smile/

Faking Unbelief by Abdelwahab El-Affendi

The quote from Niccolo Macchiavelli is from *The Prince* (HC Mansfield, trans.), Chicago University Press, 1985, p70. The Russell T. McCutcheon quote is from 'Theorizing 'Religion': Rejoinder to Robert A. Segal', *Journal of the American Academy of Religion*, Vol. 73, No. 1 (2005), pp. 215-217. The Edward Gibbon quote is from *The Decline and Fall of the Roman Empire*, 3 volumes, Modern Library, New York, 1995, 1:22. The modes of study of religion are from Jan Platvoet, 'The definers defined: Traditions in the definition of religion', *Method & Theory in the Study of Religion* 2, no. 2 (1990): 180-212 (184); the quote is from p195. The *Foreign Policy* article is by Ola Salem and Hassan Hassan, 'Arab Regimes Are the World's Most Powerful Islamophobes', 29 March 2019, available at: https://foreignpolicy.com/2019/03/29/arab-regimes-are-the-worlds-most-powerful-islamophobes/.

See also: Gregory Murry, 'Anti-Machiavellianism and Roman Civil Religion in the Princely Literature of Sixteenth-Century Europe' *The Sixteenth Century Journal*, Vol. 45, No. 2 (Summer 2014), pp. 334–335; and William James, *The varieties of religious experience*. Vol. 15. Harvard University Press, 1985.

Ancient Mechanical Horrors by Robert Irwin

E.R. Truitt, *Medieval Robots: Mechanism, Magic, Nature and Art*, (Philadelphia, University of Pennsylvania Press, 2015). 'Abd al-Latif al-Baghdadi's *Al-Ifada* was translated by Kamal Hafuth Zand and John A. and Ivy E. Videan as *The Eastern Key* (George Allen and Unwin, 1965). The deployment of statuary on the walls of Konya and other Anatolian towns is the subject of Scott Redford's 'The Seljuqs of Rum and the Antique', *Muqarnas*, vol.10, (1993) pp.148-156. Some of Ibn Zunbul's *Tuhfa al-Muluk* has been translated by E.Fagnan in *Extraits Inedits Relatifs au Maghreb*, (Algiers 1942).

On Ficino and other western thinkers on the animation of statues, Liana Saif, *The Arabic Influences on Early Modern Occult Philosophy* (Basingstoke, Hampshire, 2015), pp.121-3, 181-3, 193. The Arabic text of the *Ghayat al-hakim*, was published as *Picatrix: das Ziel des Weisen von Pseudo-Magriti* (Leipzig, 1933) and its section on magical statues is pp.309-19. Paul Kraus's magnificent, encyclopaedic survey of the treatises attributed to Jabir and of Islamic occultism more generally was published as *Jabir ibn Hayyan: contribution à l'histoire des idées scientifiques dans l'Islam*, 2 vols (Cairo, 1942-3). Marina Warner's, *Stranger Magic: Charmed States and the Arabian Nights*, (London, 2011) briefly but perceptively discusses automata considered as toys. Treatises on mechanical devices produced by the Banu Musa and al-Jazari are discussed in numerous short studies by Donald R. Hill. Al-Jawbari's *Kashf al-mukhtar fi kashf al-asrar* was translated by René R. Khawam as *Le Voile arraché: l'autre visage de l'Islam* (Paris, 1979). For the stories of the *Thousand and One Nights*, see *The Arabian Nights: Tales of 1001 Nights*, 3 vols., tr. Malcolm Lyons (London, 2008) and for those of the *Al-Hikayat al-'Ajiba*, see *Tales of the Marvellous and News of the Strange*, tr. Malcolm C. Lyons (London, 2014). The appearance of automata in the *Arabian Nights* is briskly discussed in René Khawam, 'Les statues animées dans les *Mille et Une Nuits*', *Annales, Economies, Sociétés. Civilisations*, vol.30 (1975 pp.1084-1104 and Yuriko Yamanaka, '*Les Mille et une Nuits* et les automates' in Aboubakr Chraibi et al. eds *Les Mille et Une Nuits en Partage* (Arles, 2004) pp.39-52. On automata in the medieval Arab heroic sagas, Malcolm C. Lyons, *The Arabian Epic: Heroic and Oral Story Telling* (Cambridge, 2005). Sigmund Freud's *The Uncanny*, has been translated by David McLintock (London, 2003).

AI Solutions by John A. Sweeney

This two x *Wired* article are: Glen Weyl and Jaron Lanier. 2020. 'AI Is An Ideology, Not A Technology | WIRED.' Wired. March 15, 2020. https://www.wired.com/story/opinion-ai-is-an-ideology-not-a-technology/ and Oren Etzioni and Nicole DeCario. 2020. 'AI Can Help Find Scientists Find a COVID-19 Vaccine.' *Wired*, March 28, 2020. https://www.wired.com/story/opinion-ai-can-help-find-scientists-find-a-covid-19-vaccine/;

For more concerning the advancement of AI in contemporary society, see Pranam, Aswin. n.d. 'Why The Retirement Of Lee Se-Dol, Former 'Go' Champion, Is A Sign Of Things To Come.' Forbes. Accessed March 30, 2020. https://www.forbes.com/sites/aswinpranam/2019/11/29/why-the-retirement-of-lee-se-dol-former-go-champion-is-a-sign-of-things-to-come/.

For more on COVID-19 induced displays of idiocy see Folley, Aris. 2020. 'Video of Spring Breakers Saying Coronavirus Won't 'stop Me from Partying' Sparks Viral Condemnation.' Text. TheHill. March 18, 2020. https://thehill.com/blogs/blog-briefing-room/news/488357-video-of-spring-breakers-saying-coronavirus-wont-stop-me-from and Glantz, Tracy. 2020. 'Model Who Licked Toilet Seat in Coronavirus Challenge Is 'Unbothered' by Outrage.' Miamiherald. March 17, 2020. https://www.miamiherald.com/miami-com/miami-com-news/article241270296.html.

For more on the COVID-19 pandemic and AI's applications therewithin, see Bieber, Florian. 2020. 'Authoritarianism in the Time of the Coronavirus.' *Foreign Policy* (blog). March 30, 2020. https://foreignpolicy.com/2020/03/30/authoritarianism-coronavirus-lockdown-pandemic-populism/; Chen, Sharon, Dandan Li, and Claire Che. 2020. 'Stacks of Urns in Wuhan Prompt New Questions of Virus's Toll.' *Bloomberg.Com*, March 27, 2020. https://www.bloomberg.com/news/articles/2020-03-27/stacks-of-urns-in-wuhan-prompt-new-questions-of-virus-s-toll; Chen, Stacy. 2020. 'Taiwan Sets Example for World on How to Fight Coronavirus.' ABC News. March 13, 2020. https://abcnews.go.com/Health/taiwan-sets-world-fight-coronavirus/story?id=69552462; Chun, Andy. 2020. 'Coronavirus: China's Investment in AI Is Paying off in a Big Way.' *South China Morning Post*. March 18, 2020. https://www.scmp.com/comment/opinion/article/3075553/time-coronavirus-chinas-investment-ai-paying-big-way; Dator, Jim. 1993. 'Society Is a Social Invention and You Are a Social Inventor.' http://www.futures.hawaii.edu/publications/futures-theories-methods/

SocialInventor1993.pdf; Dave, Paresh. 2020. 'White House Urges Researchers to Use AI to Analyze 29,000 Coronavirus Papers.' *Reuters*, March 16, 2020. https://www.reuters.com/article/us-health-coronavirus-tech-research-idUSKBN2133E6; Duff-Brown, Beth. 2020. 'How Taiwan Used Big Data, Transparency and a Central Command to Protect Its People from Coronavirus.' Freeman Spogli Institute for International Studies. March 3, 2020. https://fsi.stanford.edu/news/how-taiwan-used-big-data-transparency-central-command-protect-its-people-coronavirus; Dunleavy, Jerry. 2020. 'US Spy Agencies Warned Trump That China Was Lying about Coronavirus.' Washington Examiner. March 21, 2020. https://www.washingtonexaminer.com/news/us-spy-agencies-warned-trump-that-china-was-lying-about-coronavirus; Editorial. 2020. 'The Guardian View on Hungary's Coronavirus Law: Orbán's Power Grab | Editorial.' *The Guardian*, March 29, 2020, sec. Opinion. https://www.theguardian.com/commentisfree/2020/mar/29/the-guardian-view-on-hungarys-coronavirus-law-orbans-power-grab; Etherington, Darrell. 2020. 'IBM, Amazon, Google and Microsoft Partner with White House to Provide Compute Resources for COVID-19 Research.' *TechCrunch* (blog). March 23, 2020. http://social.techcrunch.com/2020/03/22/ibm-amazon-google-and-microsoft-partner-with-white-house-to-provide-compute-resources-for-covid-19-research/; Ghosh, Pallab. 2020.

To learn more about the ongoing crisis of information and knowledge see Jain, Anab. 2017. 'Can Speculative Evidence Inform Decision Making?' *Anab Jain* (blog). June 28, 2017. https://medium.com/@anabjain/can-speculative-evidence-inform-decision-making-6f7d398d201f; Christopher, Nilesh. 2020. 'We've Just Seen the First Use of Deepfakes in an Indian Election Campaign.' *Vice* (blog). February 18, 2020. https://www.vice.com/en_in/article/jgedjb/the-first-use-of-deepfakes-in-indian-election-by-bjp; Patil, Samir. 2019. 'Opinion | India Has a Public Health Crisis. It's Called Fake News.' *The New York Times*, April 29, 2019, sec. Opinion. https://www.nytimes.com/2019/04/29/opinion/india-elections-disinformation.html; Schwartz, Peter. 2001. *Inevitable Surprises: Thinking Ahead in a Time of Turbulence*. New York: Gotham Books. http://search.ebscohost.com/login.aspx?direct=true&scope=site&db=nlebk&db=nla

bk&AN=124844; and Shirky, Clay. 2019. 'Emojis Are Language Too: A Linguist Says Internet-Speak Isn't Such a Bad Thing - The New York Times.' August 16, 2019. https://www.nytimes.com/2019/08/16/books/review/because-internet-gretchen-mcculloch.html; To learn more about the Parliament project, see XML. 2016. *Parliament*. Amsterdam: XML.

Digital Ethics by Emre Kazim

For more on digital ethics see Jobin, A., Ienca, M. & Vayena, E. The global landscape of AI ethics guidelines. Nat Mach Intell 1, 389–399 (2019). https://doi.org/10.1038/s42256-019-0088-2; Hagendorff, T. The Ethics of AI Ethics: An Evaluation of Guidelines. *Minds & Machines* (2020). https://doi.org/10.1007/s11023-020-09517-8; and Burr, C., Taddeo, M. & Floridi, L. The Ethics of Digital Well-Being: A Thematic Review. *Sci Eng Ethics* (2020). https://doi.org/10.1007/s11948-020-00175-8; For more on the UK government's stance on digital ethics see Centre for Data Ethics (CDEI): 2 Year Strategy Report (March 2019) https://www.gov.uk/government/publications/the-centre-for-data-ethics-and-innovation-cdei-2-year-strategy; Artificial Intelligence and Public Standards A Review by the Committee on Standards in Public Life Chair, (February 2020) https://www.gov.uk/government/publications/artificial-intelligence-and-public-standards-report; and Regulating in a Digital World: House of Lords Select Committee on Communications (March 2019) https://publications.parliament.uk/pa/ld201719/ldselect/ldcomuni/299/299.pdf.

For the international communities view on digital ethics see White Paper On Artificial Intelligence – A European approach to excellence and trust: European Commission (February 2020) https://ec.europa.eu/info/sites/info/files/commission-white-paper-artificial-intelligence-feb2020_en.pdf; The Age of Digital Interdependence: Report of the UN Secretary-General's High-level Panel on Digital Cooperation (June 2019) https://digitalcooperation.org/wp-content/uploads/2019/06/DigitalCooperation-report-web-FINAL-1.pdf; and Recommendation of the Council on Artificial Intelligence: OECD (May 2019) https://legalinstruments.oecd.org/en/instruments/OECD-LEGAL-0449; for more NGO opinions on digital ethics see Leslie, D. (2019). Understanding artificial intelligence ethics and safety: A guide for the responsible design and implementation of AI systems in the public sector. The Alan Turing Institute. https://doi.org/10.5281/zenodo.3240529; and Whittlestone, J. Nyrup, R. Alexandrova, A. Dihal, K. Cave, S. (2019) Ethical and societal implications of algorithms, data, and artificial intelligence: a roadmap for research. London: Nuffield Foundation. https://www.nuffieldfoundation. org/sites/default/files/files/Ethical-and-Societal-Implications-of-Data-and-AI-report-Nuffield-Foundat.pdf; for the AI Now: Report (December 2019) https://ainowinstitute.org/AI_Now_2019_Report.pdf

Is It Bad to be Artificial? by Colin Tudge

Numerous editions of John Ruskin's *The Stones of Venice* (1849), Leo Tolstoy's *Anna Karenina* (1877), George Orwell's *1984* and 'Arts and Its Producers' (1818), an address by William Morris, are widely available. Other books mentioned in this essay include: Paul Mason, *Post Capitalism* (Penguin, 2019), E F Schumacher, *Small is Beautiful* (Abacus, London, 1973, 1978), Ivan Illich, *Tools for Conviviality* (Harper and Row, New York, 1973), and Amit Goswami, *The Self-Aware Universei* (Tarcher, 1995). For John Searle's ideas on AI see his collections of essays, *Expression and Meaning* (Cambridge University Press, 1979).

Four Earths by Christopher B Jones

To read more on governing evolution see Walter Truest Anderson (1987) *To Govern Evolution*, Boston, Harcourt; and John Platt, 'The Acceleration of Evolution,' The Futurist 15 (February 1981): 14-25. For more on colonising space, see Ben Finney's book chapters, (1985) 'Lunar Base: Learning to live in space' (pp. 731–756) in Wendell Mendell, ed., *Lunar Bases and Space Activities of the 21st Century*. Houston: Lunar and Planetary Institute, and (1988) 'Will space change humanity?' (pp. 155–172) in J. Schneider and M. Leger-Orine, eds., Frontiers and Space Conquest: The Philosopher's Touchstone. Bingham: Kluwer Academic Press. Concerning the posthumanism and transhumanism debate, see Donna Haraway (1991) *Simians, Cyborgs, and Women: The Reinvention of Nature*, London, Free Association Books; Raymond Kurzweil (2006) The Singularity is Near,

London, Duckworth; and Mark O'Connell (2017) *To Be a Machine: Adventures Among Cyborgs, Utopians, Hackers, and the Futurists Solving the Modest Problem of Death*, London, Granta. To learn more about Postnormal Times, see Ziauddin Sardar (ed.) (2019) *The Postnormal Times Reader*, Hendon, The International Institute for Islamic Thought. For more on Nature Deficit Disorder, see the work of Richard Louv, especially *The Last Child in the Woods* (2008). To learn more about the justification of the Dark Mountain scenario visit https://dark-mountain.net/about/manifesto/ ; and David Benatar, 'Why it is Better Never to Come Into Existence', *American Philosophical Quarterly*, 1997, volume 34, number 3, pp. 345–355. To further investigate the Collapse scenario further see Frederik Polak (1973) *The Image of the Future*, Amsterdam, Elsevier Sdentific Publishing Company; Herman Khan (2017) *On Thermonuclear War*, Abingdon, Routledge; Roberto Vacca (1974) *The Coming Dark Age,* London, HarperCollins; and Jospeh Tainter (1990) *The Collapse of Complex Societies*, Cambridge, Cambridge University Press. To explore the rationale behind Hybrid Gaia, see Donna Haraway (2016) *Staying with the Trouble: Making Kin in the Cthulucene*, Durham, Duke University Press; and James Lovelock (2019) *Novocene: The Coming Age of Hyperintelligence*, London, Penguin. To find out more on Dyson's Children see Freeman Dyson, 'Search for Artificial Stellar Sources of Infrared Radiation', *Science* 131:3414, 03 June 1960. For more on climate change see Mark Lynas (2008), *Six degrees. Our future on a hotter planet*. Washington D.C., National Geographic Society and David Wallace-Wells (2019); *The Uninhabitable Earth*. New York, Tim Duggan Books; and Alvin Toffler (1984) *The Third Wave*, New York, Bantam Books.

Faux Feminism by Esra Mirze Santesso

The two images in this article come from Ayesha Tariq, *Sarah: The Suppressed Anger of the Pakistani Obedient Daughter* (Penguin, India, 2015) and Deena Mohamed, *Qahera*, https://deenadraws.art/en/qahera. This article focusses on the three graphic novels Marjane Satrapi, *The Complete Persepolis.* (Pantheon, New York, 2007), Ozge Samanci, *Dare to Disappoint (*Farrar, New York, 2015), and Ayesha Tariq, *Sarah: The Suppressed Anger of the Pakistani Obedient Daughter* (Penguin, India, 2015); for the debate on feminism in graphic novels see Hillary Chute, *Graphic Women: Life Narrative* *and Contemporary Comics* (Columbia UP, New York, 2010), Susan Stanford Friedman, 'Wartime Cosmopolitanism: Cosmofeminism in Virginia Woolf's 'Three Guineas' and Marjane Satrapi's 'Persepolis,'' *Tulsa Studies in Women's Literature* 32 no. 1 (2013): 23-52, Janell Hobson, 'The Personal is Global: Teaching Global Feminist Consciousness,' *Transformations: The Journal of Inclusive Scholarship and Pedagogy,* 17 no 2 (2006 Fall-2007 Winter): 96-105, 'Questions for Marjane Satrapi,' abc News. Accessed March 10, 2020. https://abcnews.go.com/Entertainment/story?id=4332648&page=1, Amy Malek, 'Memoir as Iranian Exile Cultural Production: A Case Study of Marjane Satrapi's 'Persepolis' Series,' *Iranian Studies* 39 no. 3 (2006): 353-380, Golnar Nabizadeh, 'Vision and Precarity in Marjane Satrapi's *Persepolis,*' WSQ: Women's Studies Quarterly, 44 no. 1 & 2 (2016): 152-167, Hillary Chute, 'The Texture of Retracing in Marjane Satrapi's 'Persepolis,'' WSQ: *Women's Studies Quarterly*, 36 no. 1/2 (2008): 92-110, and Bhakti Shringarpure, 'This Feminist Author Wants to Get Past 'Feminism-Lite'.' Public Radio International. Accessed March 12, 2020. https://www.pri.org/stories/2018-02-23/feminist-author-wants-get-past-feminism-lite.

For more on feminism and Islam see Anouar Majid, *Unveiling Traditions: Postcolonial Islam in a Polycentric World* (Duke UP, Durham, 2000), Chandra Talpade Mohanty, 'Under Western Eyes: Feminist Scholarship and Colonial Discourses,' boundary 2 12 no. 3 (1984): 333-358, Fatema Mernissi, *The Veil And The Male Elite: A Feminist Interpretation Of Women's Rights In Islam* (Basic Books, New York, 1992, and Judith Butler, 'The Body Politics of Julia Kristeva,' *Hypatia* 3 no. 3 (1989): 104-118 and to read the veiled comic book hero Qahera see Deena Mohamed, *Qahera*, https://deenadraws.art/en/qahera.

The English Rose Who Wasn't by Hassan Mahamdallie

The quote from Matthew Goodwin is taken from *How Farage Outflanked Everyone* (May 2019) and can be found at https://unherd.com/2019/05/how-farage-outflanked-everyone/ Ann Dummett's 1973 book *A Portrait of English Racism* was published by Pelican Books. The quotes from the BBC's 'White Season', the comment article by the *Daily Express* journalist and

Anoop Nayak's research on nineteenth century attitudes to the working class can be found in the report *Who Cares about the White Working Class?* Runnymede Trust, London, 2009.

Promises, Promises by James Brooks

The following studies and news articles were used for background research for this piece: Research Europe report of European Strategy and Policy Analysis System conference 2016 (paywall) – https://www. researchprofessional.com/0/rr/news/europe/universities/2016/11/ Social-fabric-must-be-academic-focus-.html; Muck Rack report on PR officers outnumbering journalists – https://muckrack.com/ blog/2018/09/06/there-are-now-more-than-6-pr-pros-for-every-journalist; University of Leeds press release - https://www.eurekalert. org/pub_releases/2020-03/uol-sin030620.php; Phenome Centre BBC News story – https://www.bbc.co.uk/news/uk-politics-19070510; MRC press release – https://mrc.ukri.org/news/ browse/a-phenomenal-legacy-for-london-2012/; Research Fortnight story (paywall) – https://www.researchprofessional.com/0/rr/news/ uk/research-councils/2017/9/Phenome-centre-to-become-self-standing. html; The Sun report of Matt Hancock's pledges of genome testing – https://www.thesun.co.uk/news/10286545/new-nhs-dna-check-for-newborns/; Sulphur Hexafluoride BBC News story - https://www.bbc. co.uk/news/science-environment-49567197; Cobalt demand study – https://www.nhm.ac.uk/press-office/press-releases/leading-scientists-set-out-resource-challenge-of-meeting-net-zer.html; European Academies Science Advisory Council report on negative emissions technologies – https://easac.eu/fileadmin/PDF_s/reports_statements/Negative_ Carbon/EASAC_Report_on_Negative_Emission_Technologies.pdf

Through the Sea Glass by Liam Mayo

The citations mentioned in the text in order of appearance: Rushkoff, D 2014, *Present shock: When everything happens now*, New York, New York, U.S.A: Current; Nichols, T. (2017). 'How America Lost Faith in Expertise: And Why That's a Giant Problem', *Foreign Affairs*, 96, 60.; Vervaeke, J.,

Mastropietro, C., & Miscevic, F. (2017). *Zombies in Western Culture: A Twenty-First Century Crisis*: Open Book Publishers.; Ziauddin Sardar (2010). 'Welcome to postnormal times', *Futures, 42*(5), 435-444.; Foucault, M. (2005). *The Order of Things*: Routledge.; Chimisso, C. (2004). 'The Formation of the Scientific Mind', Gaston Bachelard, introduced, translated and annotated by Mary McAllester Jones. In: Taylor & Francis.; Kingsmith, A. (2017). *On Rupture: An Intervention into Epistemological Disruptions of Machiavelli, Hobbes, and Hume. The Journal of Speculative Philosophy, 31*(4), 594-608.; Eisenstein, P., & McGowan, T. (2012). *Rupture: On the emergence of the political*: Northwestern University Press.; Ravetto-Biagioli, K. (2016). The digital uncanny and ghost effects. *Screen, 57*(1), 1-20.; Freud, S. (2003). *The uncanny*: Penguin.; Morton, T. (2010). *The ecological thought*: Harvard University Press.; Morton, T. (2013). *Hyperobjects: Philosophy and Ecology after the End of the World*: U of Minnesota Press.; Morton, T. (2017). *Humankind : solidarity with nonhuman people*: London; Coole, D. (2013). Agentic Capacities and Capacious Historical Materialism: Thinking with New Materialisms in the Political Sciences. *Millennium - Journal of International Studies, 41*(3), 451-469. doi:10.1177/0305829813481006; Giri, A. K. (2013). Rethinking Integration. *Sociological Bulletin, 62*(1), 100-109.; Žižek, S. (2014). *Absolute recoil: Towards a new foundation of dialectical materialism*: Verso Trade.

The March by Naomi Foyle

With thanks to Ibrahim Hewitt at Interpal for pointing me in the right direction early on; to Hugh Dunkerley, Robert Hamberger and Joanna Lowry for comments on an early draft; to C Scott Jordan for his thoughtful editorial comments; and, for his invaluable feedback and encouragement, to Mosab Abu Toha, poet, Harvard Fellow and founder of the Edward Said Public Library in Gaza.

The character of Hamid is based on personal testimonies of people severely injured in the Great March of Return, interviewed for B'Tselem: The Israeli Information Centre for Human Rights in the Occupied Territories, and for the International Committee for the Red Cross.

https://www.btselem.org/firearms/20200130_shoot_and_abandon_in_gaza_155_amputees_and_27_paralyzed_in_two_years_of_protests; https://www.icrc.org/en/document/young-amputees-gaza-are-striving-put-their-lives-backtrack. Nur Masalha is quoted from his book *The Palestine Nakba: Decolonising History, Narrating the Subaltern, Reclaiming Memory* (Zed Books, 2012). According to Wikipedia, Haj As'ad Hassouneh, described by Saleh Abd al-Jawad as "a survivor of the [Al-Lidd and Ramle] death march", said in 1996: "The Jews came and they called among the people: "You must go." "Where shall we go?" "Go to Barfilia." ... the spot you were standing on determined what if any family or possession you could get; any to the west of you could not be retrieved. You had to immediately begin walking and it had to be to the east. ... The people were fatigued even before they began their journey or could attempt to reach any destination. No one knew where Barfilia was or its distance from Jordan. ... The people were also fasting due to Ramadan because they were people of serious belief. There was no water. People began to die of thirst. Some women died and their babies nursed from their dead bodies. Many of the elderly died on the way. ... Many buried their dead in the leaves of corn". Israeli bombs killed ninety Gazans on 20 July 2014, including sixty people in the poor and crowded neighbourhood of Shejaeeya. https://www.thenation.com/article/archive/massacre-shejaiya/;https://electronicintifada.net/blogs/ali-abunimah/massacre-shujaiya-dozens-killed-israel-shells-eastern-gaza-city-photos. Data on the Great March of Return was taken from various online sources, noting that the casualty figures given on Wikipedia were out of date.

https://en.wikipedia.org/wiki/2018%E2%80%9319_Gaza_border_protests [accessed Mar 21 2020]; https://www.middleeastmonitor.com/20191227-gaza-halts-great-march-of-return-for-three-months/; https://www.msf.org/great-march-return-depth; https://reliefweb.int/report/occupied-palestinian-territory/gaza-protests-mark-shift-palestinian-national-consciousness. A photograph of nine-year old Mohamed Ayyash, wearing the onion mask he devised for the first day of the March, went viral in 2018. https://www.aljazeera.com/news/2018/04/gaza-onion-boy-goal-grandparents-land-180405094446652.html. Although its statistics too have been superseded, the February 2019 UNHRC report on the Great March of Return comprehensively exposes the extreme and gratuitous nature of the Israeli open fire policy: https://www.ohchr.org/Documents/HRBodies/ HRCouncil/CoIOPT/A_HRC_40_74.pdf. Both Israeli and Palestinian commentators consider the BBC documentary *A Day in Gaza* to be biased toward the Israeli narrative of the conflict. The *Guardian* deemed it '. . . [as] level-headed and even-handed [as possible]. . . unfogged by endless context and historical dispute.'

https://www.middleeasteye.net/opinion/bbc-documentary-adopts-israeli-narrative-gaza-protests; https://honestreporting.com/bbc-documentary-almost-gets-gaza-right/; https://www.theguardian.com/ tv-and-radio/2019/may/13/one-day-in-gaza-review-an-almost-unwatchably-vivid-vision-of-carnage. AI 'SmartLegs' are being developed to aid better balance and functionality for amputees. Many lower limb amputees in Gaza use crutches for sport, including the team members of Heroes Football Club, formed in 2017 as an initiative of the Deir Al Balah rehabilitation centre. https://www.medgadget.com/2019/11/ smart-prosthetic-leg-uses-ai-to-make-perfect-steps.html; https://www. irishtimes.com/news/world/middle-east/gaza-strip-residents-encouraged-to-emigrate-by-israel-1.3993150; https://www.aljazeera. com/news/2018/06/playing-football-brings-hope-amputees-gaza-180618132435829.html. More information on the mental health crisis in Gaza, and Dr John Soos's efforts to support Gazan mental health professionals, can be found via these links: https://www.washingtonpost. com/world/gazans-have-survived-years-of-war-now-depression-is-killing-them/2018/06/18/e0bbfaaa-699c-11e8-a335-c4503d041eaf_ story.html; https://mondoweiss.net/2016/01/there-is-no-post-traumatic -stress-in-gaza-because-the-trauma-is-continuous/. The British bombing campaign of WWII, including of Dresden, which caused a firestorm that killed 25,000 people, is considered in many quarters to have been a war crime. https://www.theguardian.com/world/2006/dec/23/germany. secondworldwar.

COVID-19 Entertainment by Khuda Bushq

This review examined the following Netflix series: Berlanti, Greg and Sera Gamble, creators. *You.* Netflix, 2018. https://www.netflix.com/my/title/80211991; Good, Eric, dir. *Tiger King: Murder, Mayhem, Madness.* Netflix, 2020. https://www.netflix.com/my/title/81115994; Lewis, Mark, dir. *Don't F**ck With Cats: Hunting an Internet Killer.* Netflix, 2019. https://www.netflix.com/my/title/81031373; and Borgman, Skye, dir. Abducted in Plain Sight. Netflix, 2017. https://www.netflix.com/my/title/81000864.

For more on the COVID-19 pandemic and increased screentime, see Helen Davidson, 'Around 20% of global population under coronavirus lockdown,' *The Guardian.* 24 March, 2020. https://www.theguardian.com/world/2020/mar/24/nearly-20-of-global-population-under-coronavirus-lockdown. and Travis M. Andrews, 'Our iPhone weekly screen time reports are through the roof, and people are 'horrified',' *TheWashington Post.* 24 March, 2020. https://www.washingtonpost.com/technology/2020/03/24/screen-time-iphone-coronavirus-quarantine -covid/.

For more on China and Hollywood in COVID-19 times, see Scott Roxborough, Patrick Brzeski, and Pamela McClintock, 'Global Film Industry Facing $5 Billion Loss Amid Coronavirus Outbreak,' *The Hollywood Reporter.* 02 March, 2020. https://www.hollywoodreporter.com/news/film-industry-facing-5-billion-loss-coronavirus-outbreak-1282038. and Alissa Wilkinson, 'How the coronavirus outbreak is roiling the film and entertainment industries,' *Vox.* 31 March, 2020. https://www.vox.com/culture/2020/3/10/21173376/coronavirus-cancel-delay-wonder-woman-olympics-cannes-disney-ghostbusters.

Last Word: On the Disappearing Normal by Samia Rahman

For more on Carlo Rovelli's work his *The Order of Time*, (Penguin, London, 2019) and *Seven Brief Lessons on Physics* (Penguin, London, 2015).

See also, Arwa Mahdawi, 'The coronavirus crisis has exposed the ugly truth about celebrity culture and capitalism', *The Guardian* 31 March 2020, https://www.theguardian.com/commentisfree/2020/mar/31/the-coronavirus-crisis-has-exposed-the-ugly-truth-about-celebrity-culture-and-capitalism; and Aisha S Ahmad, 'Why you should ignore all that Coronovirus-inspired productivity pressure', The Chronicle of Higher Education 27 March 2020, – https://www.chronicle.com/article/Why-You-Should-Ignore-All-That/248366/?fbclid=IwAR2Qs1YErfPYSahhyP lbYl4cLVRnyuJfAEKraEp2BhMPKCCo5acTwrz451E

The List: Ten Sparks for Thought on AI
by Wendy L. Schultz

Richard Brautigan's poem, 'All Watched Over by Machines of Loving Grace', first debuted on the streets of San Francisco in 1967; more recently it was used as the title of British documentary maker Alan Curtis 2011 BBC television series. The whole poem can be read at:
[https://www.theatlantic.com/technology/archive/2011/09/weekend-poem-all-watched-over-by-machines-of-loving-grace/245251/]

Vonda McIntyre's novel *Starfarers* is published by Easton Press (1989). Numerous editions of Douglas Adam's *Hitchhikers Guide to the Galaxy* (1978) are available, alone with radio scripts, video game and a 2005 feature film. William Gibson's *Count Zero*, part of 'The Neuromancer' trilogy, is published by Arbor House (1986). The first of ten Iain Bank's culture novels, *Consider Phlebas*, was published by Macmillan in 1987. Isaac Asimov's Robot series consist of six novels, the first of which *I, Robot* was published by Gnome Press in 1950.
Peter Cochrane, 'AI Fables' article can be read at: https://www.slideshare.net/PeterCochrane/ai-fables-facts-and-futures-threat-promise-or-saviour-129689426

On 'artificial stupidity' see Michaël Trazzi and Roman V. Yampolskiy, 'Building Safer AGI by introducing Artificial Stupidity': https://arxiv.org/pdf/1808.03644.pdf; and https://thenextweb.com/artificial-intelligence

/2018/08/23/want-to-make-robots-more-human-try
-artificial-stupidity/

On halal AI, see: http://islam-today.co.uk/artificial-intelligence-the-new-
god and https://collabdeen.com/

On brain computer interface, see: https://www.theguardian.com/
science/2019/sep/22/brain-computer-interface-implants-neuralink-
braingate-elon-musk;   and   https://towardsdatascience.com/
why-many-important-minds-have-subscribed-to-the-existential-risk-of-ai-
a55cfc109cf8

On the use of big data in epidemiology, see Michael Eisenstein, 'Infection
forecast powered by big data', *Nature* 7 March 2018: https://www.nature.
com/articles/d41586-018-02473-5

For COVID-19 adds, check out: https://www.marketwatch.com/story/
wildly-popular-coronavirus-tracker-app-helps-south-koreans-steer-clear-
of-outbreak-areas-2020-03-18; and
https://www.nytimes.com/2020/04/05/opinion/coronavirus-google-
searches.html

CONTRIBUTORS

Shah Tazrian Ashrafi is a writer based in Dhaka, Bangladesh ● **James Brooks** is a science journalist and writer ● **Khuda Bushq** spends too much time watching Netflix instead of writing his dissertation on the psychology of 'Netflix and Chill' ● **Abdelwahab El-Affendi** is Dean, School of Social Sciences, Doha Institute of Graduate Studies ● **Naomi Foyle** is a well-known science fiction writer ● **Jeremy Henzell-Thomas** is a Research Associate and former Visiting Fellow at the Centre of Islamic Studies, University of Cambridge ● **Robert Irwin** is the author, most recently, of *Ibn Khaldun: An Intellectual Biography* ● **Arsalan Isa** is a London based writer ● **Christopher B Jones** is a Senior Fellow at the Centre for Postnormal Policy and Futures Studies and supervises PhD students at Walden University in the School of Public Policy and Administration ● **Emre Kazim** is a digital ethicist based in the department of Computer Science, University College, London ● **Hassan Mahamdallie** is a critic and playwright ● **Liam Mayo**, a Fellow of the Centre for Postnormal Policy and Futures Studies, works in and with communities to bring marginalised voices into the mainstream ● **Marie Michalke** is a researcher and translator who works at the Poetry Translation Centre in London ● **Samia Rahman** is the Director of the Muslim Institute ● **Esra Mirze Santesso** is Associate Professor, Department of English, Franklin College of Arts and Sciences, University of Georgia ● **Wendy L Schultz**, a renowned futurist, is Senior Fellow, Center for Postnormal Policy and Futures Studies ● **John Sweeney** is Director, Qazaq Research Institute for Futures Studies, Norxoz University, Almaty, Kazakhstan ● **Colin Tudge** is currently writing a book about the kind of changes that need to be made – in actions, infrastructure, and mindset – if we are to rescue the world from its present plight ● **Mozibur Rahman Ullah** was educated at Imperial and Cambridge and is an independent physics scholar and poet.